D0850586

PULP CULTURE

THE ART OF FICTION MAGAZINES

FRANK M. ROBINSON & LAWRENCE DAVIDSON

PORTLAND, OREGON

For Jack and Rusty and Darrell and the two Johns and all the others who loved the old magazines and helped make the collecting of them so much fun.

Principia Graphica *Design and Typography*
Ann Granning Bennett *Copy Editing*

Collectors Press books are available at special discounts for bulk purchases, premiums and promotions. Special editions, including personalized inserts or covers, and corporate logos, can be printed in quantity for special purposes. For further information contact: Special Sales, Collectors Press, Inc., P.O. Box 230986, Portland, OR 97281. 1-800-423-1848

Printed in Hong Kong
9 8 7 6 5 4 3 2

For a free catalog write to:
COLLECTORS PRESS, INC.
P.O. Box 230986
Portland, Oregon 97281

Or call toll-free 1-800-423-1848
www.collectorspress.com

Library of Congress Cataloging-in-Publication Data

Robinson, Frank M.
Pulp Culture : the art of fiction magazines / Frank M. Robinson & Lawrence Davidson. — 1st American ed.
p. cm.
Includes bibliographical references.
ISBN 1-888054-12-3 (hardcover)
1. Magazine covers—United States. 2. American fiction—20th century. I. Davidson, Lawrence, 1949- , II. Title.
NC974.R63 1998
741.6'52'0973—dc21

97-44638
CIP

Contents

Introduction

At one time the readers of pulp magazines numbered in the tens of millions and the number of titles in the hundreds. The "pulps" were the successors to the story papers of the last century and the dime novels of the beginning of the twentieth. Started in the 1890s, they reached the height of their popularity in the 1920s and 1930s and had largely disappeared by the mid-'50s—forgotten by all but a few avid collectors and cultural historians. But for many years they were the chief source of entertainment in a country that was starved for it.

At the turn of the century there were wandering minstrel shows, the chautauqua, husking bees, and church socials if you lived in the country, and occasional stage plays if you lived in one of the larger cities.

And then there was reading, the chief entertainment for a nation of readers. Newspapers came out daily, and every Saturday brought "story papers" like the *New York Ledger*, *Saturday Night*, and *Street & Smith's New York Weekly*.

During the summer, you found a lot to do, especially if you were part of a farming family—and most people were. During the winter, you had more time, allowing you hours to crowd next to the fire and read. It wasn't much different in the cities; pub-crawling and evenings at the theater during the dead of winter weren't

❶ ••••• *Bullets indicate relative value*

THE ALL-STORY

October 1912

Clinton Pettee

The most valuable pulp of all. *Tarzan of the Apes* was published complete in one issue.

❶

a favored pastime. But reading a book or magazine was. It was cheap, it was close at hand, and you didn't freeze to death walking to the bookcase and back.

Later there would be the nickelodeon for those who lived in town, and a simple radio set for everyone who could afford it—or, if money was short, you could make one from a crystal and a "cat's whisker." But magazines, a literary invention that became popular toward the end of the nineteenth century, had found a hole and filled it. They survived the nickelodeon, even after it morphed into a huge pleasure palace where the flickering images had finally learned to talk, and stayed alive, even after radio became preoccupied with the contents of Fibber McGee's closet.

Magazines were easier to handle than the daily newspaper and usually featured a carefully edited mix of articles, essays, and fiction. If slanted toward women, as was the *Ladies' Home Journal*, recipes, dress patterns, and an occasional line of poetry dominated content. Photographs and advertising, especially color ads, required use of expensive, coated paper. These "slick" magazines had to sell in the millions, both to pay their production costs and to justify what they charged for advertising.

Magazines specializing in fiction were far cheaper to produce. They carried little advertising, featured line drawings instead of photographs or wash illustrations, and were printed on inexpensive wood-pulp paper. Readers interested in adventure stories, mysteries, or westerns didn't care so long as the stories were exciting to read.

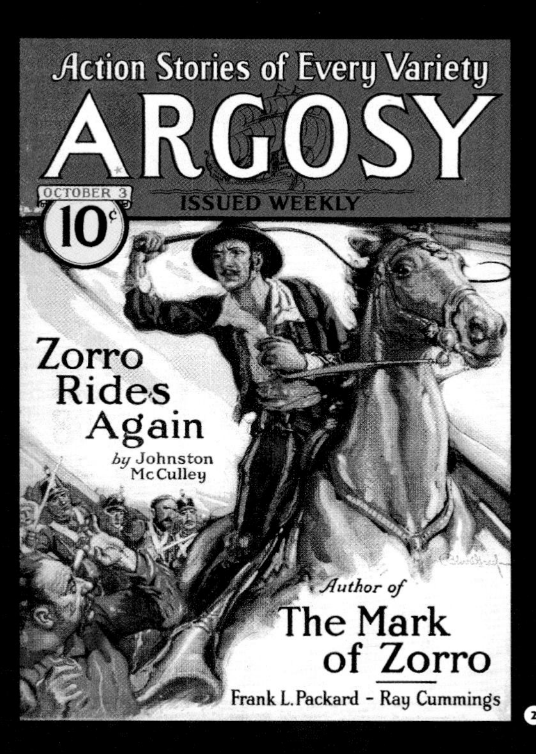

❷

❷ •
Argosy
October 3, 1931
Robert A. Graef
"Zorro" still rides high in the public imagination.

❸ •••
Weird Tales
April 1933
J. Allen St. John
The best-known cover for *Weird Tales*. Artist J. Allen St. John was probably paid one hundred dollars for it. In the late '80s a collector bought the painting for twenty-five thousand dollars.

EDMOND HAMILTON • E. HOFFMANN PRICE • CLARK ASHTON SMITH

Weird Tales

APRIL 25¢

Golden Blood
by Jack Williamson

J. Allen St. John

❸

4 •••
MAGIC CARPET
October 1933
Margaret Brundage
Magic Carpet had the most evocative logo of any pulp—undoubtedly designed and hand-lettered by artist J. Allen St. John, who probably also designed the final logo for *Weird Tales*.

6 ••
FLIGHT
October 1929
Walter M. Baumhofer
The first issue of an elegantly titled pulp.

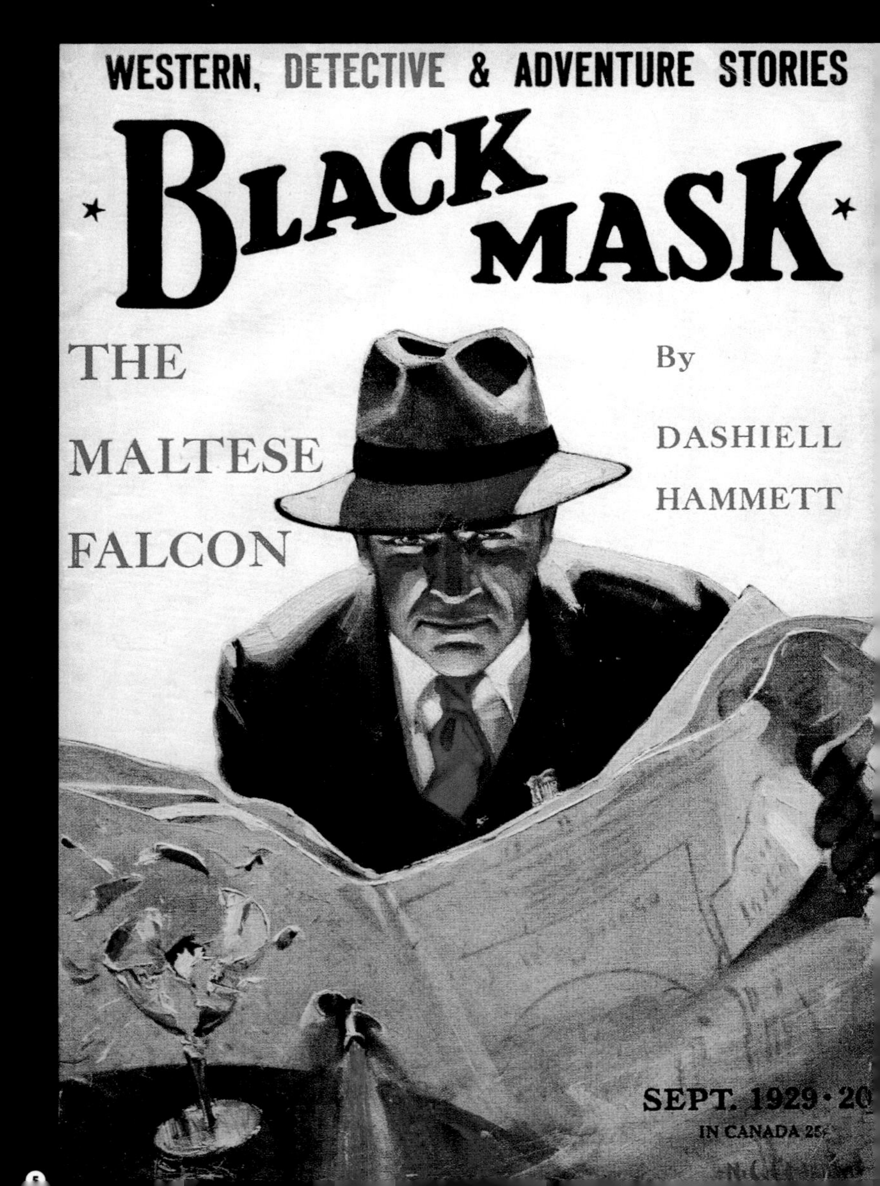

5 ••••
BLACK MASK
September 1929
H.C. Murphy, Jr.
The Maltese Falcon was one of the most famous novels to appear in a pulp.

7 •••
The Shadow
July 1932
George Rozen
The Shadow was originally intended to promote a radio show.

8 •••
Speakeasy Stories
June-July 1931
Walter M. Baumhofer
How many stories would you want to read about speakeasies?

9 •••
Doc Savage Magazine
July 1935
Walter M. Baumhofer
A "portrait" cover of Doc himself.

While magazines such as the *Saturday Evening Post*, *Collier's*, *Liberty*, *Redbook*, and the *Ladies' Home Journal* sold in the millions, the all-fiction magazines—*Argosy*, *All-Story*, *The Popular Magazine*, *Adventure*, and later titles like *Doc Savage* and *The Shadow*—sold in the hundreds of thousands. But the all-fiction magazines outnumbered their more polished cousins, and all told they probably had a far larger audience.

At the start many authors wrote for both the slicks and the all-fiction magazines. The major difference was in the amounts of their paychecks. A story that didn't find a home in the *Saturday Evening Post* eventually would be welcome at *Argosy* or *Adventure*, and frequently an author who specialized in pulp fiction "graduated" to the slicks full time.

Many cover artists had brushes in both camps as well. N.C. Wyeth and Joseph Leyendecker, popular illustrators in the early 1900s, could be found as frequently on the all-fiction magazine covers such as *The Popular Magazine* and *New Story* as they were on the *Saturday Evening Post*, *Collier's*, or *Success*. Leyendecker also became well-known as an illustrator for Ivory Soap, Kuppenheimer clothing, and Arrow shirt ads.

With time the styles of fiction began to change. Subject matter in the slicks was generally reality-based; in the all-fiction magazines, the stories became more imaginative and veered toward the sensational. You could find H.G. Wells in *Cosmopolitan* and Sherlock Holmes in *Collier's*, but it was *All-Story* that printed *Tarzan of the Apes* and *Black Mask* that was to feature Dashiell Hammett's *The Maltese Falcon*.

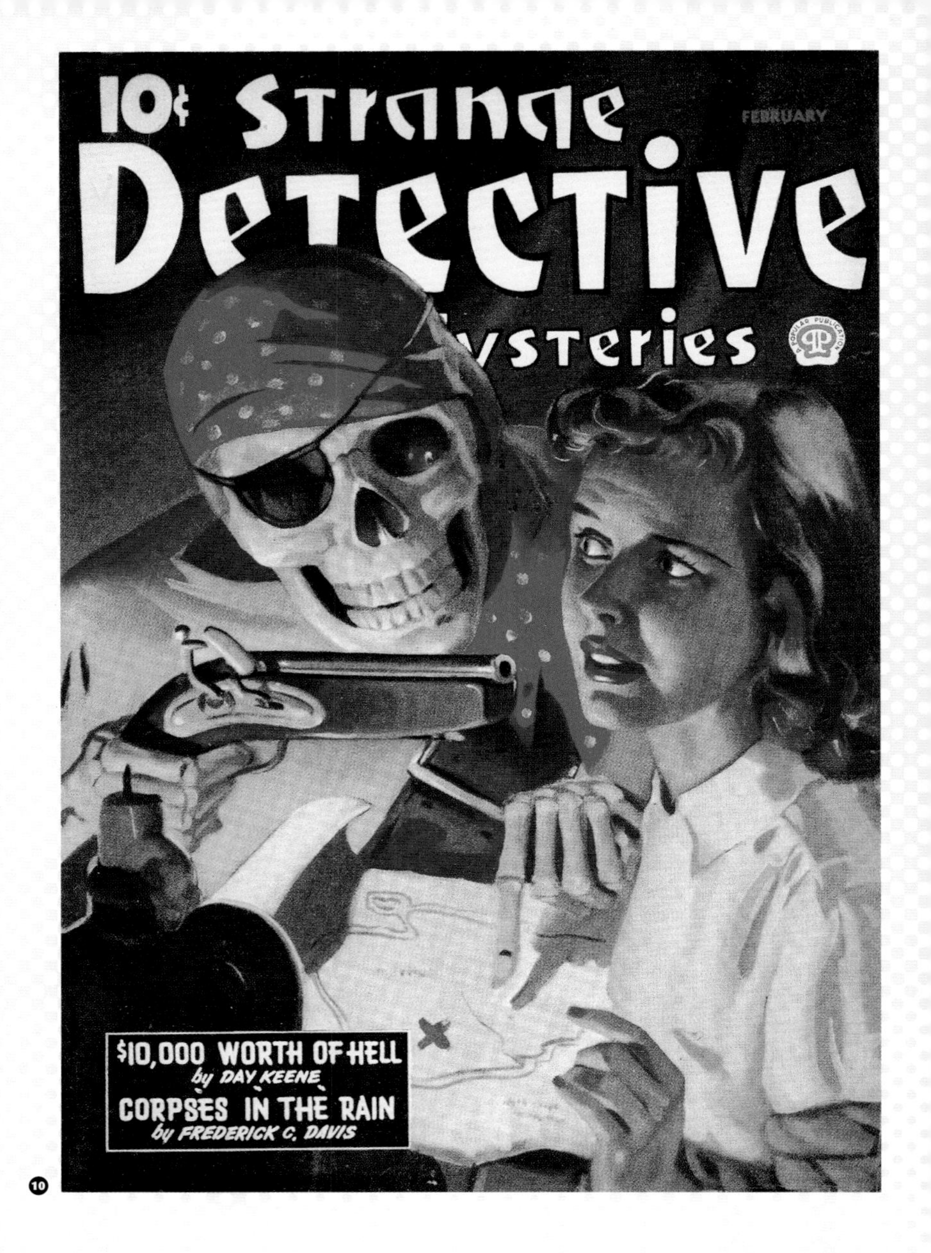

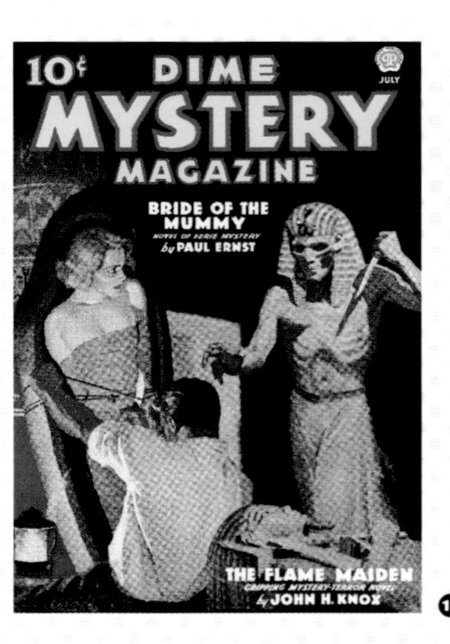

10 ••
Strange Detective Mysteries
February 1943
Unknown
Covers for Canadian editions were usually redrawn by Canadian artists and were sometimes more striking than the originals.

11 ••
Dime Mystery Magazine
July 1936
Tom Lovell
It was the curse of Ra once again.

The all-fiction magazines—soon nicknamed "pulps" because of the rough wood-pulp paper on which they were printed—were more influenced by Rudyard Kipling, Robert Louis Stevenson, and Edgar Allen Poe than they were by Frances Hodgson Burnett, author of *Little Lord Fauntleroy* and *The Secret Garden*, the latter a popular serial in *American Magazine*. And while the slicks didn't ignore western, mystery, or adventure stories, they could hardly afford to put all their fictional eggs in one basket. It remained for the pulps to introduce titles devoted to a single genre for those who loved stories of western sheriffs and outlaws or tales about the cops and robbers who lived and died on the streets of the big cities.

Much like the "story papers" of the last century, the pulps had their occasional literary star. The *New York Ledger*, a popular story paper of the 1850s and 1860s, once paid Charles Dickens $5,000 in 1859 dollars to keep company on its pages with "The Doom of Deville or, The Maiden's Vow" by E.D.E.N. Southworth, the leading sob-sister of her day when it came to fiction.

Seventy years later the pulps paid considerably less for Dashiell Hammett, Ray Bradbury, Raymond Chandler, and a score of others to add a touch of class to their magazines.

As the stories in the pulps became more sensational, so did the paintings on their front covers. The slicks sold their millions of copies through a combination of newsstand and, primarily, subscription sales. In the '30s many boys even had magazine routes for the *Saturday Evening Post* and *Liberty*, much like a newspaper route.

⓬ •
Detective Fiction Weekly
April 20, 1935
Unknown
A classic detective magazine cover.

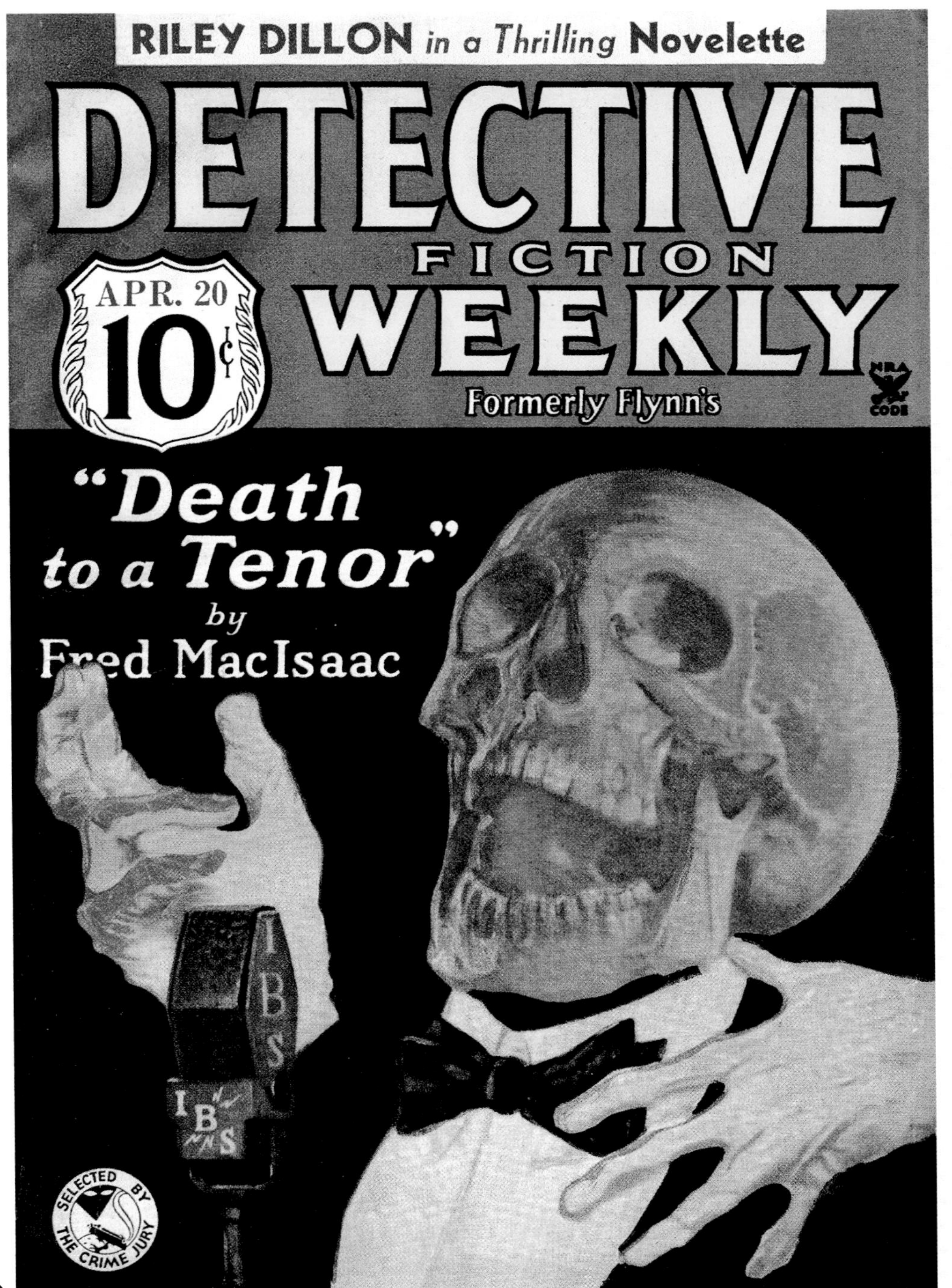

⓬

Pulps seldom had extensive subscription lists. They mainly sold off the newsstand. This meant they competed with dozens of other titles and required covers that grabbed the potential buyer's attention at a glance.

In the beginning there were relatively few pulps. Covers tended toward the sedate, showcasing minor works of art by N.C. Wyeth, Joseph Leyendecker, or Harvey Dunn (like Wyeth, a famous artist of the Howard Pyle school). Even early covers for Street & Smith's *Western Story Magazine* were relatively bucolic—an Indian astride his pony, a gold miner leading his mule, cowboys reading a magazine outside a bunkhouse.

⓭ ••
ASTOUNDING STORIES
January 1934
Howard V. Brown
One of the most striking science-fiction covers ever published.

⓮ •
WONDER STORIES
September 1935
Frank R. Paul
Menacing robots were a staple of science-fiction covers.

15 ••
FIFTH COLUMN STORIES
January 1941
Unknown
During World War II the country worried about a "fifth column" of spies and saboteurs.

15

18 ••
THE POPULAR MAGAZINE
September 1, 1930
Howard V. Brown
Call the Orkin man...

19 •
TOP-NOTCH
April 1, 1930
Robert A. Graef
Lester Dent was a favorite pulp author and the writer of most of the *Doc Savage* novels.

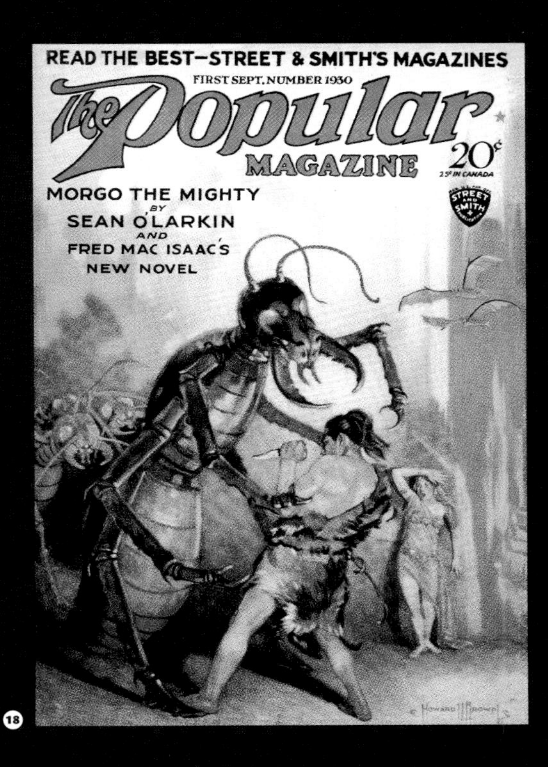

18

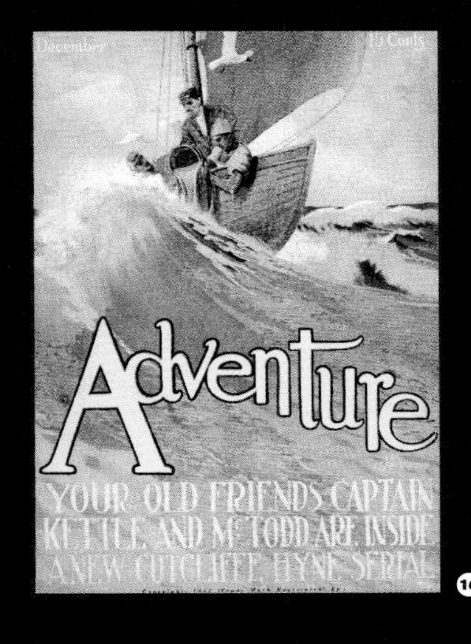

16

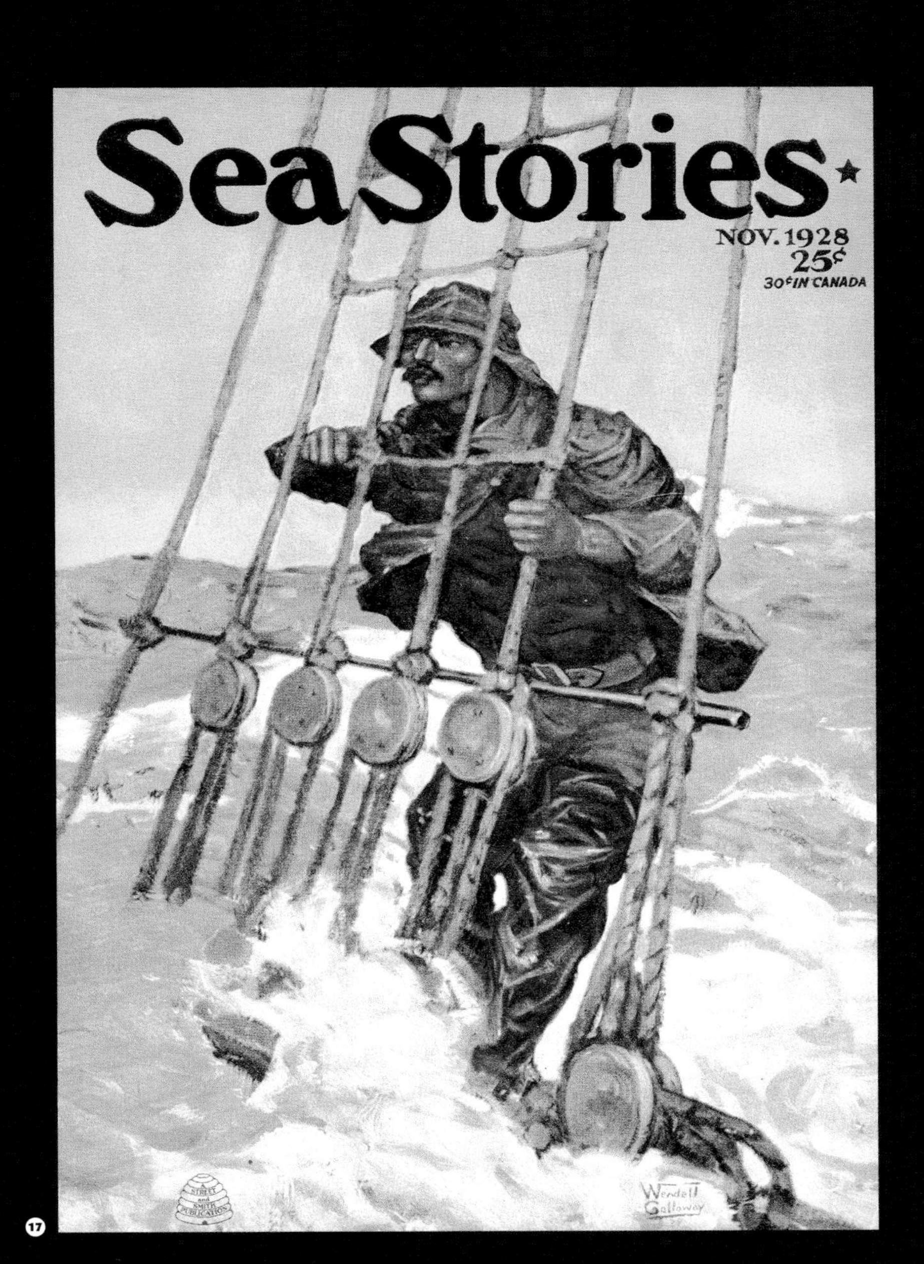

17

16 ••
ADVENTURE
December 1911
Lejaren Hiller
Probably the only issue of a magazine to run its title at the bottom.

17 ••
SEA STORIES
November 1928
Wendell Galloway
Sea Stories published some of the more evocative pulp covers.

19

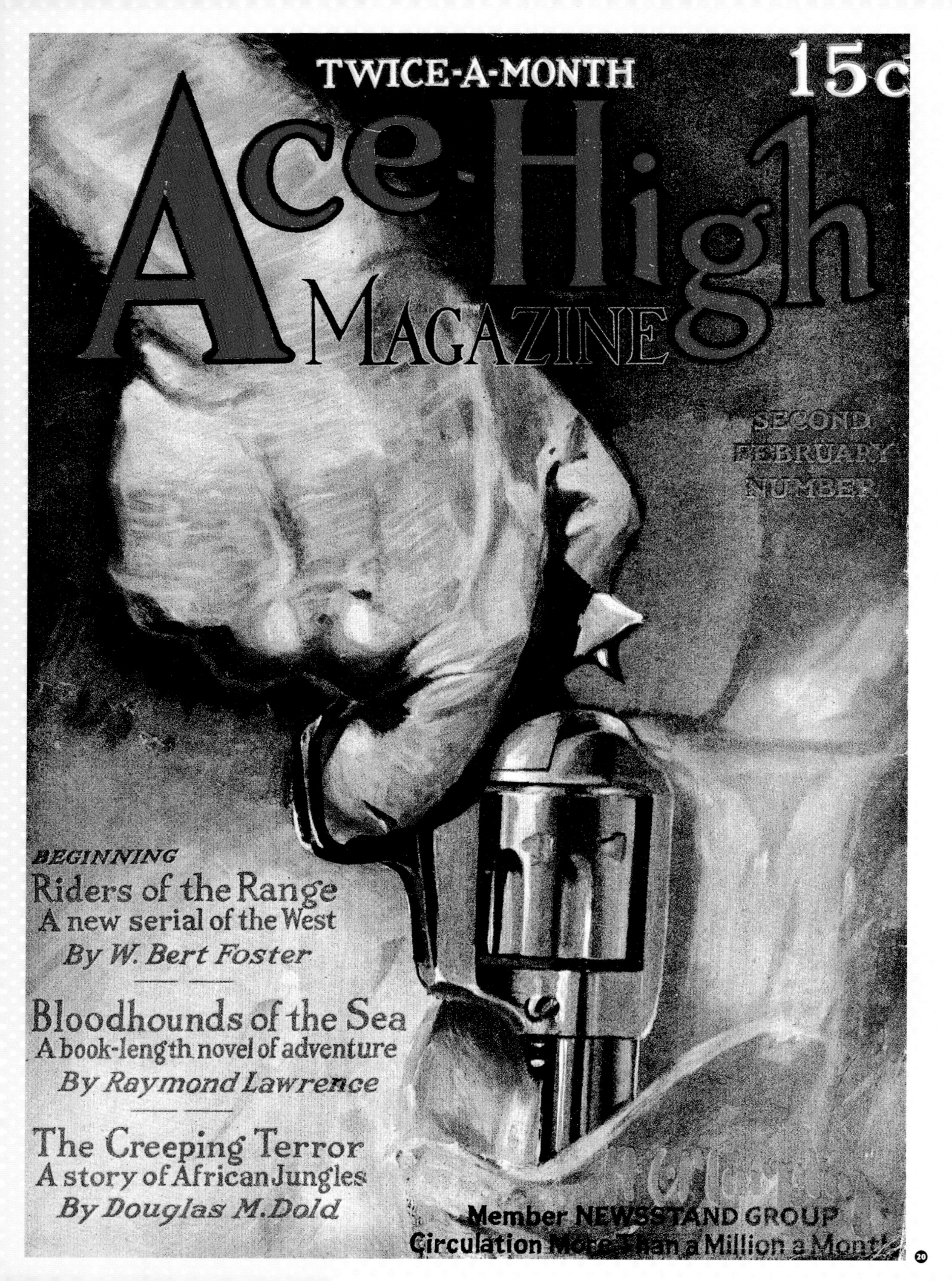

20

21 •••

SPICY MYSTERY STORIES
July 1936
H.J. Ward

The inspiration for the cover was probably the movie *King Kong*.

21

20 ••

ACE-HIGH MAGAZINE
February 2, 1923
H.C. Murphy

A surprisingly artistic study of a man and his gun.

The proliferation of titles and genres coupled with intense competition quickly changed this situation. Artists were as prized for their ability to depict action and strange or horrifying scenes as were the writers of the stories for their unique talents. Norman Rockwell made his name with his "small-town" covers for the *Post*. Walter M. Baumhofer was to gain his reputation with covers for western and adventure magazines; John Newton Howitt for the "shudder pulps"; Frank R. Paul and Howard V. Brown for science-fiction publications; George Gross for sports magazines; Frederick Blakeslee and Frank Tinsley for air pulps; plus a host of other talented painters who became identified with particular genres.

For the publisher the newsstands were a jungle out there, and he expected the cover artist to clear a path for his magazines.

When pulps finally died in the early '50s, many cover artists drifted to the slicks or into the paperback field. Not surprisingly a number went into portrait painting and fine art. The pulps had contributed more than their share to America's golden age of illustration, and what was left behind were the covers the artists had painted, snapshots of a portion of popular culture that had vanished forever.

Many of the cover paintings were junked, thrown into an alley for the garbageman to pick up. A very few by the more famous artists found their way into museums. Collectors of the old pulps purchased a large number, or they were auctioned off at various conventions. In fact, probably more science-fiction and fantasy art is available now simply because it was auctioned at conventions from the '40s on.

But the covers themselves remain a chronicle of the past, as important as the stories they illustrated and the magazines they promoted. In one sense we can compare the old covers to the special effects in contemporary movies. They were what grabbed the eye, made you buy the magazine, and stayed with you in your imagination as you read the story.

No history of the old pulp magazines can be complete without a gallery of the cover art that enticed the reader and sparked the imagination. It's our hope that we've presented such a gallery: one that's not only a history but a feast for the eye and a guide to what thrilled and beguiled the readers of yesteryear.

Frank M. Robinson and Lawrence Davidson

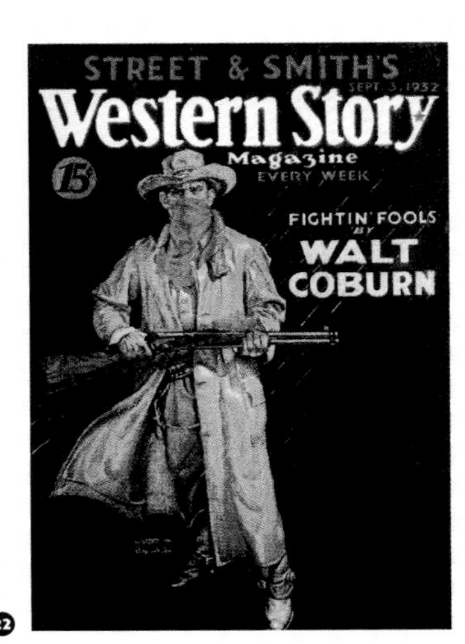

22

22 •
Western Story Magazine
September 3, 1932
Walter M. Baumhofer
Artist Baumhofer could paint in almost any genre but was particularly good at covers for Western pulps.

In the Beginning

The pulp magazines were born at the turn of the century and flourished in a country where entertainment was a scarce commodity. It was a simpler life then, one in which the family used the parlor only on Sunday and the bathroom was an outhouse in the backyard.

Its entertainment was simple as well. The most common and the cheapest was reading. At the top of the list was the newspaper. In 1900 New York City alone boasted sixteen dailies. Following close behind were the mass-circulation magazines such as *Cosmopolitan*, *Munsey's*, and *McClure's*, plus the "story papers" and dime novels.

The story papers were once-a-week newspapers. Most, like the *New York Ledger* and *New York Fireside Companion*, published family fiction, while others, *The Boys of New York* and *Street & Smith's New York Weekly* among them, serialized more exciting stories starring Buffalo Bill or Nick Carter, as well as epics such as "One More Unfortunate; or, Nelly the Newsgirl."

The story papers faded toward the end of the century. The general magazines replaced the family-oriented papers, and dime novels such as *Pluck and Luck*, *Brave and Bold*, and *Secret Service* substituted for those papers designed for boys. The general size of today's "golden age" comic books, they featured a single, self-contained story along with a colorful, comic-book type cover.

1 ••
HE ARGOSY
ctober 1896
nknown
he first issue of the first pulp magazine published.

2 ••
HE ARGOSY
ctober 1905
nknown
he first issue of *Argosy* to use front-cover painting.

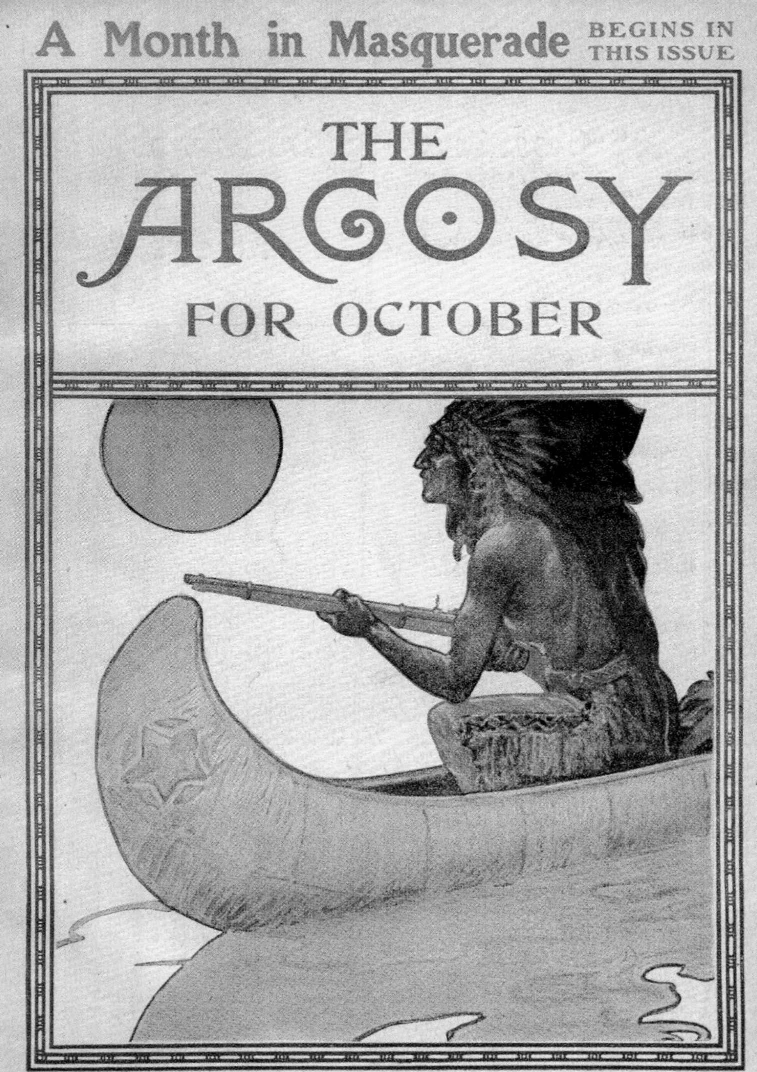

By the end of the century, the story papers had largely disappeared, but the dime novels sold in the millions. Twenty years later they, too, were gone, and the magazine field had expanded to include the "pulps," all-fiction magazines that specialized in short stories and serials running the gamut from westerns and mysteries to love stories and science-fiction. Everybody read them, from young women entranced by romantic tales that invariably ended happily to teenage boys who smuggled the magazines into bed at night to read about the Wild West or the mountains of Mars.

Almost all the pulps at the start were intended for family reading and were distinguished from general magazines primarily by the paper they were printed on

3 •
THE ARGOSY
June 1915
Modest Stein
H. Bedford-Jones was to become a leading writer for the pulps in the '30s.

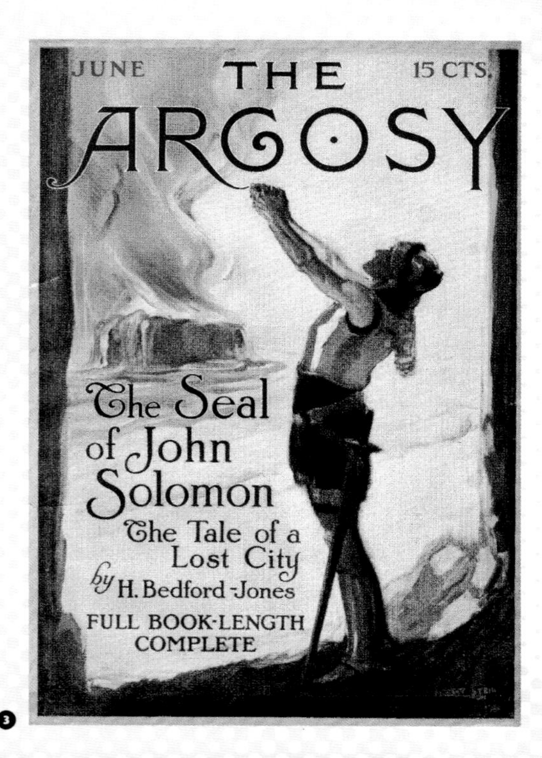

and by their emphasis on fiction. Many authors wrote for both, though the pulps preferred far more action and simpler plots than the slicks were comfortable with.

With time, especially during the Depression, the pulps became more sensational. They reached their peak in the '20s and '30s, declined in popularity after World War II, and finally died in the early '50s, their readership split among those preferring the even more sensational comic books, the convenience of paperbacks, or the soap operas, dramas, and comedies television provided for free.

The creation of the first pulp probably was as much a move of desperation as a stroke of publishing genius. Frank A. Munsey, a farmer's son from Maine, had founded *The Golden Argosy*, a boy's weekly, in 1882. Munsey personally wrote much of the material and even sold the ads. The magazine staggered along for thirteen years through various size and title changes with little enduring success.

In 1889 Munsey launched *Munsey's Weekly*, a twenty-five cent magazine the size of today's *National Geographic*. It was printed on coated stock and carried photographs along with an editorial mix of articles and fiction. Unfortunately it, too, was a mediocre success until Munsey slashed the price to ten cents in 1893. The low-priced *Munsey's Magazine*, now a monthly, was an immediate bestseller. Munsey may have been unsure of just what the public wanted, but he had a very good idea of what the public was willing to pay for it.

4

4 •
THE ARGOSY
September 1914
Modest Stein
Zane Grey was one of the most popular authors of his day.

5 •

The Popular Magazine
November 15, 1909
N.C. Wyeth
The most famous of the covers for *Popular* by artist N.C. Wyeth.

5

Success for *Argosy* came three years later. By 1896 the magazine had evolved from a slim, youth-oriented weekly, with a page size similar to that of *Time*, to an anemic monthly imitator of *Munsey's*. Like the latter, the contents were a mix of essays and articles—some illustrated with photographs, poems, and fiction—all printed on "slick" paper.

The mix worked well for *Munsey's Magazine* but failed to do much for *Argosy*, which continued to founder. Munsey was faced with combining *Argosy* with *Munsey's* (later he became notorious for coupling failing titles with successful ones), publishing it as cheaply as he could, hoping it would at least break even, or folding it and servicing the subscription list with copies of *Munsey's*.

Effective with the October 1896 issue, and with no prior announcement whatsoever, *Argosy* dropped its articles and photographs, switched to a low-cost pulp paper, and featured only fiction.

What remained was the cheapest package possible to produce. It was also far less inviting to read: page after page of columns of solid type running the full width of the magazine, broken up only by the occasional bit of poetry. The yellow cover was bare except for the title, date, subscription rates, address, and slogan: "The biggest magazine in the World. A Dollar's worth of reading for Ten Cents."

The magazine had only one thing going for it. It was 192 pages of pure fiction, and fiction was what the readers really wanted. They would not miss the bland travel essays and articles with their equally bland and badly printed photographs.

6 •
The Popular Magazine
March 1909
J.C. Leyendecker
A romantic cover by the creator of the Arrow Collar Man.

7 •
The Popular Magazine
November 1, 1909
J.C. Leyendecker
Artist Joseph Leyendecker had a flair for painting football players.

8 •
All-Story Cavalier Weekly
January 16, 1915
Unknown
Sometimes early pulps had stylized covers.

9 •
All-Story Weekly
January 24, 1920
Modest Stein
The "Golden Atom" stories by Ray Cummings were classics of the fantastic.

8

10¢ PER COPY SATURDAY JAN. 24 BY THE YEAR $4.00
ALL-STORY WEEKLY
The People of the Golden Atom
by Ray Cummings
A Sequel to "The Girl in the Golden Atom."

9

10

10 •••
All-Story Cavalier Weekly
May 16, 1914
F.W. Small
One of the first of many sequels to *Tarzan of the Apes*.

The magazine doubled in circulation, stabilizing at eighty thousand for a few years, then suddenly doubling and doubling again. At its heyday in the teens, *Argosy* had a circulation of seven hundred thousand, the high-water mark for any pulp.

Munsey had the all-fiction field to himself until 1903. *The Popular Magazine* was a slim entry from Street & Smith, known primarily for its story papers and dime novels. It wasn't much competition—ninety-six pages of fiction aimed primarily at boys—though it did have a full-color cover, which *Argosy* wouldn't adopt for years.

Street & Smith got serious when it discovered more men than boys were reading the magazine. It increased the pages to 192 and included "name" authors to pump its circulation. In 1905 Munsey added *All-Story*, and the Story Press Corporation of Chicago brought out *The Monthly Story Magazine*, soon to evolve into *Blue Book*. A few years later, Munsey launched *Cavalier* as still another all-fiction, pulp-paper magazine. In 1912, *Cavalier* became the first weekly pulp.

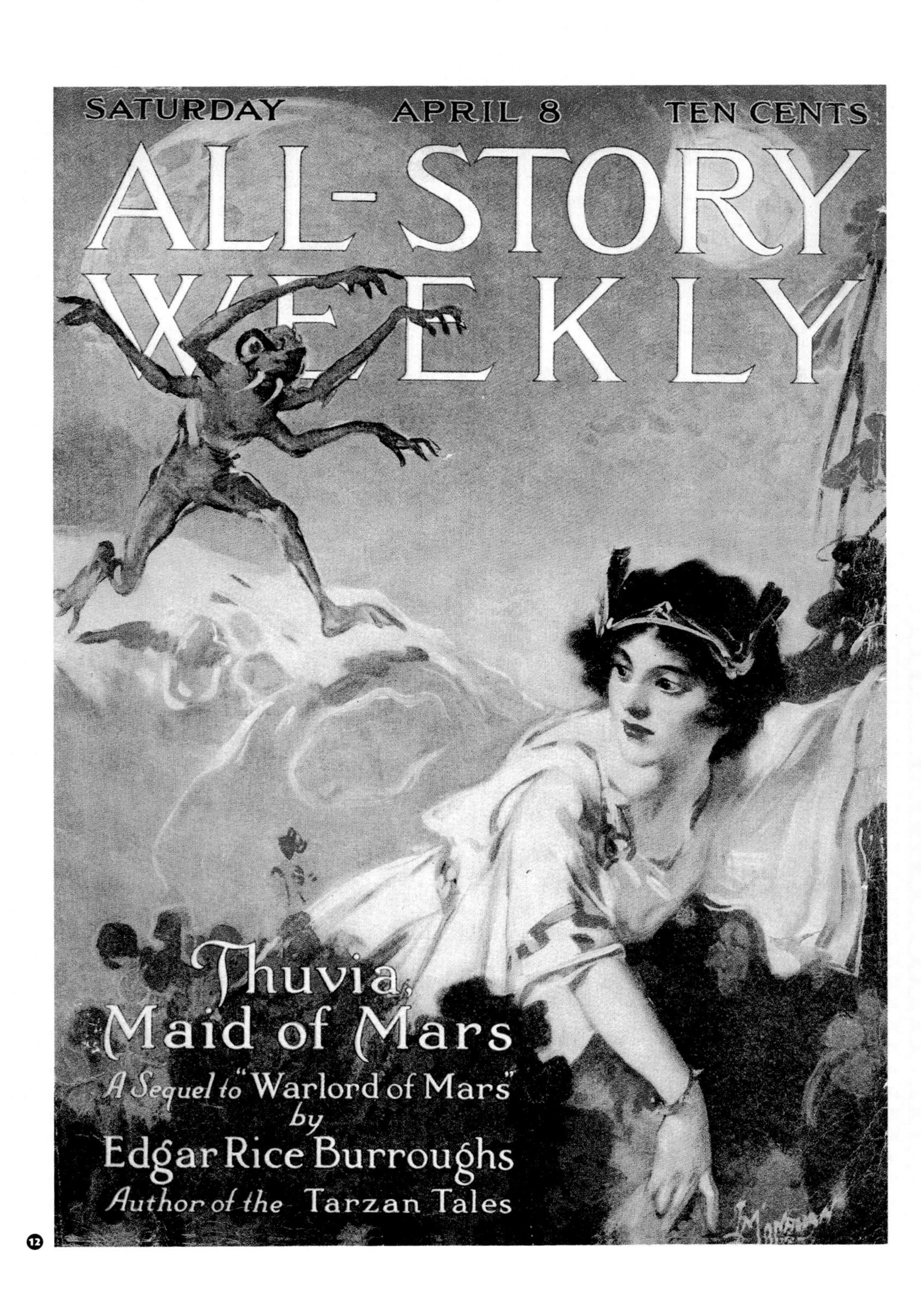

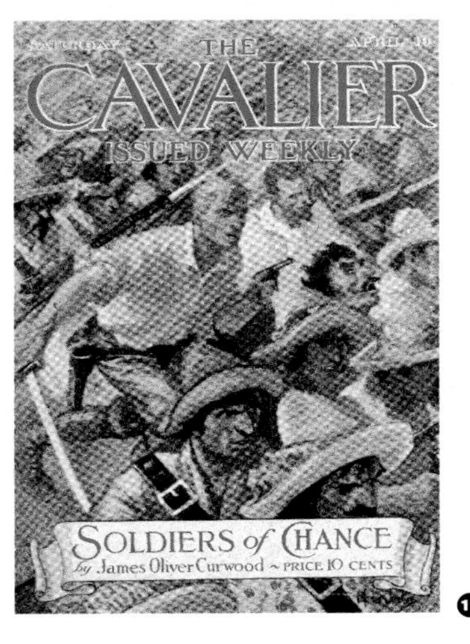

⓫ •
THE CAVALIER
April 19, 1913
Martin Justice
The Cavalier was the first weekly pulp magazine.

⓬ ••
ALL-STORY WEEKLY
April 8, 1916
P.J. Monahan
Edgar Rice Burroughs's stories about Mars were reader favorites.

13 •
Tip Top Semi-Monthly
November 25, 1915
Unknown
Another dime novel that changed into an early pulp.

14 ••
Wild West Weekly
August 13, 1927
Remington Schuyler
The last dime novel to convert to a pulp. The lead story was about young Billy "Wild" West.

15

WESTERN STORY MAGAZINE
January 8, 1921
Nick Eggenhofer
A "gag" cover by artist Eggenhofer. The boys in the bunkhouse are reading a copy of—you guessed it—*Western Story Magazine*.

16

17

16 •
WESTERN STORY MAGAZINE
April 23, 1921
Lon Megaree
One of the few realistic covers of a Native American before Indians were stereotyped as savages complete with war bonnets and tomahawks.

17 •
WESTERN STORY MAGAZINE
April 2, 1921
Unknown
Ride 'em, cowboy!

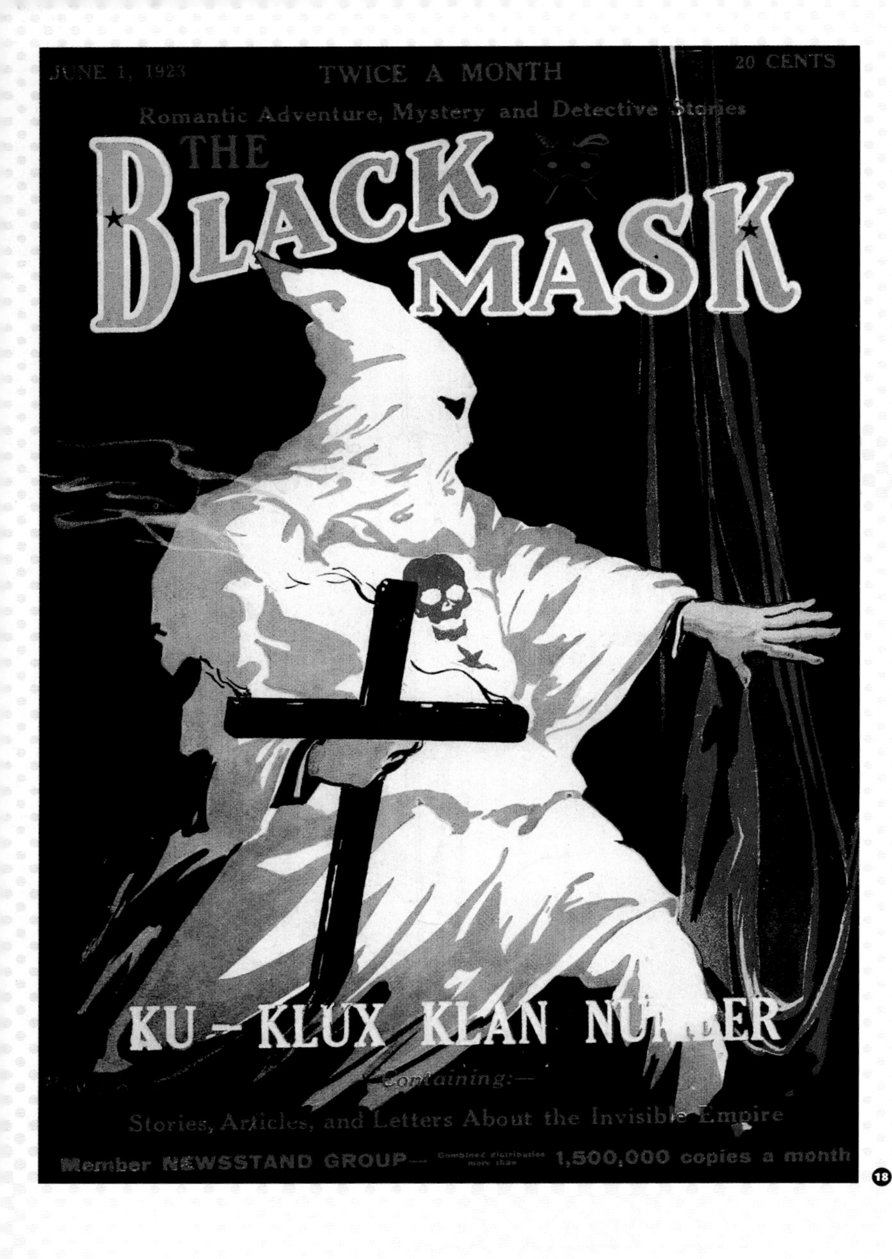

18 •••

The Black Mask
June 1, 1923
L.L. Balcom

"Race Williams," the first "private eye," appeared in this issue. The magazine, incidentally, was subtly supportive of the Klan.

19 •••

The Black Mask
December 1, 1923
L.L. Balcom

The early covers for *Black Mask* sometimes had an element of the fantastic.

20 •••

New Story Magazine
February 1914
N.C. Wyeth

Newell Convers Wyeth was a fine illustrator and a great art teacher—the only one his son, Andrew Wyeth, had.

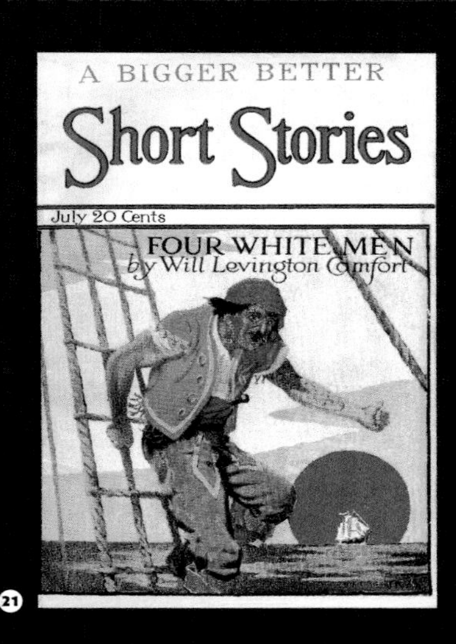

23 •••••
Weird Tales
March 1923
Richard R. Epperly
The first issue of a magazine that later introduced Tennessee Williams, Robert E. Howard, H.P. Lovecraft, Robert Bloch, and many others.

24 ••
Ace-High Magazine
November 1921
William C. McNulty
An early adventure pulp that later specialized in Westerns.

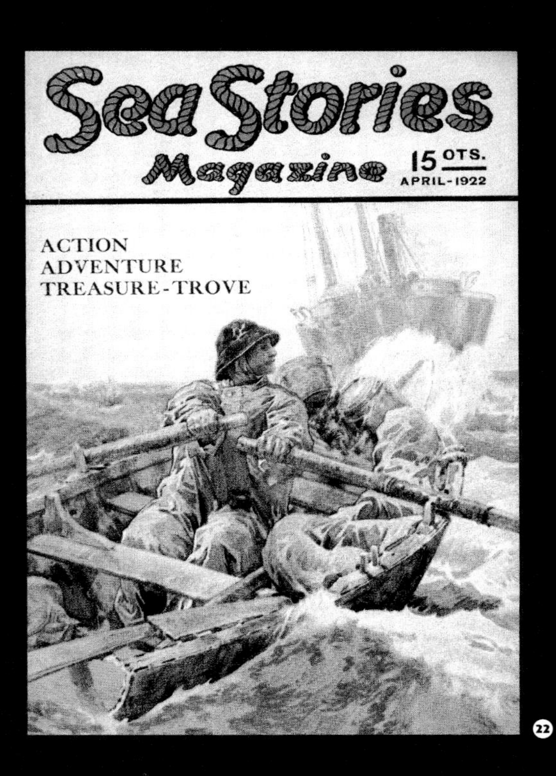

25 •
Action Stories
February 1924
H.C. Murphy
An early adventure title that lasted until the '50s—but it never, ever paid ten grand for story plots.

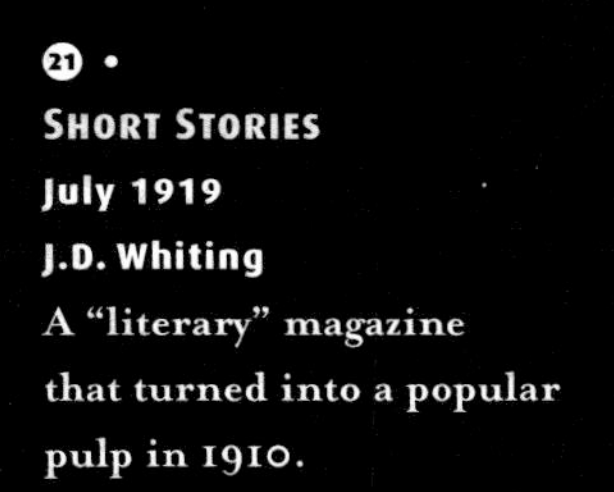

21 •
Short Stories
July 1919
J.D. Whiting
A "literary" magazine that turned into a popular pulp in 1910.

22 ••
Sea Stories Magazine
April 1922
Anton Otto Fischer
The rope logo was a distinctive touch.

26 • •
THE RAILROAD MAN'S MAGAZINE
October 1906
Unknown
The first issue of the first specialized pulp published, relying solely on type to advertise fact and fiction for the railroad buff.

27 • •
RAILROAD MAN'S MAGAZINE
November 16, 1918
Unknown
It must have startled the readers—a serial about the Vikings!

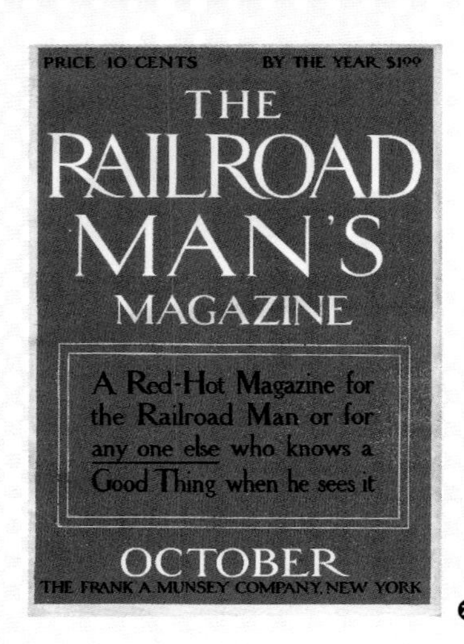

26

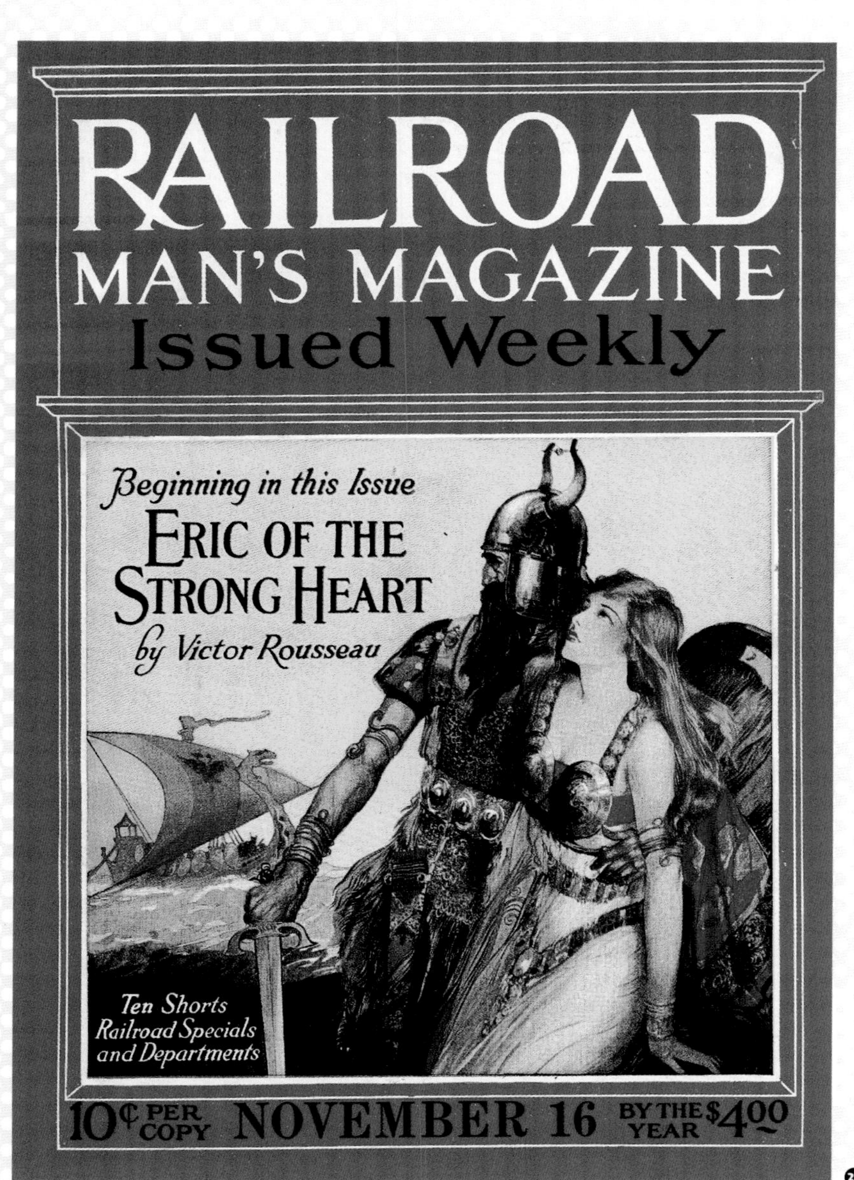

27

The last major competitor to *Argosy* was *Adventure*, started in late 1910. *Adventure* cost fifteen cents and definitely was an upscale magazine with an interior illustration and hand-lettered title for each story. The first five issues were printed on high-quality book paper; then the magazine reverted to cheaper wood-pulp stock.

Almost as significant as Munsey's conversion of *Argosy* to an all-fiction format was his decision to publish magazines specializing in specific subjects. He started *The Railroad Man's Magazine*, devoted to fiction and fact about railroading, in 1906. He followed it with *The Ocean*, an attempt to do the same thing for life on the bounding main, in 1907. *The Ocean* sank within eleven issues, but *Railroad Magazine*, its final title, continued until the late '70s.

The next step was further specialization within a strictly fiction format. Street & Smith converted its dime novel *Nick Carter Stories* into the pulp *Detective Story Magazine* in 1915. *Buffalo Bill Weekly* became *Western Story Magazine* in 1919. *Wild West Weekly*, a dime novel published by Frank Tousey, didn't make the transition to pulp format until Street & Smith bought it in 1927. Street & Smith added still more pulp titles with *Love Story*, *Sea Stories*, and *Sport Story Magazine* in the early '20s.

More than most publishers, perhaps because of its early involvement with dime novels and story papers, Street & Smith was well aware that cover art had potent sales appeal. Its *New Story*, *All Around*, and *Popular Magazine* featured covers by Joseph Leyendecker and N.C. Wyeth (father of Andrew), as well as other famous illustrators of the period.

28 •••

Detective Story Magazine
October 5, 1915
Unknown
The first issue of the first all-fiction specialized pulp, formerly the dime novel *Nick Carter Stories*.

29 ••

Detective Story Magazine
May 14, 1927
John A. Coughlin
It was a shock to the loyal reader—but Nick Carter returned, not only in *Detective Story* but later in his own magazine.

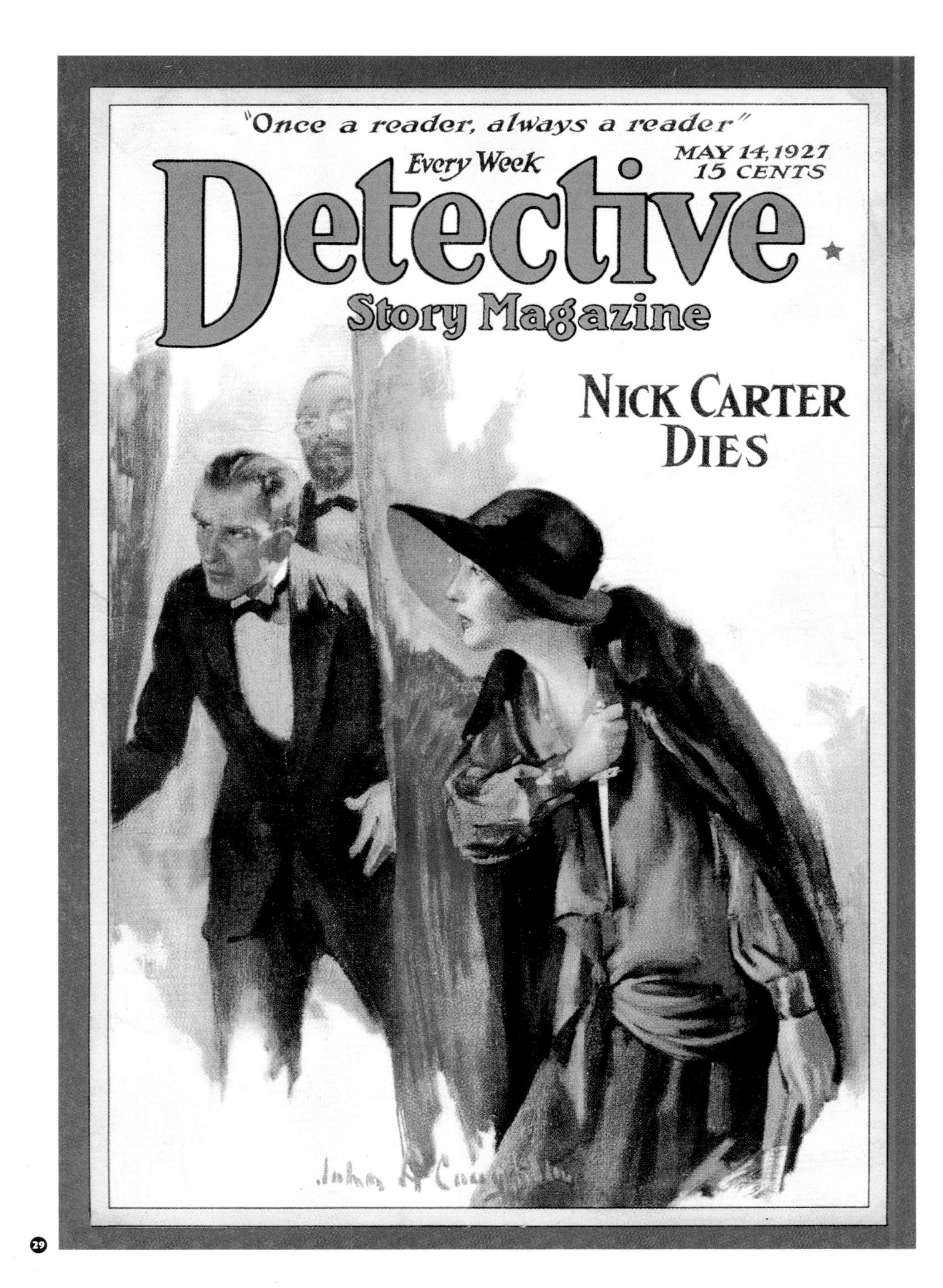

30 ••

Mystery Magazine
January 1927
Fred T. Everett
Mystery Magazine specialized in gorgeous art deco covers, but they didn't help sales.

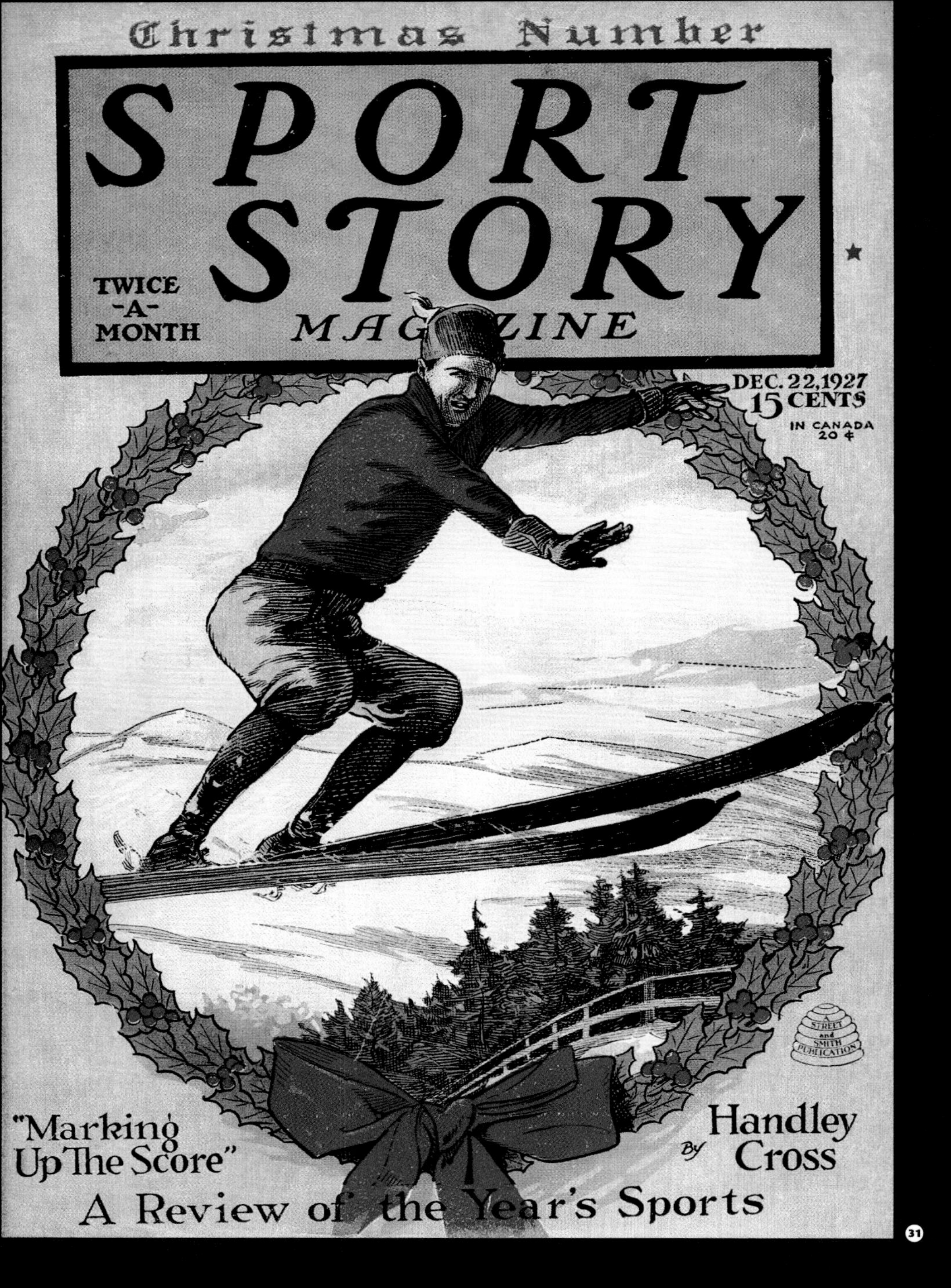

31

33

33 •
Top-Notch Magazine
March 15, 1916
Unknown
An unusual cover for a magazine—one with great poster appeal.

32

31 •
Sport Story Magazine
December 22, 1927
Unknown
A Christmas cover for the first of the sports pulps.

32 •
Sport Story Magazine
May 22, 1924
Unknown
The first sports title—and by far the most diversified in the different sports it covered.

34 ••
Adventure
July 1913
Sidney Riesenberg
The most unusual color scheme ever published for a magazine title.

35 •
Top-Notch Magazine
July 15, 1920
Unknown
An update of Jules Verne's *Around the World in Eighty Days.*

Leyendecker went on to paint numerous covers for the *Saturday Evening Post* and became famous as the creator of the "Arrow Collar" man. Wyeth was to have an illustrious career as a children's book illustrator, creating the definitive illustrated versions of Robert Louis Stevenson's *Treasure Island* and *The Black Arrow*, as well as James Fenimore Cooper's *The Deerslayer* and Marjorie Kinnan Rawlings's *The Yearling*, all for Charles Scribner's Sons.

With time cover art for the pulps became as sensational as the contents, and the schism between pulps and slicks became even deeper. The slicks favored bucolic versions of American life by artists like Norman Rockwell. The pulps of the late '20s through the '30s preferred action scenes with the type

36 ••
Adventure
November 1911
Charles B. Falls
Riflemen in planes were on covers eight years after Kitty Hawk.

of jut-jawed heroes that Walter M. Baumhofer painted for *Doc Savage* and *Western Story*, or with the graphic sadism of a John Newton Howitt for *Terror Tales* or Tom Lovell for *Dime Mystery*.

At the same time more publishers began to move in, not so much to compete with the general pulps, such as *Argosy* or *Popular Magazine*, as with the genres of western, love, or mystery. In some cases, they even created niche markets unique to their own publication. Starting a pulp magazine was a far less risky proposition than starting a slick, and many entrepreneurs tried their hand at publishing one. *Ace-High*, *Triple-X*, and *Action Stories* appeared in the early '20s, as did *Black Mask*, which, at least initially, combined detective tales with western and aviation stories.

The future lay in specialization, and by the time the pulps finally died, more than twelve hundred different titles had appeared, exploiting every human endeavor from making love to making money, from throwing a football to flying a Zeppelin.

The *Saturday Evening Post*, *Collier's*, and *Liberty* printed a variety of fiction appealing to the entire family. The pulps, on the other hand, became more and more dedicated to the reader who preferred only westerns or mysteries—or, for that matter, only stories taking place in African jungles or chronicling the adventures of urban firemen.

37 •
THE BLUE BOOK MAGAZINE
October 1907
Unknown
In 1907 this passed for a beautiful and sexy cover.

38 •
THE BLUE BOOK MAGAZINE
November 1921
Laurence Herndon
Both Oppenheim and Agatha Christie wrote for the early *Blue Book*.

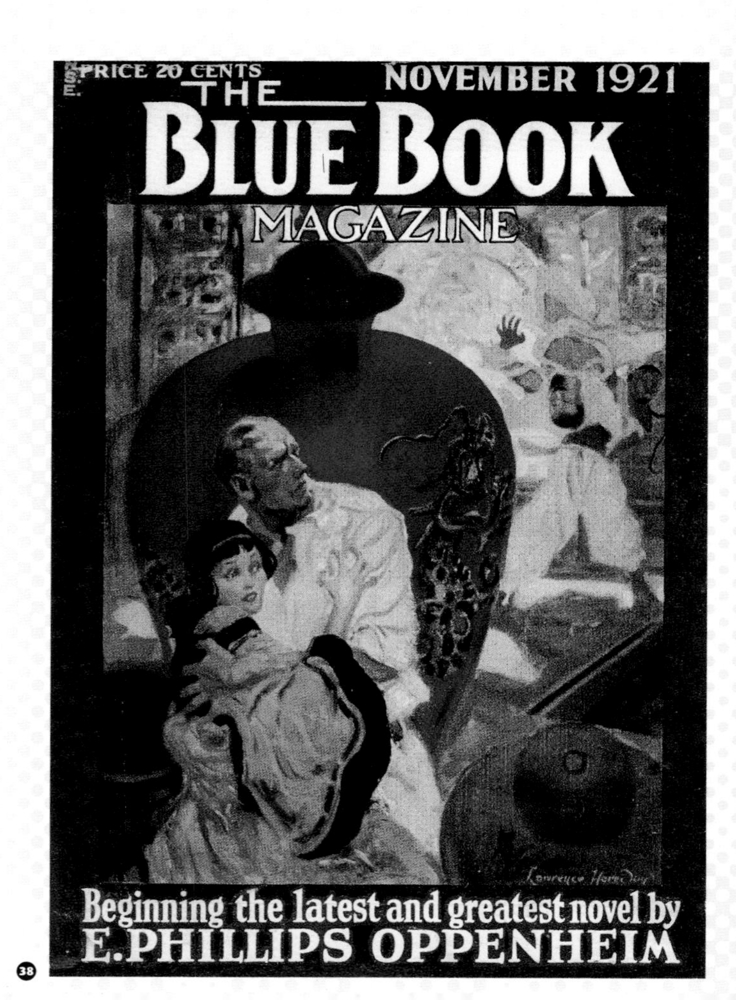

39 •

Women's Stories
September 1914
Robert A. Graef
The first all-fiction women's magazine didn't last long.

39

40

40 • •

All Around Magazine
September 1916
Francis Miller
All Around was an early pulp designed for the entire family.

41 •

Snappy Stories
October 25, 1921
Nathan R. Gould
Snappy Stories should have been called *Flapper Stories*.

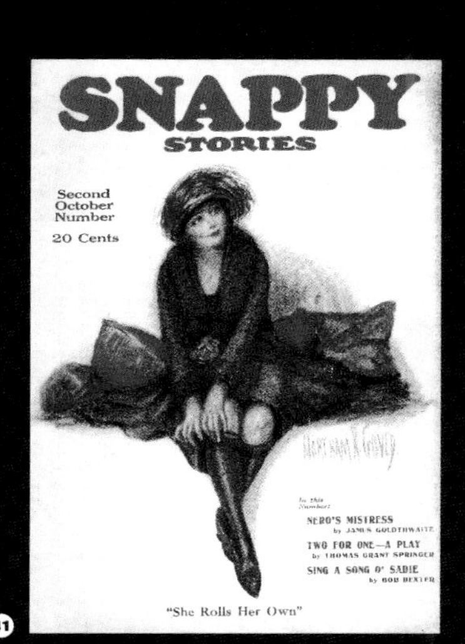

41

Tales of Timbuktu

Adventures in Exotic Lands

One of the first and most successful areas of specialization for pulp magazines was adventure. Early pulps quickly became action-oriented, and action implied adventure and exotic locales. Even the "family" pulps like *Argosy*, *Blue Book*, and *Popular Magazine* embraced the action formula.

The most successful of the pure adventure magazines was the original *Adventure* called, on its Silver Anniversary in 1935, "The No. 1 Pulp" by *Time* and "Dean of the Pulps" by *Newsweek*. *Adventure's* first issue was published in November 1910, and for most of its life the magazine maintained a standard of quality that no other pulp in its field, with the possible exception of *Argosy* or *Blue Book*, ever equaled.

Despite its title the magazine was more of a general pulp with no departments and the occasional bit of fiction slanted for women readers. That direction changed quickly when Arthur Sullivant Hoffman replaced Trumbull White as editor in 1912. During the early years Hoffman had as his assistant a young Sinclair Lewis, in 1930 the first American writer to win the Nobel prize.

Hoffman devoted as much time to the magazine's departments as he did to its fiction, even creating an "identity card" for the readers. The magazine assigned each reader requesting one a card with a serial number printed on it. The intent was that if he or she were killed or injured while carrying the card, the individual

2 •
ADVENTURE
October 15, 1931
Gerard C. Delano
Asian villains were stereotypes with skull caps and pigtails.

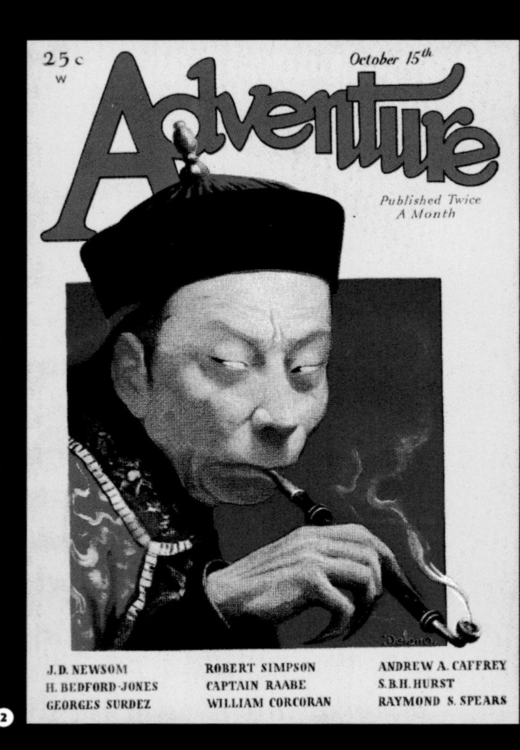

1 •
ADVENTURE
June 1, 1929
V.E. Pyles
Darkest Africa was always the perfect setting for adventure.

coming upon the accident would notify the magazine, which in turn would notify the next-of-kin. Since many of the magazine's readers were genuine soldiers of fortune, the card was immediately popular. Card bearers struck up friendships, eventually resulting in formation of The Adventurers Club of New York.

The magazine also was largely responsible for creation of the American Legion. In 1915 many people worried about the country's lack of preparedness for war, and patriotism soared to a fever pitch. The Adventurers Club even threw out several members

4

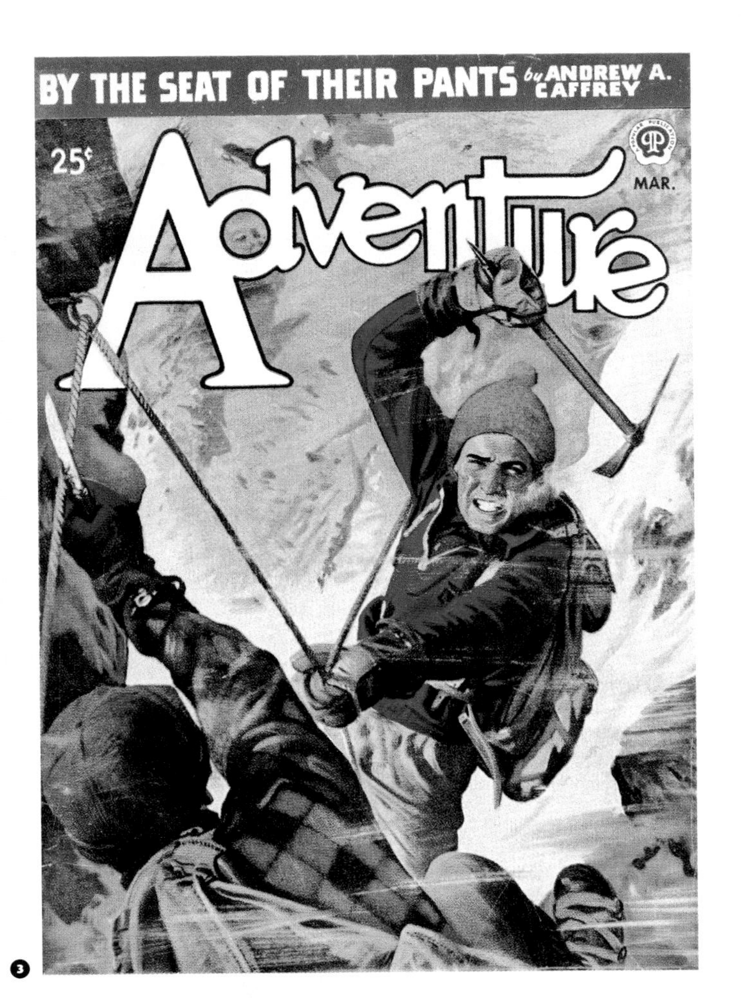

3

3 •
ADVENTURE
March 1947
Peter Stevens
Everest had yet to be conquered, but mountain climbing was still high adventure.

4 •
ADVENTURE
November 1939
Wesley Neff
This effective cover was probably a photograph the artist had doctored.

for making speeches considered disloyal. (Reports were that one of the excommunicated members was Sinclair Lewis, Hoffman's former assistant.)

Through the magazine, members could enroll in an organization named the Legion, which boasted Theodore Roosevelt as one of its vice-presidents and Hoffman, editor of *Adventure*, as secretary. Noted on membership cards were the owner's skills and specialties. The magazine forwarded card holders names and stated abilities to the War Department once the U.S. declared war, and the government used this information in forming two regiments of aviation mechanics. After the war the Legion became an organization of veterans—the American Legion.

The magazine's letter column, "The Camp-Fire," was a forum where readers could argue whether an author was correct with the facts in his or her story. Readers were anything but casual in their analysis of the fiction and countless lines of type were expended on the historical accuracy, type of weapons the characters used, geography and terrain where the stories occurred, and so forth.

The biggest brouhaha took place when popular author Talbot Mundy wrote a long letter essentially attacking the character and morals of Julius Caesar, causing a debate that raged for months in the column.

Another popular column was "Lost Trails," which helped readers find lost family members and friends. Anticipating the personals in today's *Soldier of Fortune* magazine, "Wanted—Men and Adventurers" was a column where readers could advertise their qualifications for jobs on the riskier side of life—or offer jobs in the same area.

Then there was "Ask Adventure," where readers could write in asking questions about practically anything and receive a personal response from an expert in the field. And among the writers and readers of *Adventure*, there was no end of experts.

Departments continued to proliferate. One was titled "Various Practical Services Free to Any Reader," listing, for example, places to write for advice on the best fishing in North America or for details about firearms. Another suggestion by Hoffman was that readers establish "Camp Fire Stations" where they could meet other readers of the magazine, a precursor to the science-fiction fan clubs that came along years later. By the mid-'20s hundreds of Camp Fire Stations were scattered around the world.

Adventure was no longer just a magazine; it had become a way of life. It was, as Richard Bleiler states in his *Index to Adventure Magazine*, "the most important pulp magazine in the world."

5 ••
Blue Book Magazine
February 1932
Laurence Herndon
In the early '30s *Blue Book* was a large-format pulp—but one still featuring stereotypical Asian villains.

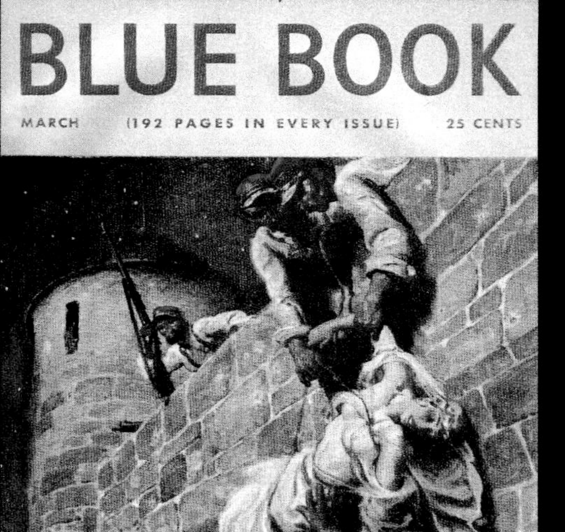

6

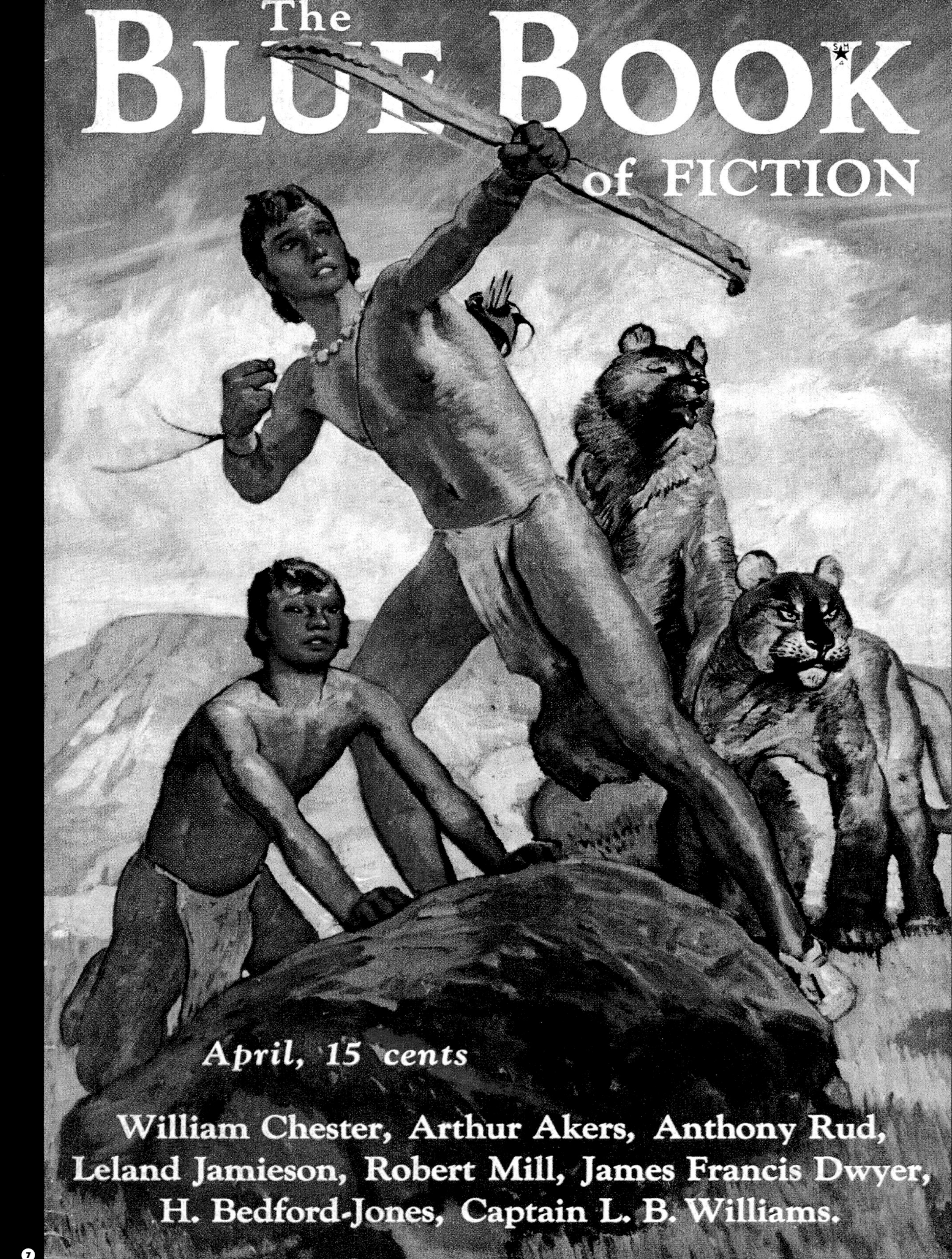

6 •
Blue Book
March 1940
Herbert Morton Stoops
A surprisingly nude cover for the usually conservative *Blue Book*.

7 •
Blue Book
April 1937
Herbert Morton Stoops
The "hawk of the wilderness," featured on the cover, was a white boy adopted by Indians.

7

8

Argosy

March 2, 1929

Robert A. Graef

A beautiful mermaid and a violinist—how lyrical could a pulp cover get?

9

Argosy

February 6, 1937

V.E. Pyles

Zombies on the outside and Edgar Rice Burroughs and L. Ron Hubbard on the inside. What more could the reader want?

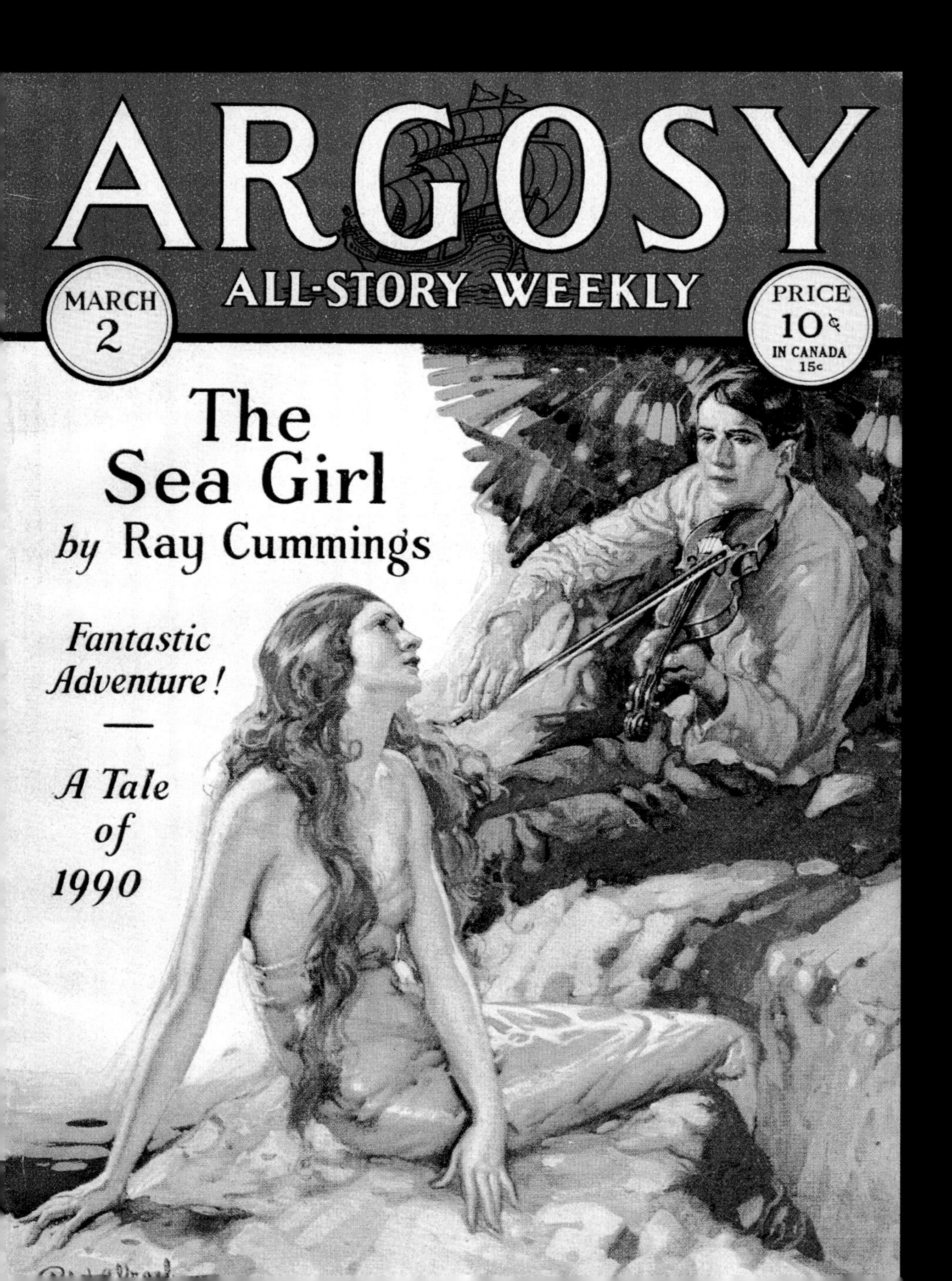

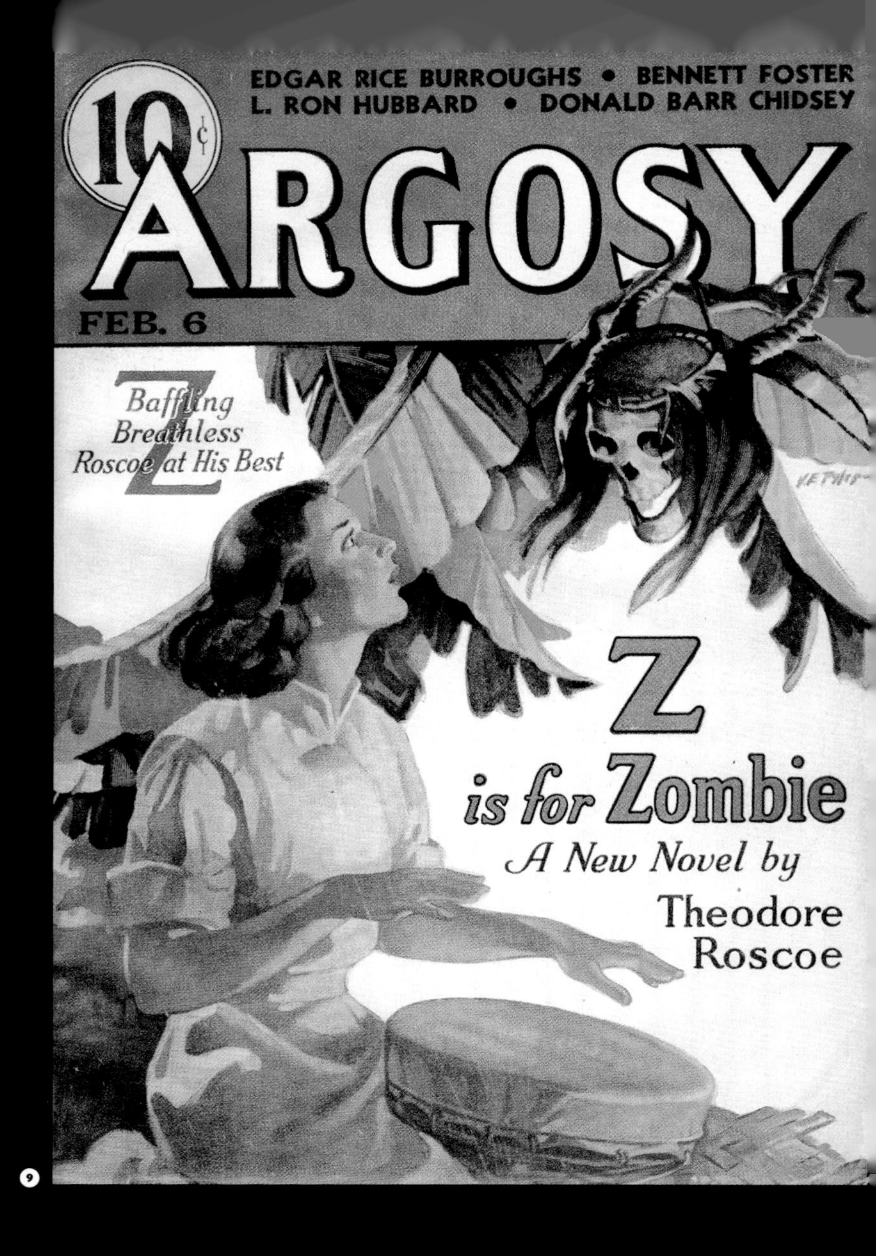

9

10 •

Argosy

April 16, 1932

Robert A. Graef

Giant bugs were always popular on pulp covers

Argosy also featured adventure stories, as did *Blue Book* and *Short Stories*. *Action Stories* was exclusively adventure, as were *Red Blooded Stories* and *Danger Trail*. *Top-Notch*, *Complete Stories*, *Short Stories*, and *Five-Novels Monthly* were among other magazines specializing in adventure stories, though none equaled the original. *Adventure*, usually costing a nickel more than the competition for much of its life, was expensive. But then you got far more than just a magazine; you actually were buying a membership in a select brotherhood. More than most editors, Arthur Sullivant Hoffman was adept at selling the sizzle as well as the steak. It was obvious in the time and thought lavished on the magazine that for editor Hoffman, the magazine was much more than just a magazine.

Many authors who wrote for *Adventure* based their stories on personal experience. Arthur O. Friel had explored the jungles of the Orinoco in Venezuela. W.C. Tuttle, famed for his western stories, was the son of the sheriff of Dawson County, Montana, while author Gordon MacCreagh explored Abyssinia in 1927, searching for the lost Ark of the Covenant (shades of *Raiders of the Lost Ark*!).

The most popular author for *Adventure* was Talbot Mundy, with more than 160 entries in the Bleiler *Index*. Mundy was born in London in "respectable circumstances" but later ran away to India and Africa where he became "an all-around cad, bounder, and swindler" and did jail time more than once. It's of more than passing interest that Major W.R. Foran, an assistant district superintendent of the British East African Police, once arrested Mundy in Lake Victoria in 1908. Four years later Major Foran also became a contributor to *Adventure* but never revealed Mundy's background.

Adventure, which paid well for its fiction, also paid well for its artists and was one of the first of the pulps to make a real effort to illustrate stories with something more than sketchy scrawls. Frequently the publication would assign a single artist the entire magazine to illustrate. Rockwell Kent was perhaps the most famous artist to adorn its pages, and John R. Neill, popular illustrator for the "Oz" books, also contributed interiors and at least one cover.

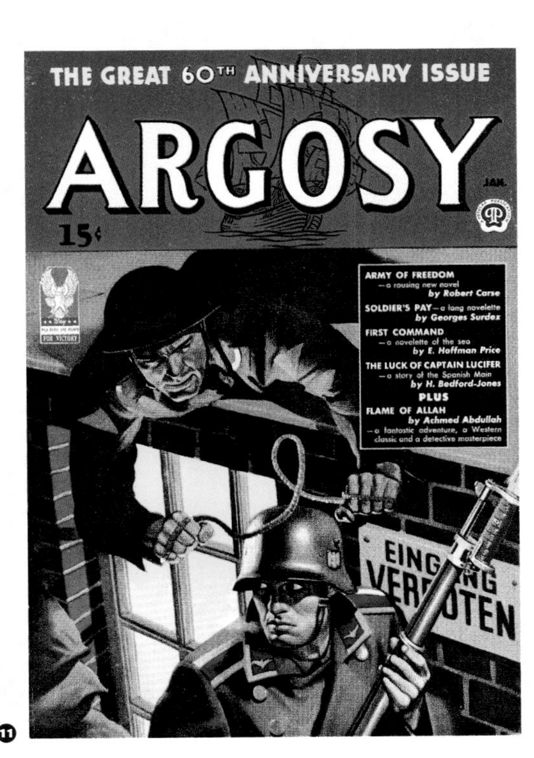

⓫ •
ARGOSY
January 1943
Peter Stevens
Several issues later *Argosy* became a large-format men's "slick" magazine to compete with *True*.

⓬ • •

ALL ACES
April 1936
Malvin Singer
The first issue of a general pulp with a cover that would make most readers think it was a detective magazine.

⓭ • • •

RED BLOODED STORIES
November 1928
Unknown
Sixty years later "Chaka" was immortalized in a TV series.

⓭

⓬

⓯

⓰

⓮ • • •

TALES OF DANGER AND DARING
March 1929
Unknown
Red Blooded Stories changed both title and later its format to become a short-lived, large-format slick paper magazine.

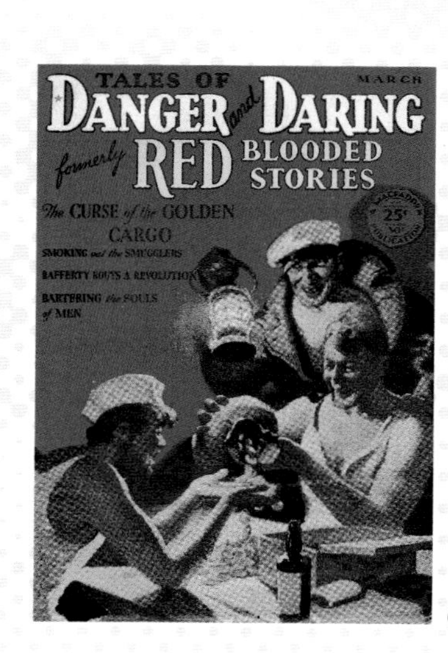

⓮

⓯ • •

ALL-FICTION
March 1931
H.W. Reusswig
Another short-lived competitor to *Argosy* and *Adventure*.

⓰ • •

DYNAMIC ADVENTURES
October 1935
Norman Saunders
Another rare, short-lived adventure magazine.

⓲ ••

Star Magazine
March 1931
Gerard C. Delano
An effective "Yellow Peril" cover by artist Delano.

⓱ •••

Man Stories
June 1931
Eric Lundgren
No messing around. The title was as macho as they get.

⓱

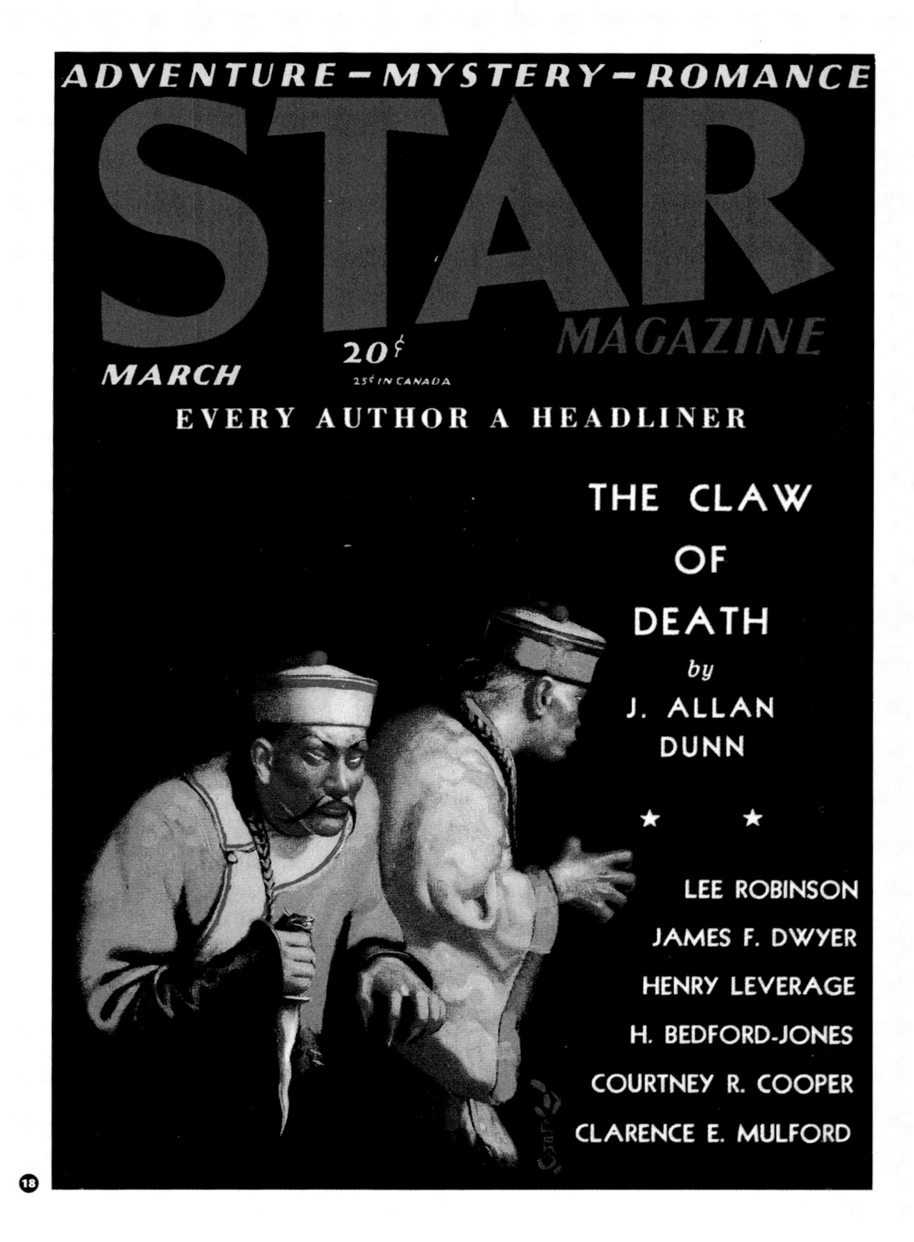

⓲

⓳

⓳ •••

Excitement
January 1931
Jerome Rozen
Artist Rozen was one of twin brothers—Jerome and George. George was best known for his covers for *The Shadow*.

20 •
Short Stories
October 10, 1925
James C. McKell
Short Stories was a strong competitor to *Argosy* and *Adventure*.

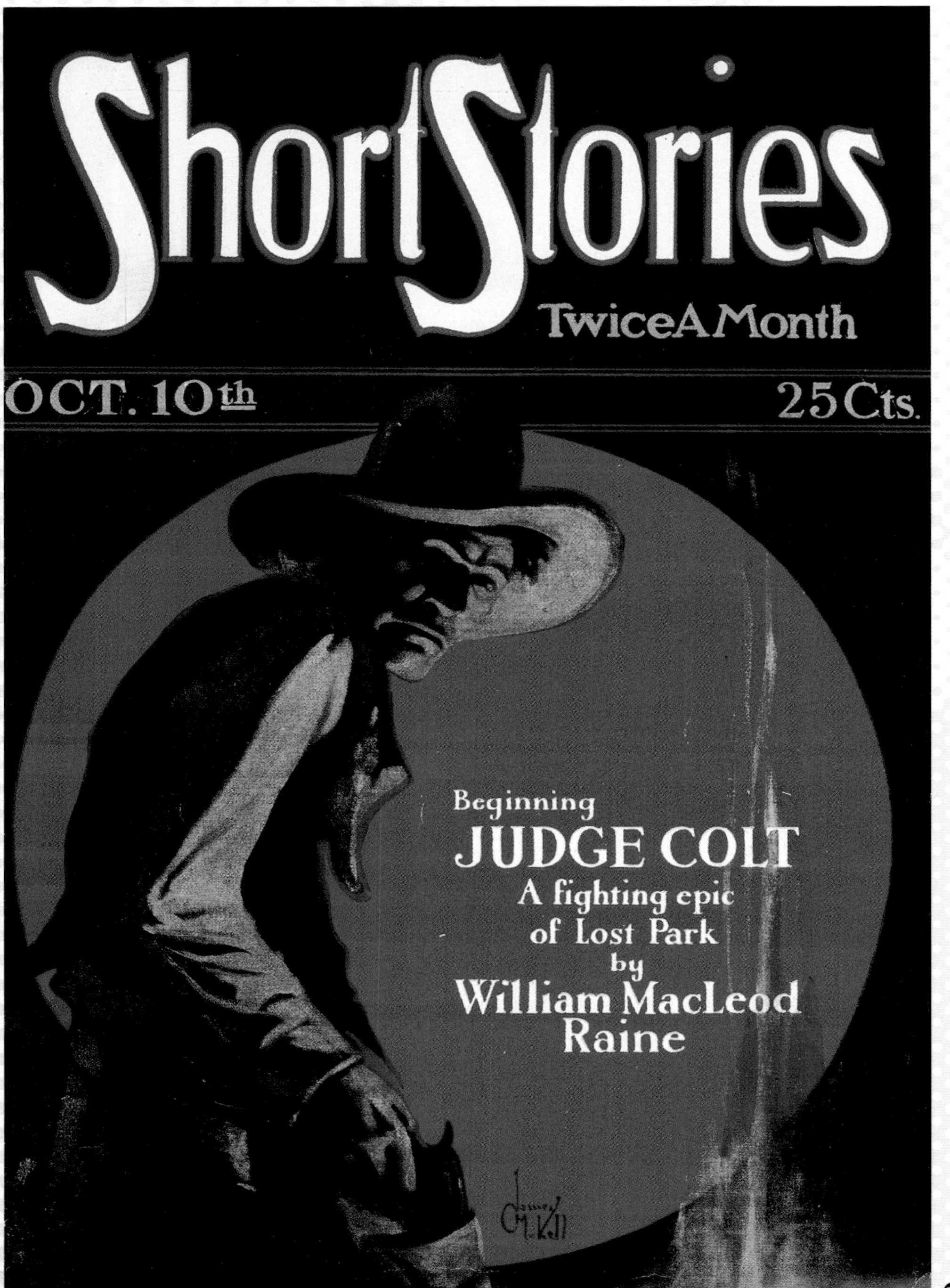

20

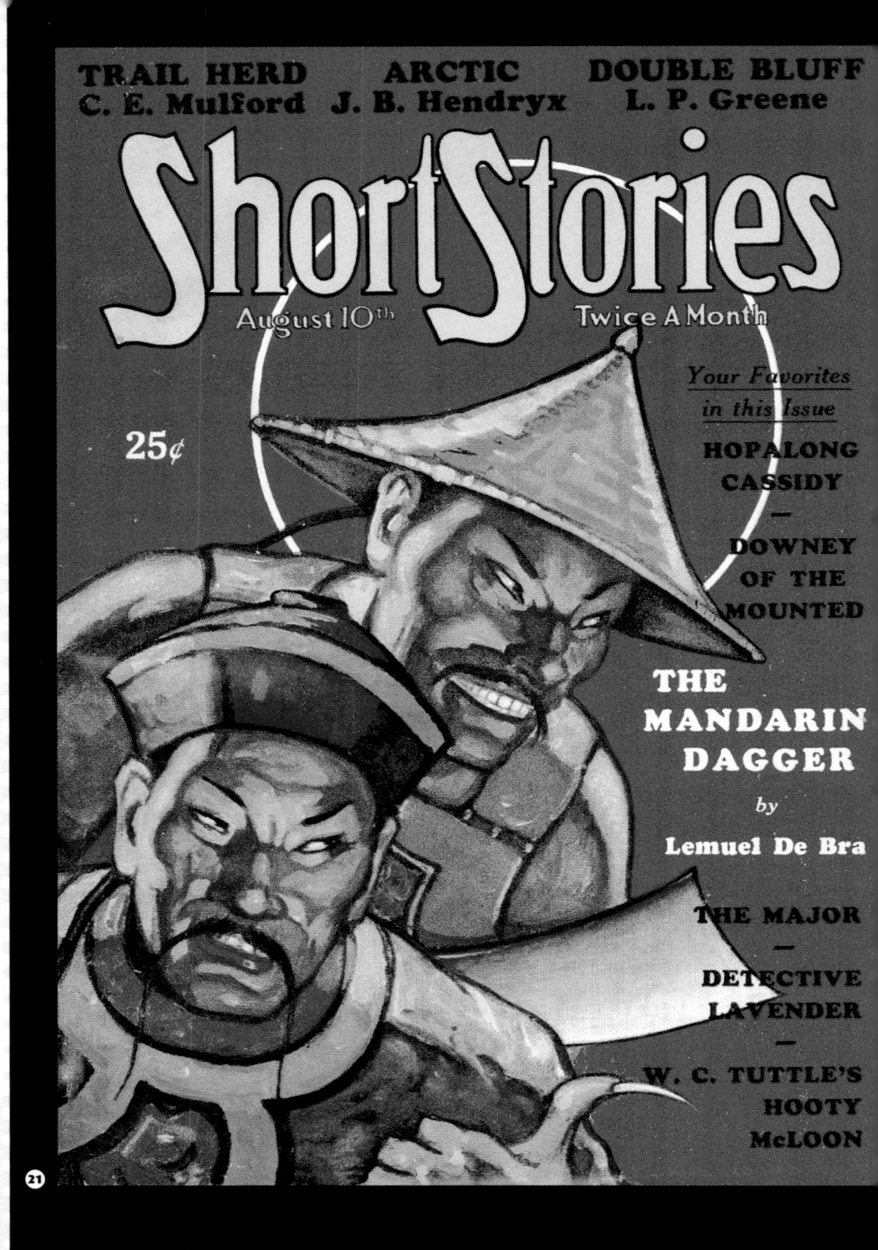

21

21 •
Short Stories
August 10, 1933
Duncan McMillan
Artist McMillan had a knack for portraying vicious Asian villains.

22 •
Short Stories
March 25, 1930
Edgar Franklin Wittmack
He was no one you would want to meet in a dark alley—or a jungle.

22

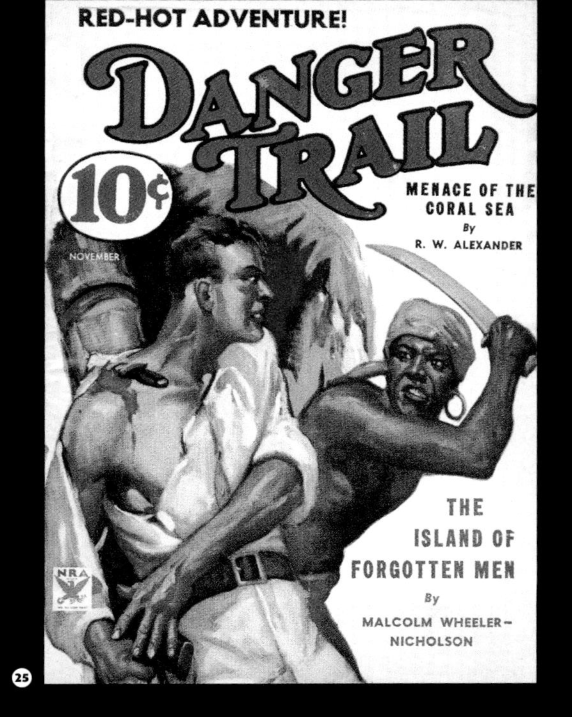

23 • • •
Soldiers of Fortune
December 1931
Jerry Delano
The bowman of Muscovy
was right out of *Robin Hood*.

24 • •
The Danger Trail
August 1927
Elliott Dold
The "danger trail" led from the
China Seas to the sands of Araby.

25 • •
Danger Trail
November 1933
Sidney Riesenberg
Danger Trail was sold to a new
publisher but saw few issues.

26 •
Complete Stories
October 1, 1931
Gayle Hoskins
An octopus on the cover
was a real reader grabber.

27 •
Complete Stories
February 15, 1933
H.W. Scott
Calling Indiana Jones!
What could be more scary than
a rattler in your lap?

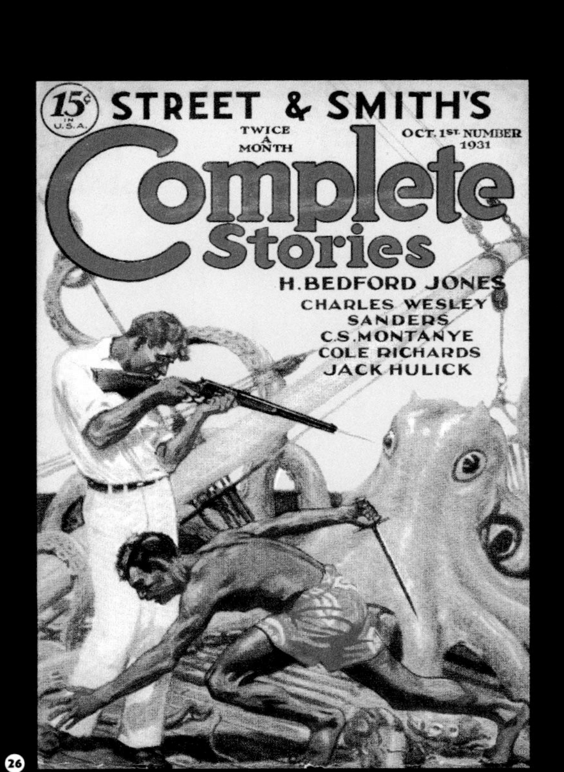

29 • •
TROPICAL ADVENTURES
June 1928
Unknown
A short-lived adventure pulp that never had the pizzazz of the other titles in the field.

30 • • •
DIME ADVENTURE MAGAZINE
December 1935
Hubert Rogers
A short-lived and cheaper competitor to *Adventure*—one that featured both L. Ron Hubbard and Luke Short.

28 • •
RED STAR ADVENTURES
August 1940
H.J. Ward
A late, short-lived adventure pulp featuring a Tarzan imitation.

Perhaps the strangest cover that *Adventure* ever printed was the August 18, 1921, issue by John Held, Jr., the chronicler of the Jazz Age. From the cover, it's apparent that Held was uncomfortable and unfamiliar with the genre. Held's "Sheiks and Shebas" and assorted flappers later slinked and shimmied across the covers of *Life* and *Judge* and *College Humor*. In the '30s Held wrote novels and short stories and did woodcuts for *The New Yorker Magazine*.

But it's doubtful that editors of the other publications knew of Held's one fling with *Adventure*.

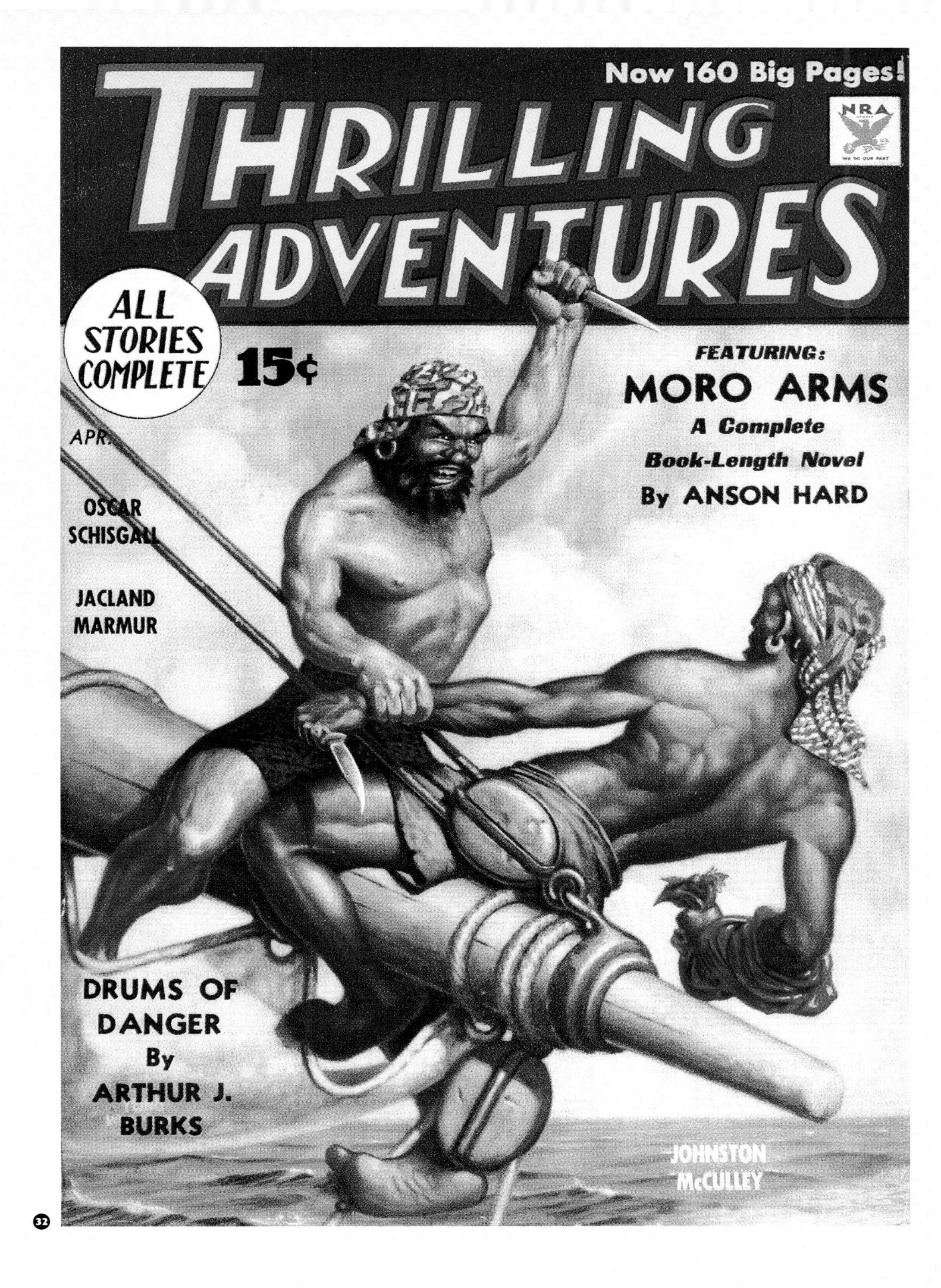

31 •
Mammoth Adventure
May 1947
Robert Gibson Jones
A late entry in the adventure field.

32 ••
Thrilling Adventures
April 1934
Unknown
Thrilling Adventures was a successful title, lasting to the middle of World War II when the paper shortage killed it.

33 ••
ACTION STORIES
December 1940
Unknown
Cavemen and dinosaurs were a natural for a pulp cover.

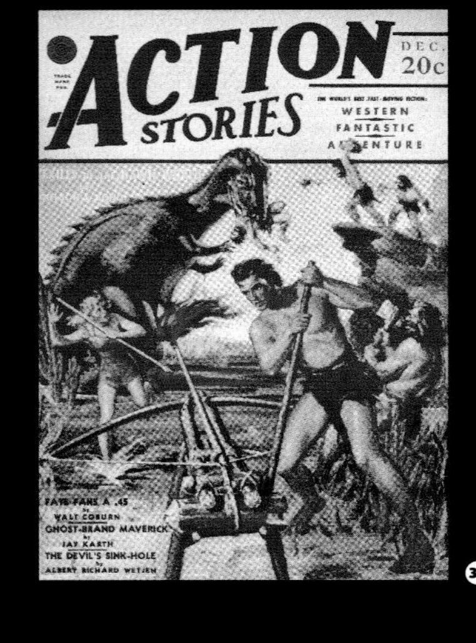

33

34 •••
EXCITEMENT
November 1930
Jerome Rozen
Formerly *Sea Stories*, the magazine sank for good during the Depression.

34

35 •
THE POPULAR MAGAZINE
September 2, 1930
Howard V. Brown
The only time any magazine featured a giant chicken as the menace, but vicious rabbits were never portrayed.

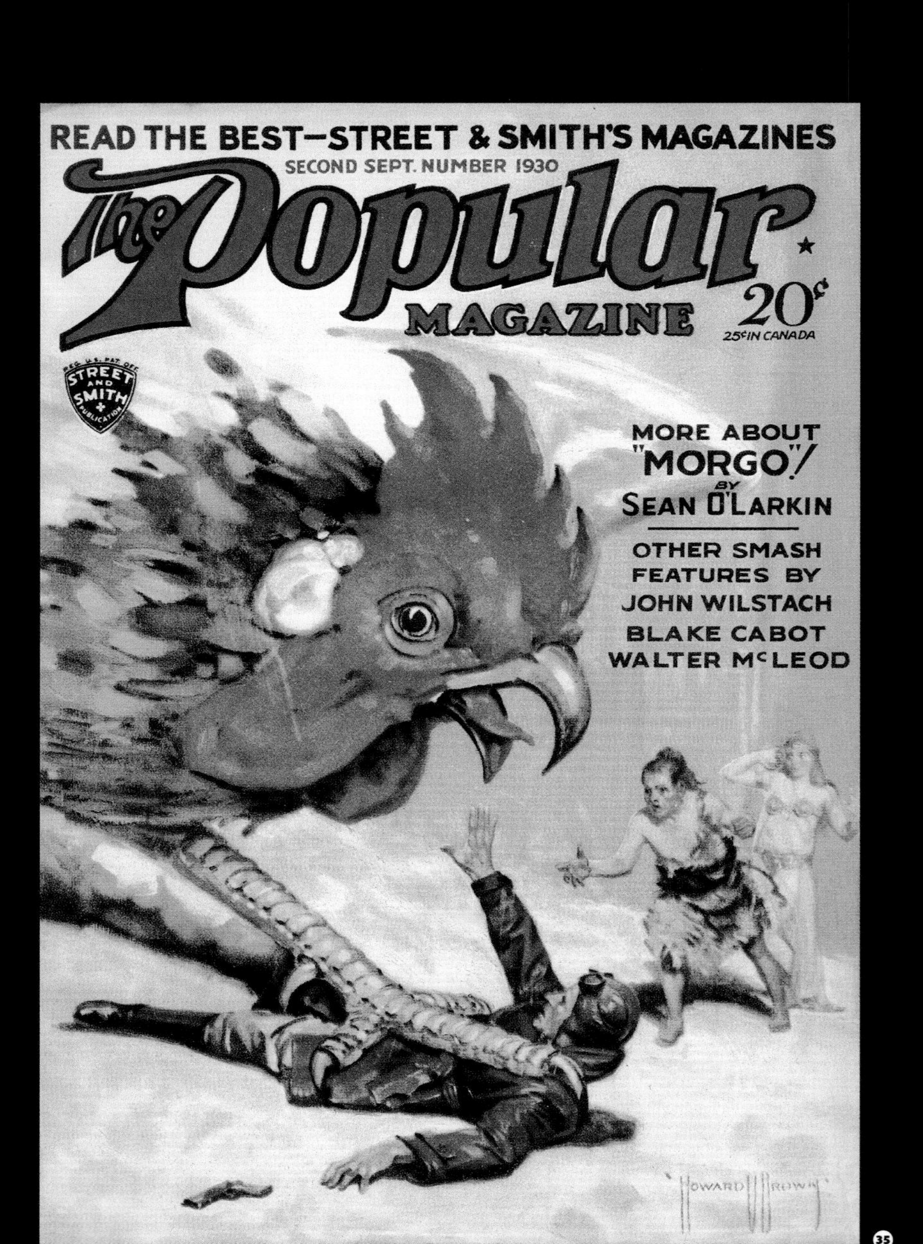

35

36 •
THE POPULAR MAGAZINE
January 2, 1929
Edgar Franklin Wittmack
A country Christmas back in 1929...

36

37 ••
POPULAR FICTION
December 1931
Eric Lundgren
Popular Fiction often used metallic inks on the cover to get attention.

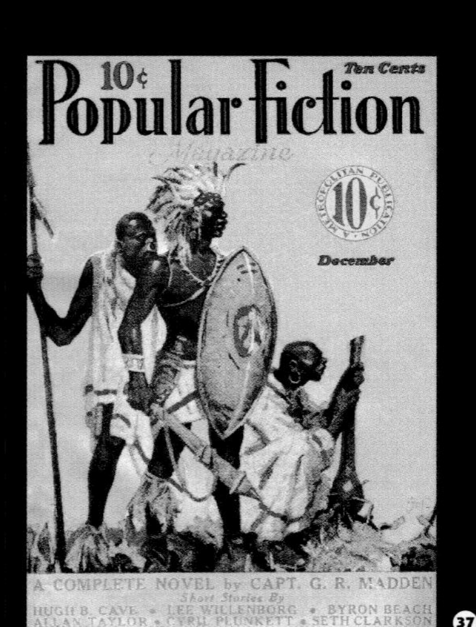

37

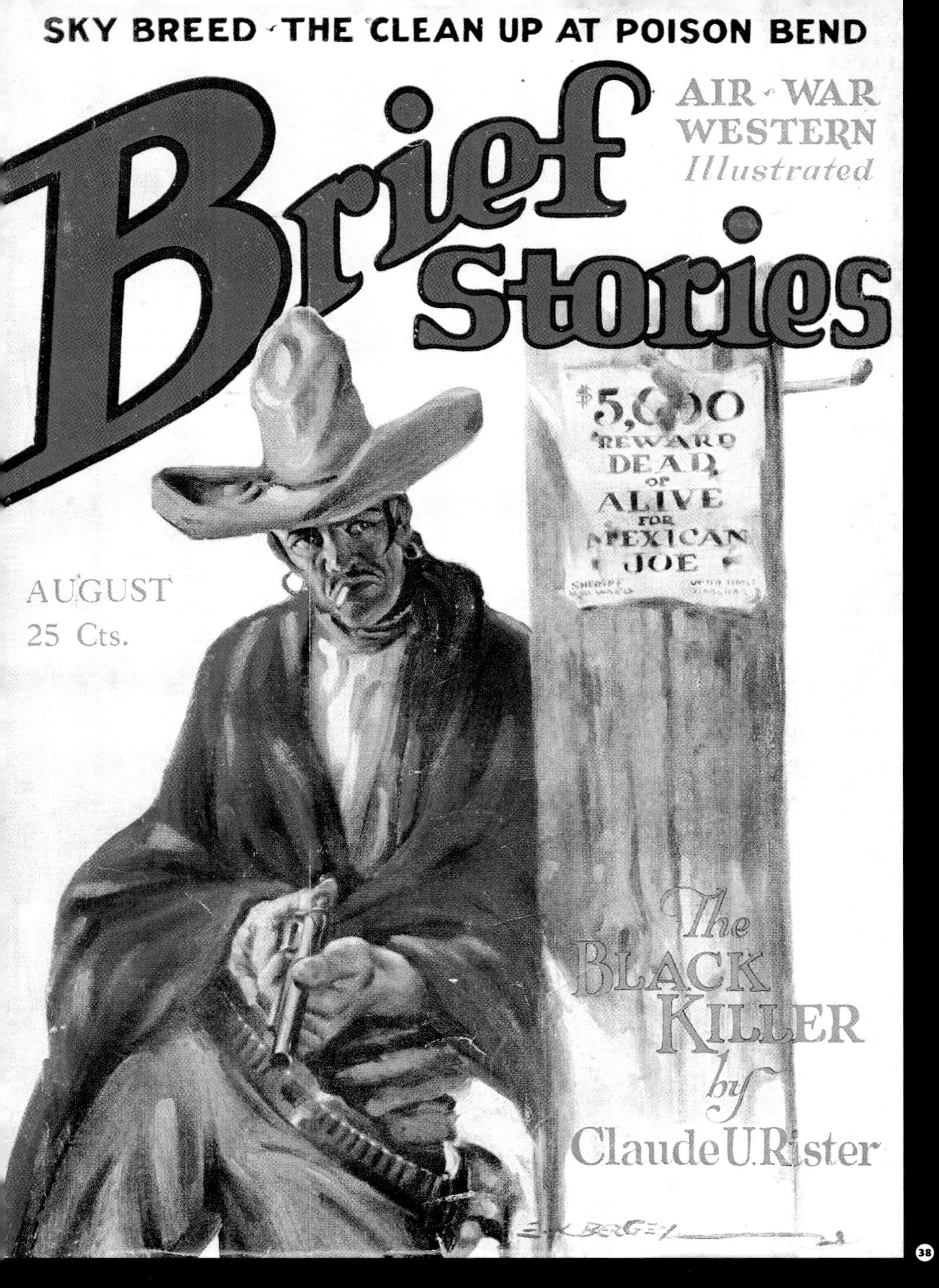

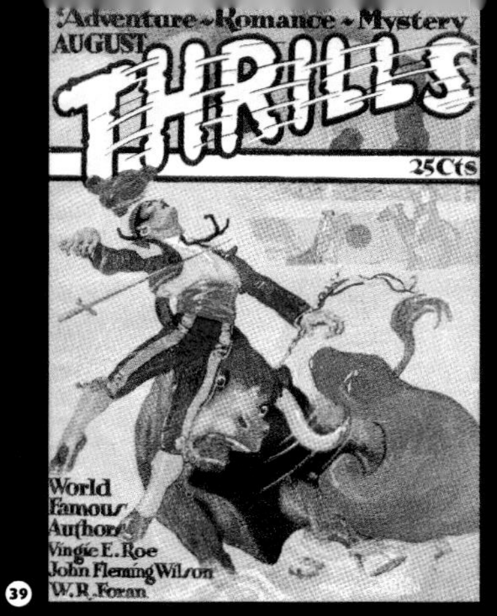

39 ••

THRILLS

August 1927

Jack Warren

Thrills was another *Adventure* imitator that never made it.

40 ••

EVERYBODY'S COMBINED WITH ROMANCE

August 1929

Duncan McMillan

Romance, a companion magazine to *Adventure*, featured stories by women, an advice-to-the-lovelorn column, the mostmature attitude toward sex of any of the pulps—and an adventure novel by Talbot Mundy on its cover!

38 ••

BRIEF STORIES

August 1928

Earle K. Bergey

Brief Stories was a casualty of the Depression.

Strangely enough Edgar Rice Burroughs, one of the most popular pulp writers of all time, never sold a story to *Adventure*—though he tried—but became a mainstay of *All-Story*, *Argosy*, and *Blue Book*. (Robert E. Howard, another popular pulp-adventure writer and creator of "Conan," never sold to *Adventure* either.) One suspects that readers would have torn to shreds Burroughs's view of Africa, a continent he had never visited and which he populated with tigers in *Tarzan of the Apes*, though they never were found there. Burroughs never repeated his mistake in subsequent novels (he never bothered to revise *Tarzan* either), but the damage probably had already been done.

Burroughs first published in *All-Story* with *Under the Moons of Mars*, using the pen-name of "Norman Bean." He shot to fame with *Tarzan of the Apes*, published complete in the October 1912 issue. He was the first pulp-magazine superstar, and his name on the cover automatically meant a hefty increase in circulation.

Collectors eagerly seek adventure pulps, though complete files of them, especially of *Adventure*, are rare. But the most valuable single pulp of all is the issue of *All-Story* containing *Tarzan of the Apes*. Copies of it in fine condition have gone for thousands of dollars at auction, far more than Burroughs ever received for the story itself.

41 •
Top-Notch Magazine
June 1, 1930
Robert A. Graef
The magazine tried a story with a theme song. You read it, then you sang it. Not so strange: today's films popularize their sound tracks.

42 ••
Top-Notch
March 1935
Tom Lovell
Top-Notch celebrated its silver anniversary, then died two years later.

43 •
Top-Notch Magazine
June 1, 1931
H.T. Fisk
Some cover paintings had overtones of fine art. This one by Fisk showed influences of Thomas Eakins, a renowned American artist.

GALS, GATS, AND GUMSHOES

You've Gotta Have a Gimmick

At one time the most popular fiction genre of all was that of mystery and detective stories. Edgar Allan Poe has been credited with the invention of the genre, but it was "Nick Carter" who popularized it. He first appeared in *Street & Smith's New York Weekly* in 1886, beating Sherlock Holmes into print by a little more than one year.

Detective tales were popular in the story papers and general magazines, and it wasn't long before Nick Carter had his own magazine, as did his chief competitors: Old Sleuth, Old Cap Collier, and King Brady.

But by 1915 Street & Smith had become convinced that *Nick Carter Stories* was tired and had lost its spark. The solution was to change it from a dime novel into a pulp titled *Detective Story Magazine* with "Nick Carter" as the editor, a pretense that didn't last very long. *Detective Story Magazine* was the first all-fiction pulp to specialize in a particular genre.

The twice-a-month *Detective Story Magazine* soon became a weekly. It had the field substantially to itself until the birth of *The Black Mask* (April 1920), which specialized in neither detective stories or mysteries but included them as part of the editorial mix featuring, in addition, *Adventure, Romance, and Spiritualism* (the latter for the first issue only).

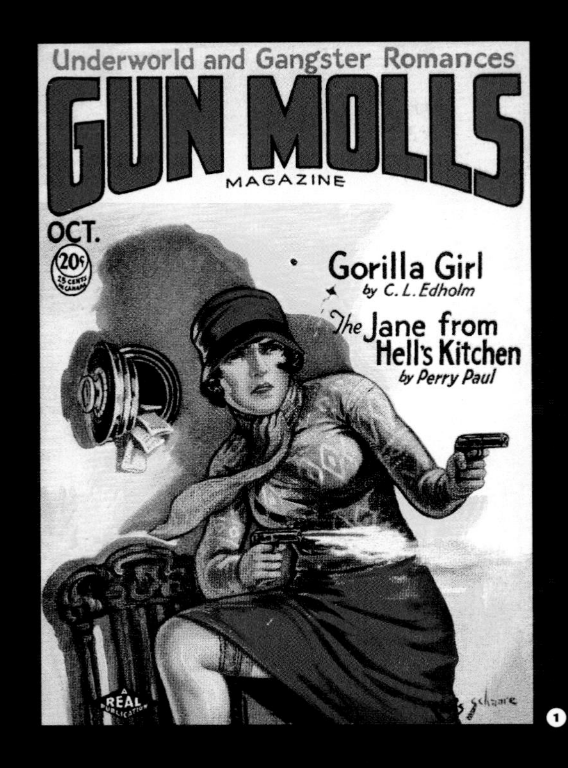

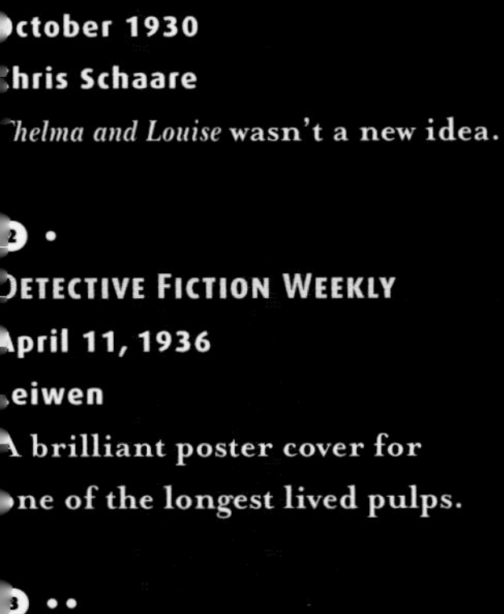

❶ •••
Gun Molls Magazine
ctober 1930
hris Schaare
helma and Louise wasn't a new idea.

❷ •
etective Fiction Weekly
pril 11, 1936
eiwen
 brilliant poster cover for
ne of the longest lived pulps.

❸ ••
ublic Enemy
ecember 1935
orman Saunders
uring the dark days of the
epression the G-men were
he nation's heroes.

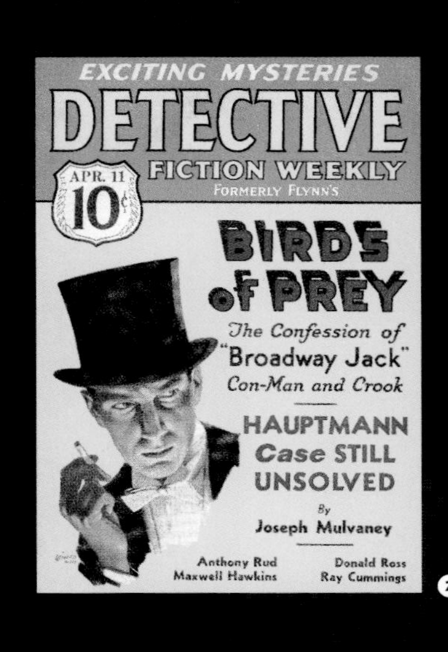

❷

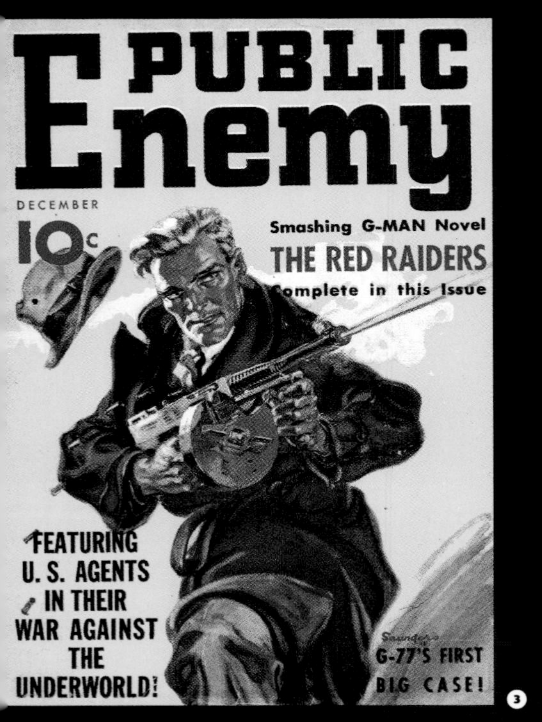

❸

❹

❺

❹ •••
The Underworld
May 1927
Unknown
The first issue of the magazine
that started the gang genre.

❺ •••
Black Bat Detective Mysteries
October 1933
Unknown
Despite the title the *Black Bat*
wasn't a "hero" pulp.

The Black Mask was the brainchild of H.L. Mencken and George Jean Nathan, co-editors and part owners of *The Smart Set*, a magazine of upscale fiction, stylized satire, and reviews aimed at the sophisticated reader. It was subtitled *A Magazine of Cleverness*. The difficulties were two-fold: There simply weren't that many "sophisticated" readers, and the magazine frequently went over the heads of those who considered themselves as such. *The Smart Set* was a money-loser.

The solution was to go slumming in the more popular venues of publishing and put out some "louse," as Mencken described them, magazines strictly for the money. Nathan and Mencken were relatively successful with their first efforts, *Parisienne* and *Saucy Stories*, and even more successful with *The Black Mask*. Predictably, they hated the magazine and, as soon as it was making money, sold it for a handsome profit.

In its early years the magazine was an uneasy combination of mystery, western, and adventure stories with no notable efforts in any of them. The first editor—neither Mencken nor Nathan would soil their hands with actually editing it, or even allow their names to appear on the masthead—was officially "F. Osborne," better known around the office as Florence Osborne. She was an associate editor of *The Smart Set*, and Wyndham Martyn, another associate editor, was her assistant. In contrast to the usually dull fiction, the covers were striking, verging on the fantastic and art deco.

With a new publisher and under a new editor, George Sutton, *Black Mask* began to shape up. Most agree on the seminal issue; it was dated June 1, 1923, and known as the "Ku-Klux-Klan Number." The issue, which subtly approved of the Klan, introduced "Race Williams," fiction's first "private eye."

Well, not quite. Author Carroll John Daly had tried his hand at a private eye before, one Terry Mack, hero of "Three Gun Terry" in the issue preceding the Klan number. But it was Race Williams who made Daly's name and, largely, the fortune of the magazine.

It was an odd coincidence of publishing that editor Sutton had been on vacation when an assistant bought the first two Race Williams stories. After Sutton returned, there was a long silence before he

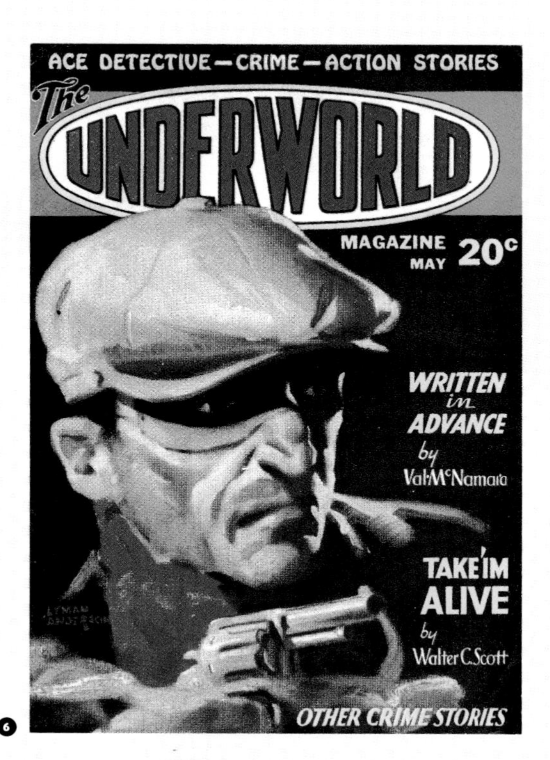

6 ••
The Underworld Magazine
May 1933
Lyman Anderson
The gang magazines took a slug with the repeal of Prohibition.

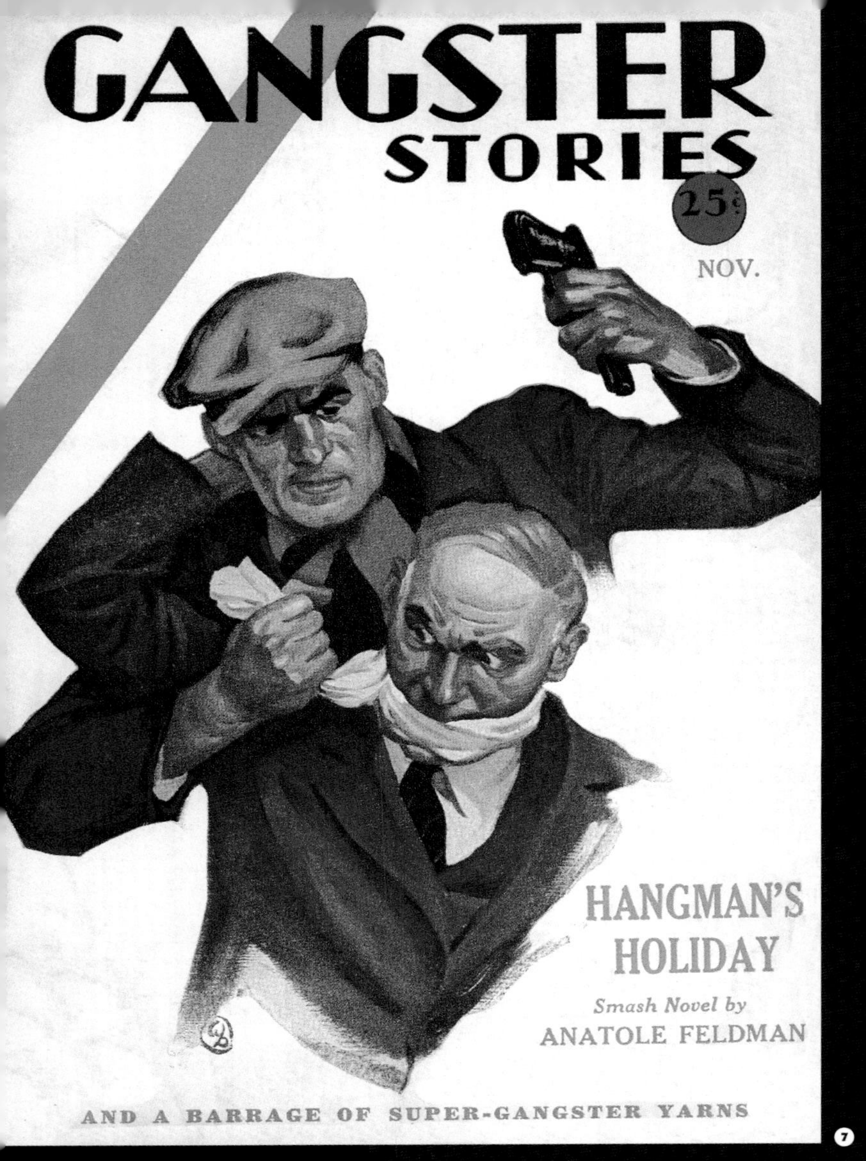

7 • • •
Gangster Stories
November 1932
Walter M. Baumhofer
The publisher identified his magazines with the candybox stripe.

8 • • •
Prison Stories
November 1930
C. Wren
A *Sing Sing Stories* or *Alcatraz Stories* would have been a natural.

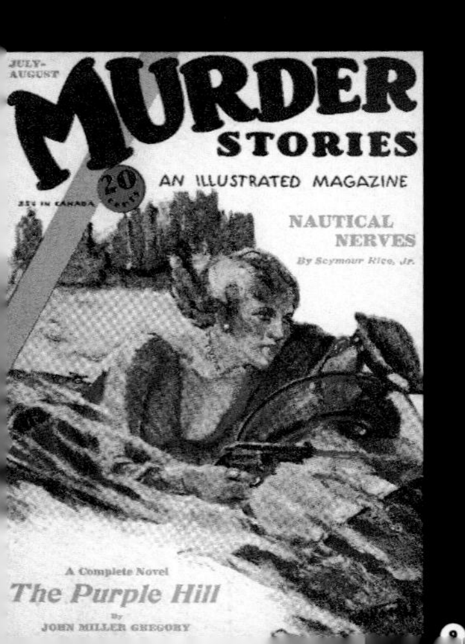

9 • • •
Murder Stories
July-August 1931
R.C. Wardel
Murder was what the gang magazines were really about. Right?

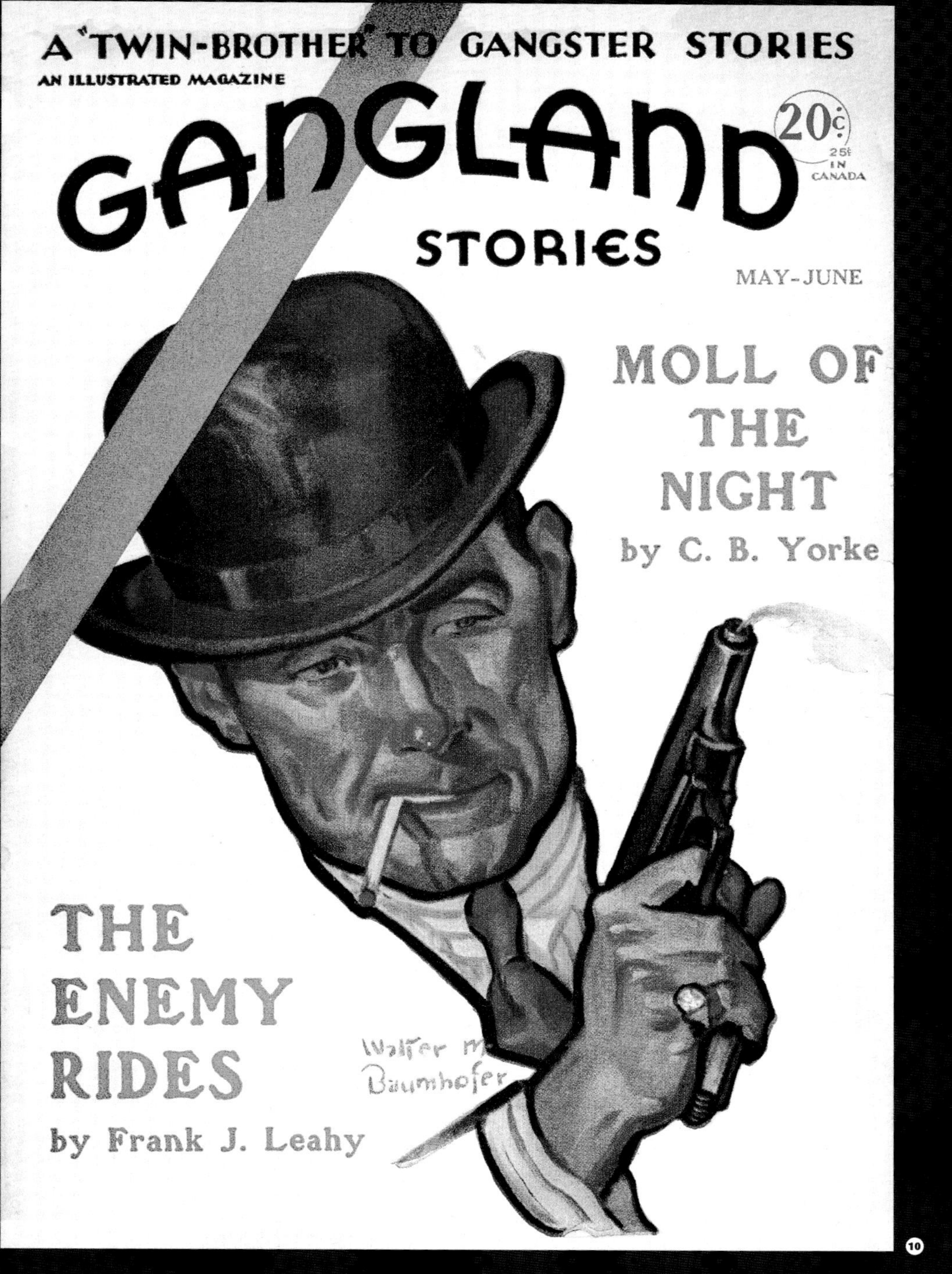

10 ••
Gangland Stories
May-June 1931
Walter M. Baumhofer
The model for Baumhofer's cover could have been actor Edward G. Robinson.

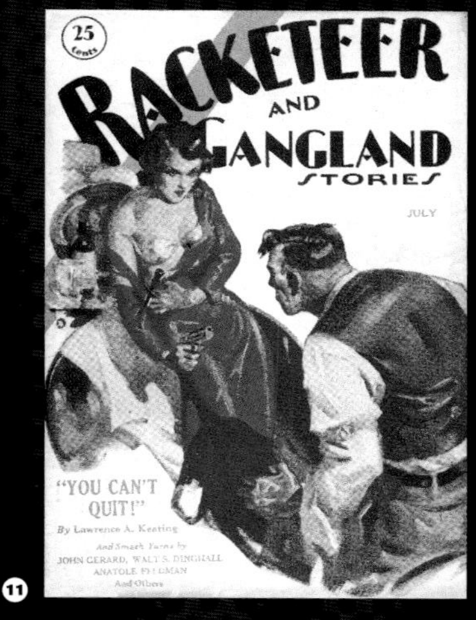

11 ••
Racketeer and Gangland Stories
July 1932
Tom Lovell
Publishers combined titles when the gang magazines began to decline.

12 ••
Detective Trails
February 1930
W.C. Brigham
The "map" cover became popular in paperbacks years later.

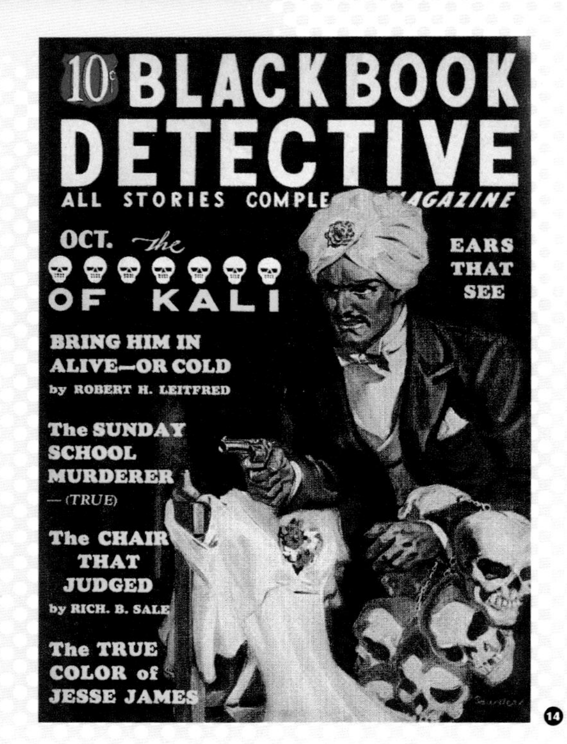

13 •

Clues Detective Stories
September 1939
Modest Stein
Not what you would want to see when shaving in the morning.

14 ••

Black Book Detective Magazine
October 1936
Norman Saunders
The title of the story was, of course, "The Seven Skulls of Kali."

15 •

Mobsters
December 1952
Robert Stanley
The last new crime title to appear—and one of the last of the pulp magazines. Artist Stanley later made a name for himself in the paperback field.

16 •

Detective Story Magazine
July 1941
Unknown
By the early '40s *Detective Story* had become an upscale pulp.

17 ••

Black Book Detective
June 1933
Unknown
If they had been making Bruce Lee movies in the '30s, the story probably would have featured an Oriental hero rather than a villain.

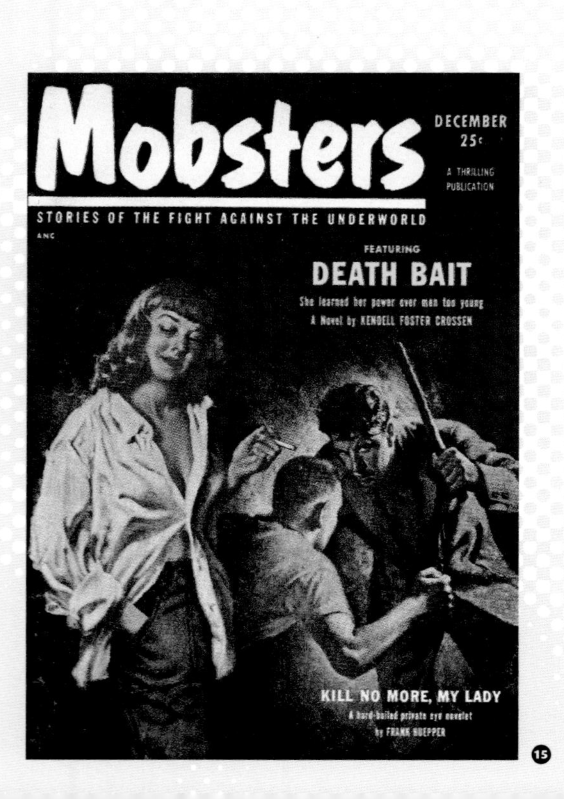

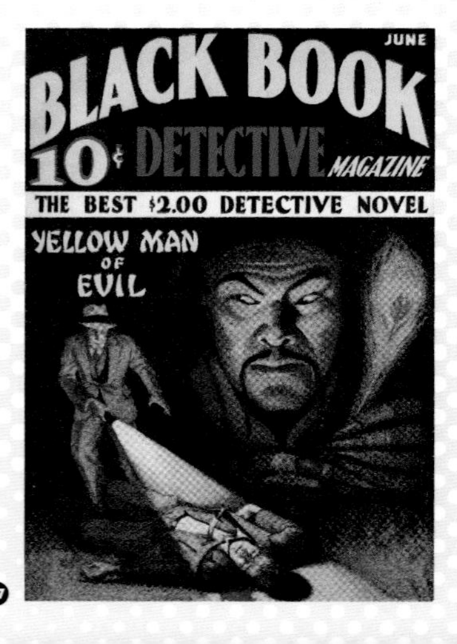

told Daly the reason why. It seemed Sutton hated Race Williams and never would have bought the stories on his own. According to Ron Goulart in *The Dime Detectives*, Sutton told Daly how much he hated the stories and despised the characters. But by the time four months had passed, circulation figures had come in, and Race Williams was an obvious hit with the readers. In the future the printing of Daly's name and "Race Williams" on a cover could add fifteen percent to the magazine's circulation.

The private eye was born, and Daly had the green light to write more stories about him.

Dashiell Hammett was next up with a private eye, one with no name, simply known as the "Continental Op," introduced in the October 1, 1923, issue. A new editor, Phil Cody, loved Hammett's work and so, especially, did his successor, Joseph T. Shaw, better known as "Cap" Shaw. (He had been an Army captain during the Great War.) *Black Mask* published all the stories about the Op and also serialized *The Maltese Falcon*, featuring Sam Spade, *The Glass Key*, and the various stories that made up *Red Harvest*, and *The Dain Curse*.

Under Shaw, *Black Mask* pioneered the hard-boiled school of detective writing, publishing stories by Hammett, Erle Stanley Gardner, Raymond Chandler, Frederick Nebel, Raoul Whitfield, Lester Dent, and many others. It wasn't very long, of course, before other publishers began investigating the possibility of publishing detective and mystery magazines.

18 •••
All Detective Magazine
January 1935
Norman Saunders
Sometimes it was a fine line between the mystery and horror genres.

19 • •
Complete Gang Novel Magazine
November 1931
Walter M. Baumhofer
Reports were the publisher sometimes used artist Baumhofer's sketches as finished covers.

20 • • •
Black Mask
December 1927
Fred Craft
Black Mask was also a "he-man's magazine"—whatever that was.

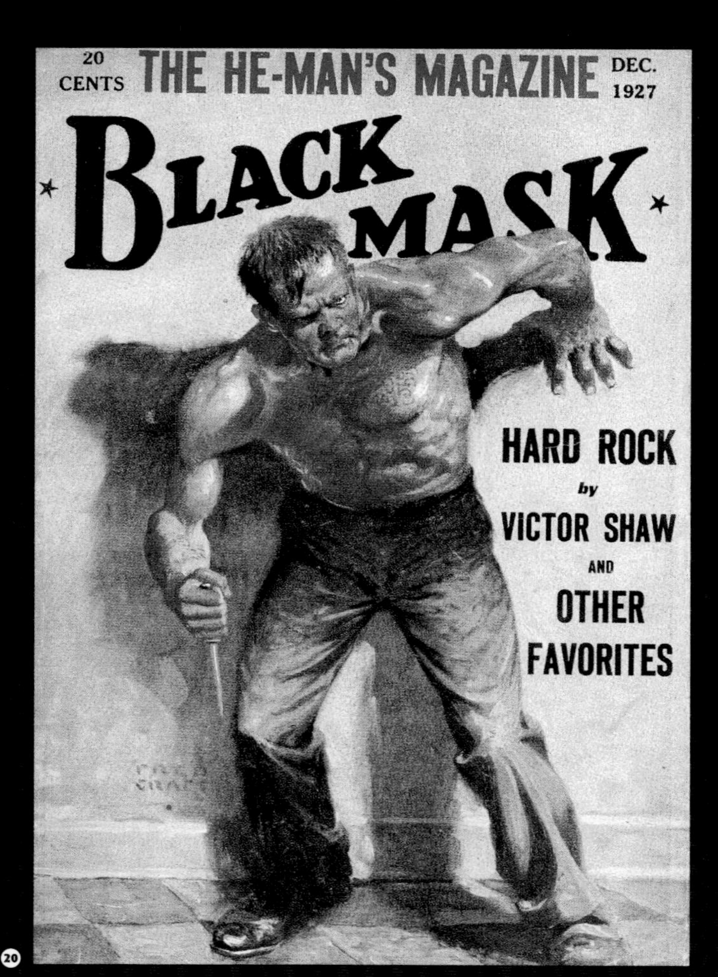

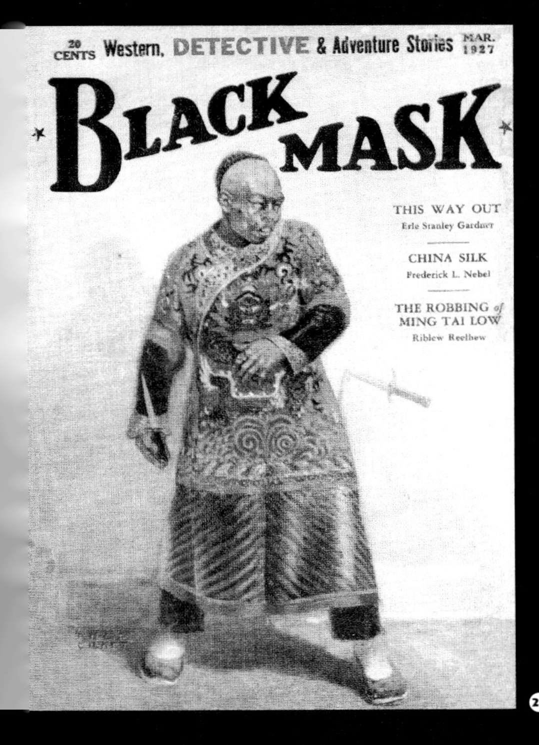

21

WESTERN, DETECTIVE & ADVENTURE STORIES

BLACK MASK

DEATH IN A BOWL

By RAOUL WHITFIELD

SEPT. 1930 · 20¢
IN CANADA 25¢

ALSO

FREDERICK NEBEL E. AND M. SCOTT

RAMON DECOLTA J.-J. DES ORMEAUX GUTHRIE BROWN

22

21 •••
Black Mask
March 1927
Fred Craft
Mandarin robes and stilettos in a Chinatown that never existed.

22 ••
Black Mask
September 1930
J.W. Schlaikjer
Black Mask was adept at depicting gangsters who had character.

23 ••
AMAZING DETECTIVE TALES
September 1930
John Ruger
Science didn't sell, so *Scientific Detective Monthly* became *Amazing Detective Tales* complete with "Yellow Peril."

24 ••
MYSTERY STORIES
January 1929
F.R. Glass
Despite the title the magazine published other genres as well.

25 ••
CRIME BUSTERS
February 1939
Unknown
Probably a combination photograph and painting. The skeletal hand looks far too real.

26 ••
DETECTIVE ACTION
August-September 1937
Charles De Feo
The "Godfather" lurking behind death's head mask.

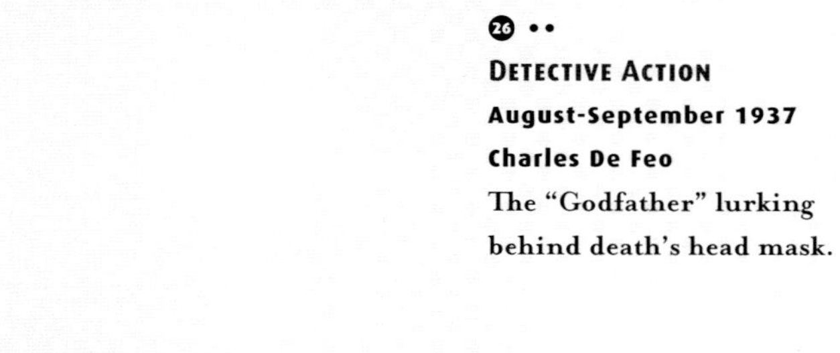

27 ••
SCIENTIFIC DETECTIVE MONTHLY
January 1930
John Ruger
The latest advance in scientific detecting—a lie detector.

28 •

MAMMOTH DETECTIVE
February 1945
Richard R. Epperly

"John Evans" was the pen name for editor Howard Browne, who later became justifiably famous for his television scripts for crime shows. Artist Epperly, incidentally, painted the first cover for *Weird Tales*.

30 •••

STRANGE DETECTIVE STORIES
February 1934
Clifford Benton

In the small type you can see why this magazine is a collector's item: "Fangs of Gold" by author Robert E. Howard, creator of "Conan."

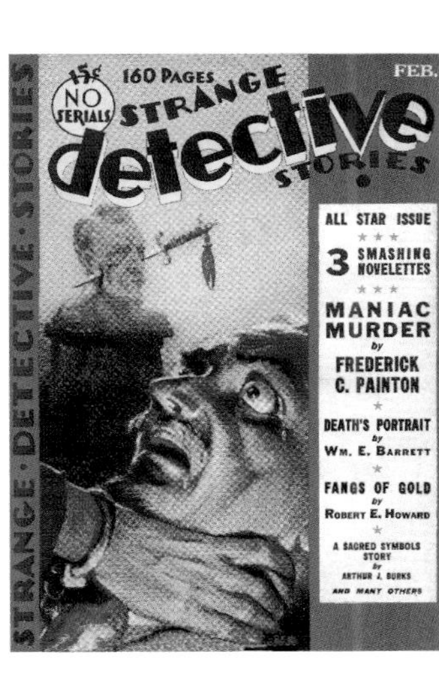

30

29 ••

MYSTERY NOVELS MAGAZINE
Summer 1934
Rudolph Zirn

Author J.S. Fletcher, of course, has no connection to "Jessica Fletcher" of television's *Murder, She Wrote*.

31 ••
The Feds
June 1937
Unknown
In the '30s J. Edgar Hoover was the most popular man in the U.S.

First out of the gate was *Flynn's*, a ten-cent weekly companion to *Argosy*, named after and presumably edited by William J. Flynn, a former chief of the Secret Service. It appeared in 1924. The late '20s were also the Roaring Twenties. Prohibition had been the law of the land since the end of World War I, bootlegging was common, and with it the growth of the underworld and magazines that chronicled it. The first of them, *The Underworld Magazine*, was a predictable success.

With the start of the Great Depression, interest in crime and crime fiction increased enormously. Real competition for *Black Mask* came from *Dime Detective*. It published stories by Raymond Chandler, who had left *Black Mask* when "Cap" Shaw protested a wage cut and resigned, and Cornell Woolrich, who wrote "It Had to be Murder" (later filmed as *Rear Window*) in the February 1942 issue. Woolrich became famous not only under his own name but also as "William Irish."

By the late '30s there were dozens of detective magazines, and private eyes soon came in all sizes, shapes, and genders. There was Bob Larkin (Erle Stanley Gardner), who used a billiard cue as a weapon; Vee Brown (Carroll John Daly), a "gumshoe" who also wrote pop songs; Ken Carter (Norvell Page), a former professional juggler; Oliver Quade (Frank Gruber), the "human encyclopedia"; Carrie Cashin (Theodore Tinsley), the most popular of the female private investigators; a hemophiliac op known as "the Bleeder" (Ejler Jacobson), "the world's most vulnerable dick";

33 ••
Ace G-Man Stories
May-June 1936
Malvin Singer
By the middle '30s "G-men" magazines had replaced the gang pulps.

32 •
G-Men Detective
April 1946
Rudolph Belarski
More gangsters escaped Alcatraz in the pulps than in real life.

32

33

❹ • •
Popular Detective
April 1937
Unknown
This cover was as grisly as you could get. Guaranteed to sell to teenagers.

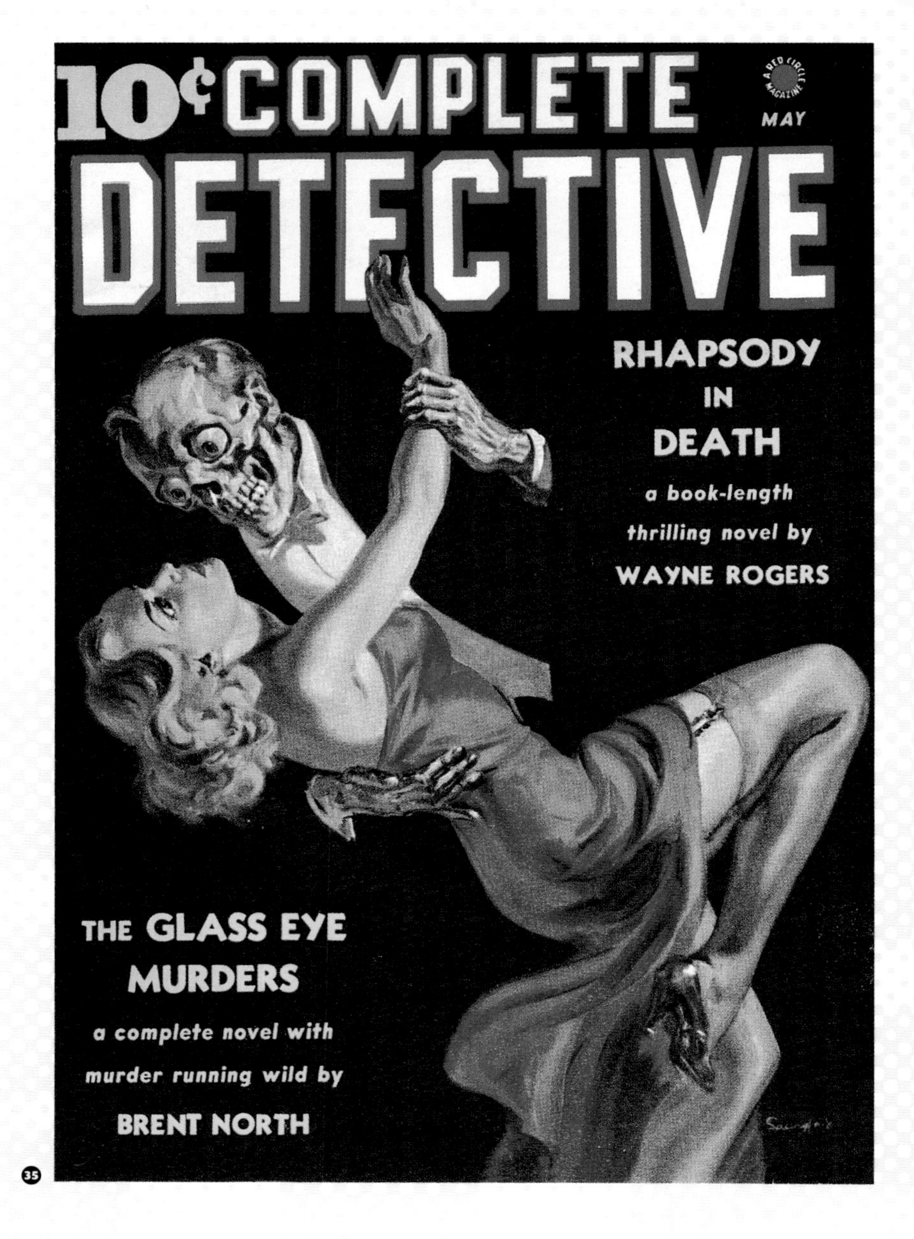

❺ • •
Complete Detective
May 1938
Norman Saunders
A dance with death...

❻ • • •
Double Detective
March 1943
Unknown
Under a different publisher the magazine had been billed as *Fiction and True Stories*. By 1943 it was all fiction.

37 • •

DETECTIVE TALES
March 1936
Tom Lovell
The magazine was undeniably successful, lasting into the '50s.

38 • •

DIME DETECTIVE
February 15, 1934
John Newton Howitt
The magazine's covers were almost always eye-catching and creative.

37

38

39 • •

NICKEL DETECTIVE
March 1933
Eric Lundgren
Half the magazine for half the price. But readers didn't buy it.

39

40

40 • •

SUPER-DETECTIVE
October 1940
H.J. Ward
The first issue;
the magazine lasted until 1950.
It couldn't lose, not with covers by H.J. Ward and with Robert Leslie Bellem hiding under the name of "John Grange."

41 • •

LONE WOLF DETECTIVE
December 1940
Norman Saunders
Still another hero in the mystery field...

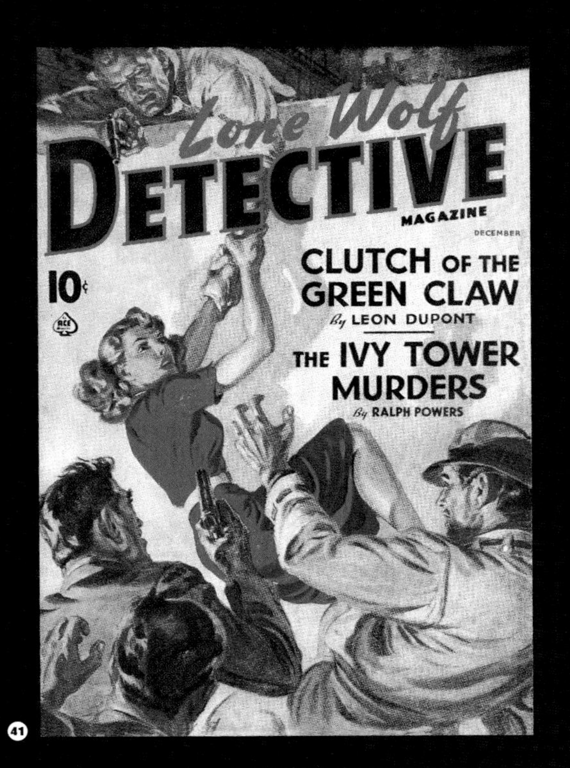

41

44 ••

Gang World

September 1931

William Reusswig

Cops vs. criminals was the theme of *Gang World*.

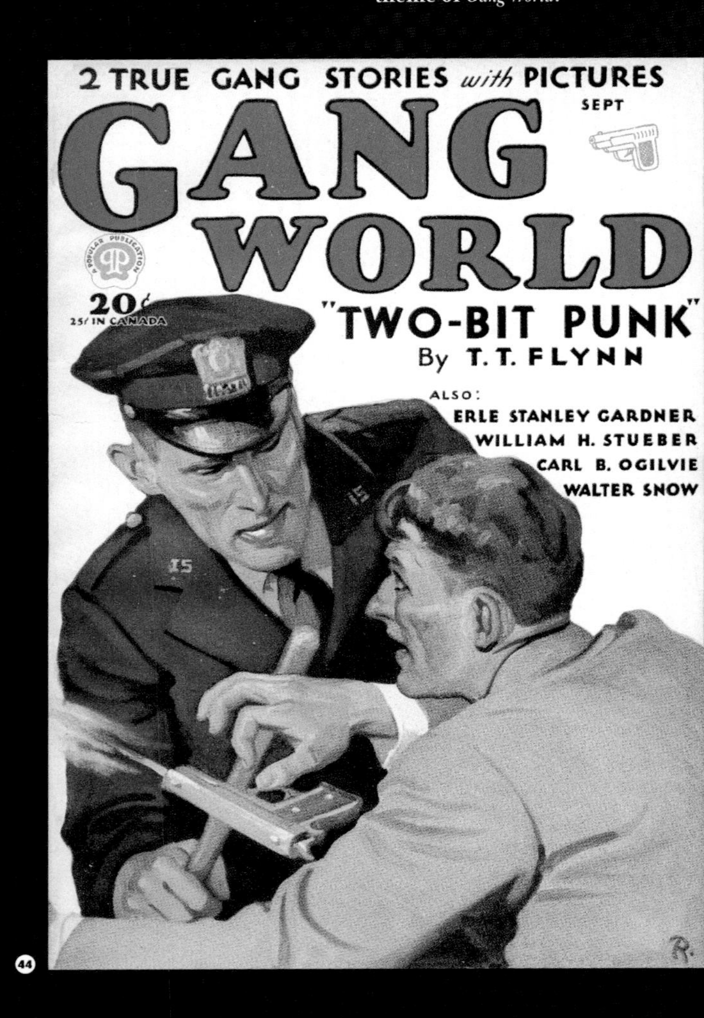

44

42 43

42 ••••

Blue Steel Magazine

March 1932

43 ••

Gang World

February 1932

William Reusswig

One of the scarcest of all pulps. *Blue Steel* was *Gang World* with the cover stripped off and a *Blue Steel* cover glued on to avoid New York City's ban on gang-related titles.

45 •••
BLACK ACES
April 1932
George B. Cutts
One of the early imitators of *Black Mask* that didn't make it. The *Mask*'s authors stayed loyal to editor "Cap" Shaw.

46 ••
STAR NOVELS MAGAZINE
September 1934
Howard Parkhurst
The biggest newsstand bargain during the Depression: two hundred fifty-six pages for twenty-five cents. But *The Saint* novel wasn't really a novel.

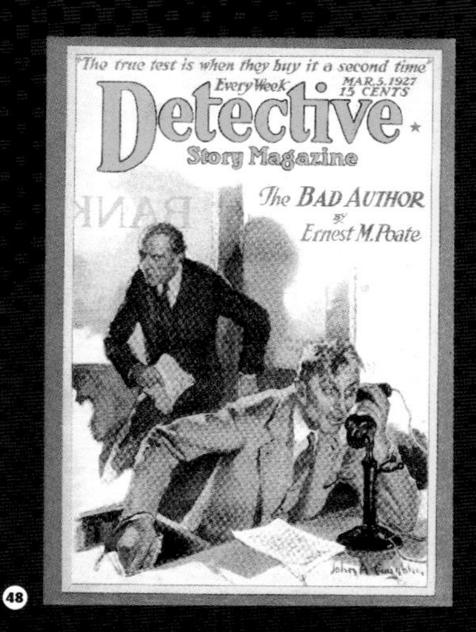

48

48 •
DETECTIVE STORY MAGAZINE
March 5, 1927
John A. Coughlin
Every editor's favorite cover.

49 ••
THE DRAGNET MAGAZINE
April 1929
W.C. Brigham
The reverse swastika had nothing to do with Nazi Germany.

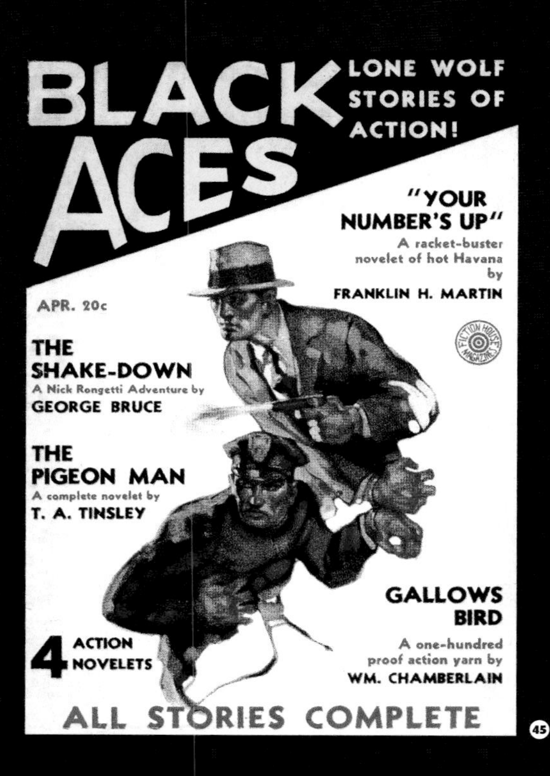

45

47

49

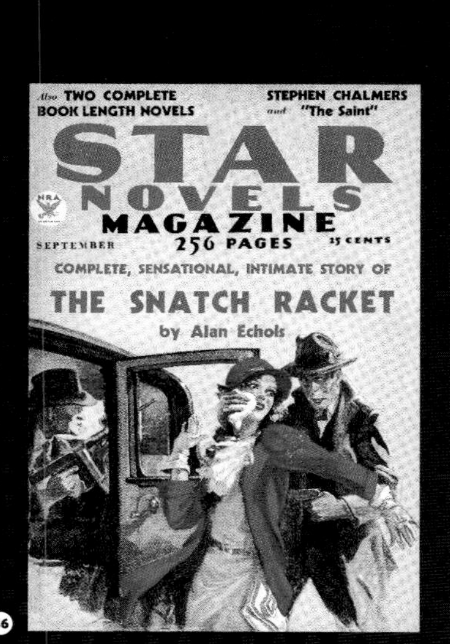

46

47 ••
GREATER GANGSTER STORIES
August 1933
Tom Lovell
Dealers sold gang magazines under the counter in Capone's Chicago.

50

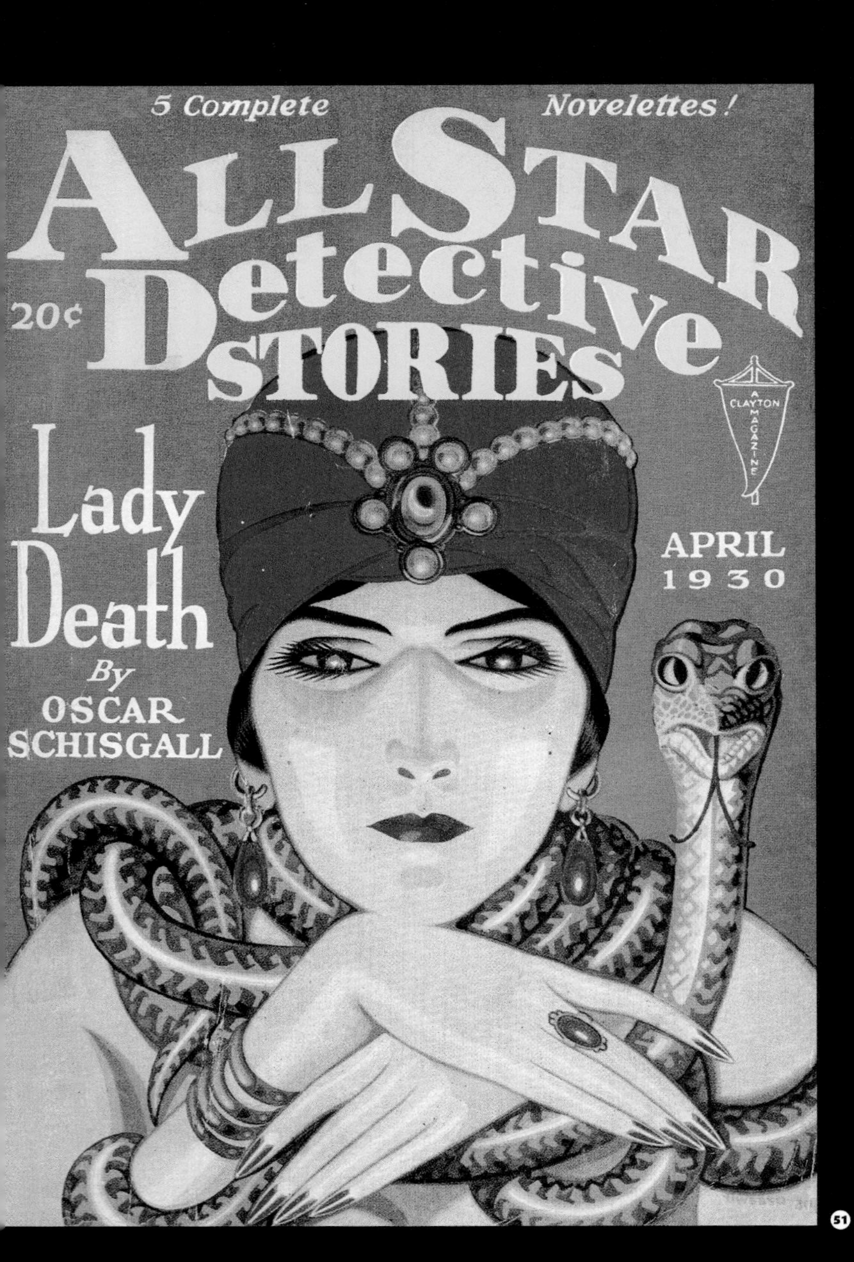

51

Harlan Dyce (Arthur J. Burks), three feet tall and weighing sixty pounds; and Violet Dade (Cleve Franklin Adams), a former circus fat lady who ran a detective agency along with Nevada Alvarado, a pretty Hispanic P.I.

Those were just some of the heroes, all distinct from each other. As Gypsy Rose Lee once said, "You've gotta have a gimmick!" It's just as true today for mystery books and television series, though lawyers seem to dominate the former and police the latter.

There were sub-genres in the mystery and detective field as well: one devoted to gangsters—*Gang World*, *Racketeer Stories*, *Gangster Stories*, *Gun Molls*, *Speakeasy Stories*, and so forth; and one concentrating on the F.B.I. and other government agencies—among them, *The Feds*, *Ace G-Man Stories*, *G-Men Detective*, and *F.B.I. Detective Stories*.

During the late '20s and early '30s, newsstands sold the gang pulps under the counter in Chicago; Al Capone was a power in the city, and no news dealer wanted to offend him. Coincidentally sales of the gang magazines plummeted with the end of Prohibition and the jailing of Capone. The glamour had faded for gangsters but not, it seemed, for the F.B.I. and J. Edgar Hoover, the country's new hero. The F.B.I. magazines took over where the gang magazines left off.

One author invented his own sub-genre, that of the Hollywood detective. Robert Leslie Bellem, a prolific pulp writer, created Dan Turner, a private eye who was to appear in each and every issue of *Hollywood Detective*.

Bellem, who later wrote scripts for television shows, never bothered with the niceties of style and the depths of human emotion. He was content writing tale after tale of his hard-boiled creation, who drank barrels of Vat 69, lusted after female suspects with "creamy-white thighs," and never referred to a revolver as a gun but always as a "gat" or a "roscoe," one that seldom fired but always "barked."

It remained for latter-day critics to spoil the fun by suggesting that when it came to Dan Turner, Bellem was only kidding.

52 ••
10-Story Detective
January 1938
Unknown
A first issue. The year 1938 was a hot one for new titles in the detective field.

53 ••
Dime Detective
May 1932
William Reusswig
The most successful competitor to *Black Mask*.

Writers of the Purple Sage

Westward Ho!

Few branches of fiction have been as popular as the western story or have as long a tradition in America. James Fenimore Cooper's *The Last of the Mohicans* was published in 1826, and Owen Wister's *The Virginian* in 1902. Acclaimed as American literary classics, they represent two of the best-known early "westerns."

(A case could be made for calling *The Last of the Mohicans* an "eastern" since the story takes place around Lake Champlain between Vermont and upstate New York during the French and Indian wars. However, it certainly was a "western" in atmosphere and plot, if not in location.)

But the most popular westerns of all and the most enduring certainly with teenage boys were Ned Buntline's stories of Buffalo Bill, a staple of *Street & Smith's New York Weekly* beginning in 1869. The cowboys of *The Virginian* and Natty Bumppo of Cooper's *Leatherstocking Tales* may have become literature, but Buffalo Bill became legend.

"Ned Buntline" really was Edward Zane Carroll Judson, a writer who had led a life as exciting as that of any character he wrote about. Author of four hundred dime novels, he was a well-known duelist, an organizer for the infamous "Know-Nothing" political party, and a former member of the Union Army, dismissed during the Civil War for drunkenness. William Frederick Cody owed the name of

Western Story
Every Week Magazine Mar. 23, 1929
15¢
20¢ IN CANADA
STREET AND SMITH PUBLICATION
Features by
ROLAND KREBS ~
SETH RANGER ~
JOHN FREDERICK ~
ARTHUR PRESTON HANKINS

1 •
Western Story Magazine
March 23, 1929
George H. Wert
A longhorn takes the cook for a ride.

2 •
Western Story Magazine
November 19, 1927
William F. Soare
A great touch. Note the bullet cutting the surface of the water.

3 •
Western Story Magazine
May 9, 1931
Gayle Hoskins
Probably the first "graphic novel." Artist Hoskins told a story in twenty-four consecutive cover paintings. This is number eighteen.

"Buffalo Bill" to Buntline. He was a buffalo hunter hired by the Union Pacific Railroad to kill buffalo to feed the men spanning the continent with steel tracks.

Both men had a talent for self-promotion. Cody went on to create *Buffalo Bill's Wild West Show*, while Judson concocted story after story about him. When Judson died of old wounds and a bad heart, Colonel Prentiss Ingraham, author of the competing "Pawnee Bill," took over the "Buffalo Bill" stories.

Buffalo Bill eventually had his own dime novel, and when, by 1919, interest in his adventures had faded, *New Buffalo Bill Weekly* became the semi-monthly *Western Story Magazine*. (Street & Smith had tried to sell the original title, but nobody wanted it.) Within a few years *Western Story* was selling half a million copies a week. Competition soon followed, and Street & Smith itself published a number of them: among them, *Far West*, *Wild West Weekly* (the magazine, formerly a dime novel, had been bought from another publisher), and *Cowboy Stories* (bought from the old Clayton Publishing Company). The two real winners were *Western Story Magazine* and *Wild West Weekly*, magazines that prospered for years.

The western also was a staple of more general pulps like *Argosy*, *Adventure*, and *Blue Book*, as well as the slicks. Some writers became identified with the western, though many of them were equally at home with adventure or mystery. Ernest Haycox, whose *Stage to Lordsburg* was made into the film *Stagecoach*, and "Luke Short" (Frederick Glidden) started in the pulps and eventually graduated to the slicks, as had Zane Grey.

Walt Coburn and W.C. Tuttle, the sheriff's son, were popular, as was William Colt MacDonald (his middle name was all the western expertise he needed) and Johnston McCulley, creator of "Zorro." Louis L'Amour was a latecomer to the pulps and wrote for *Thrilling Adventures* (usually under the pen name "Jim Mayo"), *Sky Fighters*, *West*, and *Detective Tales* among others. Elmore Leonard specialized in westerns, switching to mysteries only when westerns had faded.

The proliferation of western-story magazines didn't really begin until the late '20s but continued well into the '30s. *Ace-High* and *Triple-X Magazine*, both creations of the early '20s, began as general pulps, gradually switching over to a western format. *Dime Western*, *10-Story Western*, *.44 Western*, *Pioneer Western*, *Western Rangers*, *Mavericks*, and so on, were all products of the '30s.

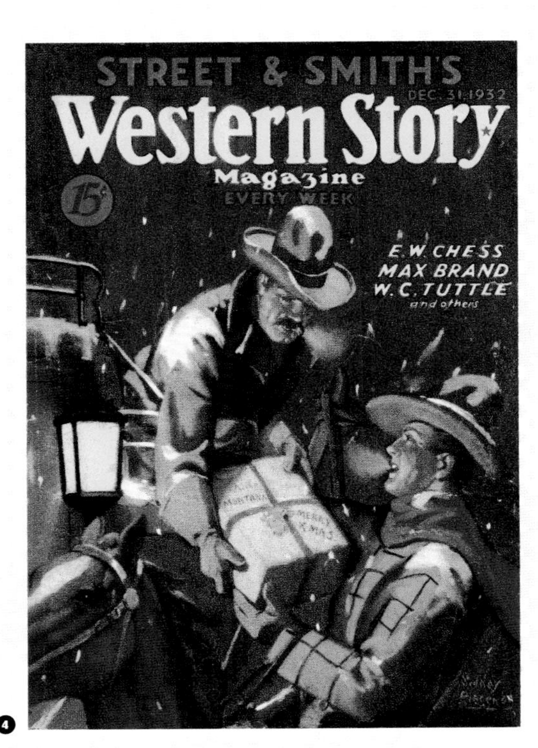

❹ •
Western Story Magazine
December 31, 1932
Sidney Riesenberg
For years the holiday issues of Street & Smith's magazines featured a Christmas cover.

The standard western story cover of the late '20s and the '30s was typically one of the gunfighter or cowboy in a crouch with both guns blazing. *Western Story Magazine* of the early '20s, on the other hand, featured covers far removed from portraits of the typical gunslinger. As we've said, some were almost pastoral: a gold miner leading his donkey, a cowpoke and his horse in the dead of winter "riding the line," a mountain man aiming his gun at a cougar crouching on the roof of his cabin, a farmer and his son walking away from a trout stream with a full catch of fish...

Those early covers owed much to the paintings of Frederic Remington and Charles Russell. They were nostalgic in mood, and, while they may not have mirrored reality, the West they portrayed was alive and well in the imagination of the reader. The slogan of *Western Story* was "big, clean stories of outdoor life," and the covers conveyed exactly that.

Toward the middle and end of the '20s competition crept into the field, and violence and gunfighting became the order of the day when it came to covers. For the better magazines, the covers didn't suffer at all. Walter M. Baumhofer, Gayle Hoskins, R.G. Harris, Nick Eggenhofer, George Wert, Edgar Franklin Wittmack, Fred Craft, Gerard Delano, and H.W. Scott, among others, frequently made the covers of the western pulps artistic standouts on the newsstands.

With the proliferation of titles also came a proliferation of authors, many of whom knew nothing of the West beyond what they had gleaned in the stacks of the New York Public Library. But the readers of westerns

5 ••
Far West Illustrated
March 1927
H. Fisk
Early Western pulps usually had the best painted and most evocative covers of all the pulps.

6 •
The Lariat Story Magazine
January 1926
Elliott Dold
Artist Dold painted covers in a cartoonish style.

ar West Stories
une 1930
oward V. Brown
hanges in cover design and
itle were common in the pulps.

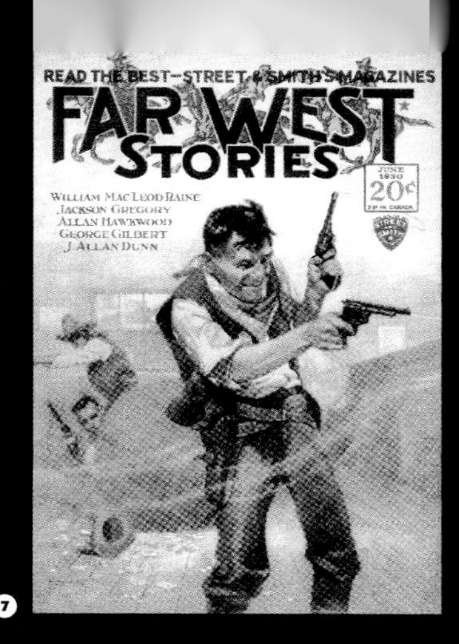

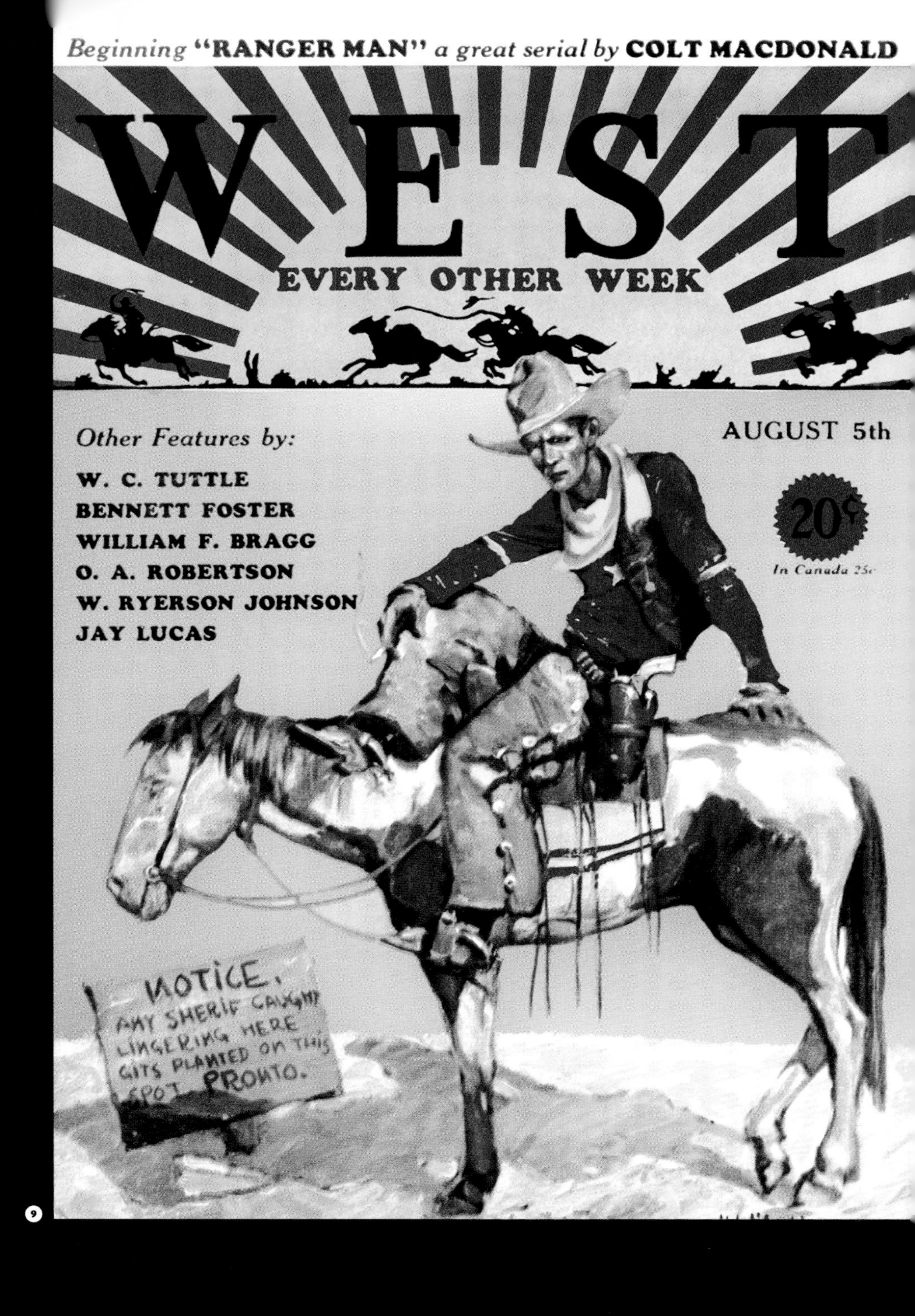

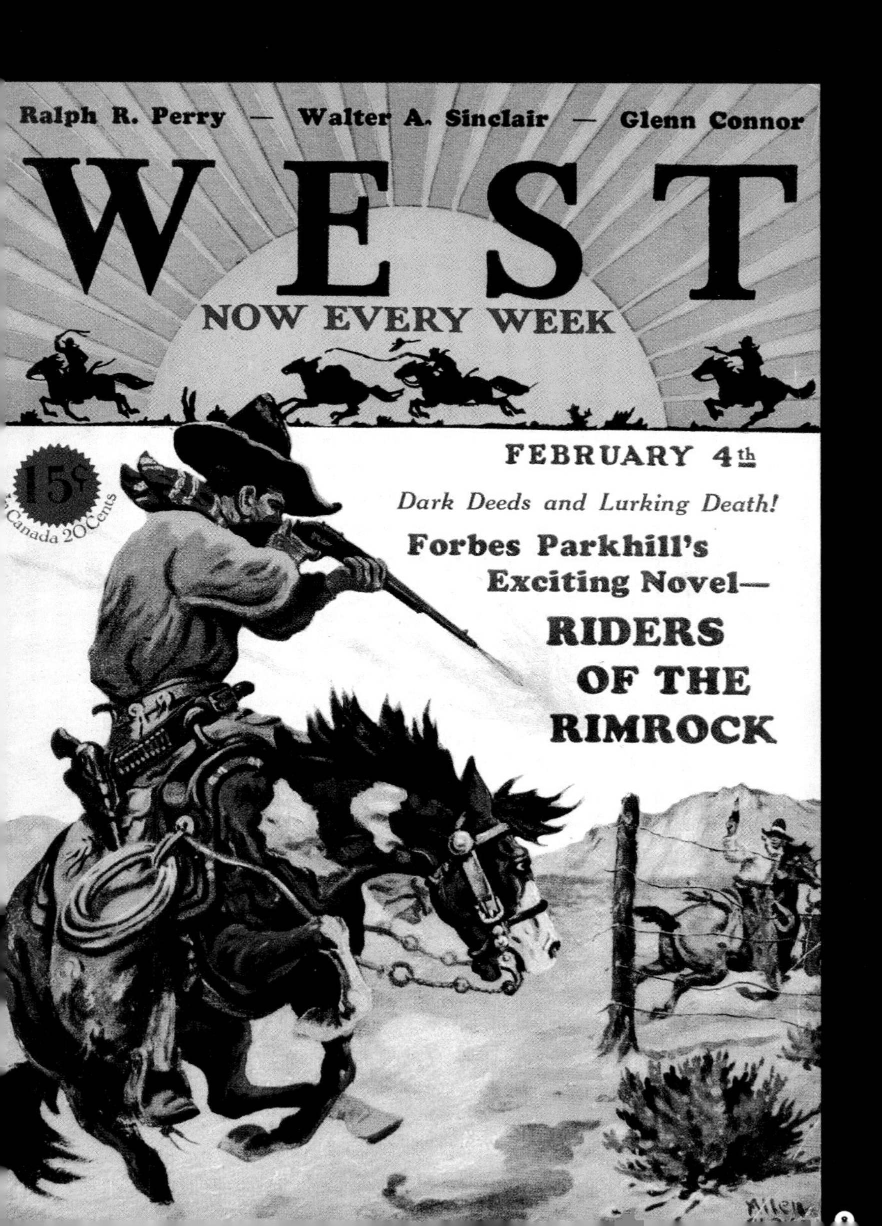

8 •
West
February 4, 1928
Allen Store
One of the oldest and most popular of the Western pulps.

9 •
West
August 5, 1931
H.C. Murphy
Another chuckle or two for the Western story reader.

⑩ •

.44 Western Magazine

January 1938

Gerard Delano

Sometimes two guns didn't help...

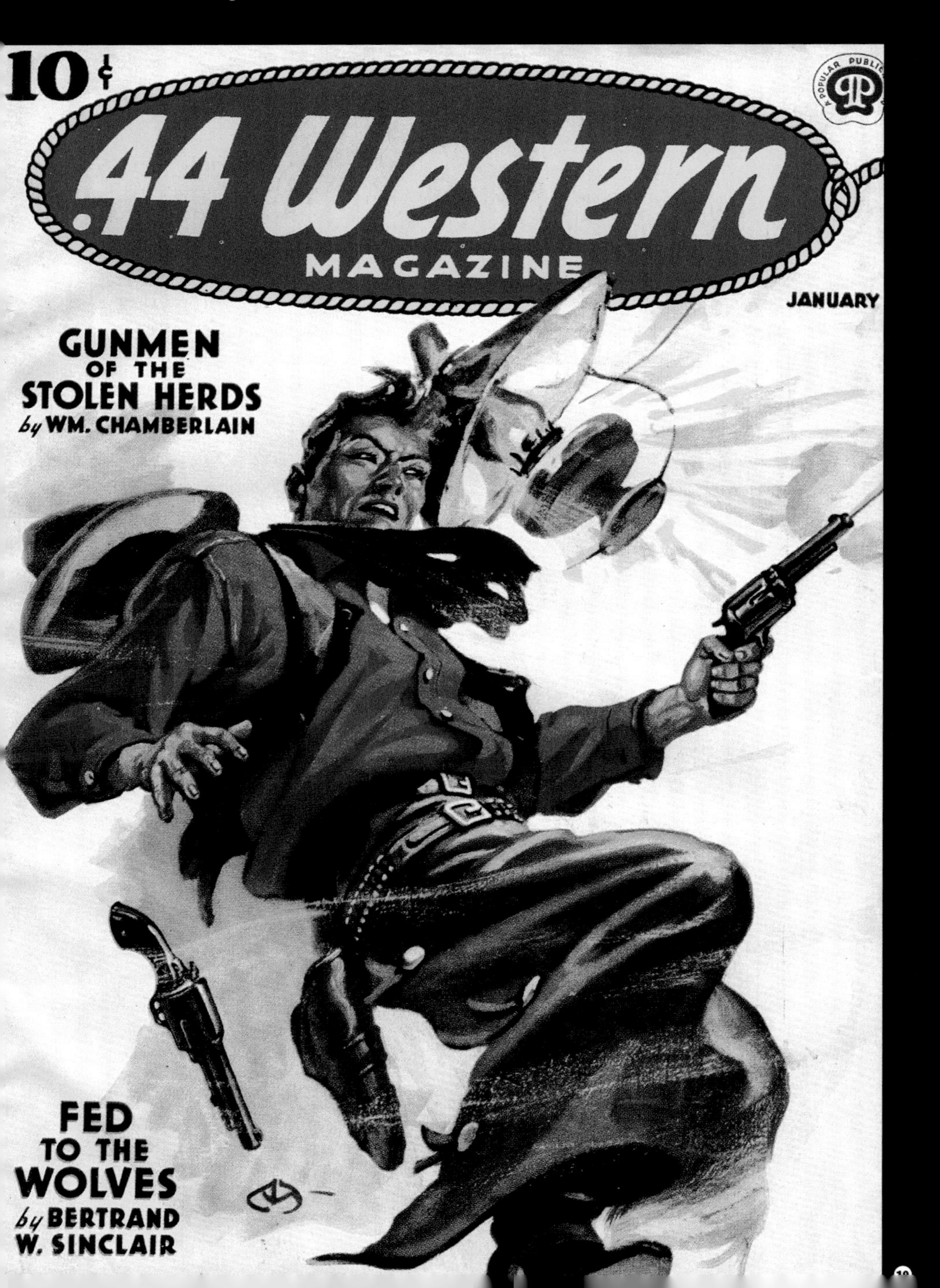

⑪ •

Lariat Story Magazine

May 1927

H.C. Murphy

Real cowboys read the Western pulps all right, but only a few of the writers had ever seen the West.

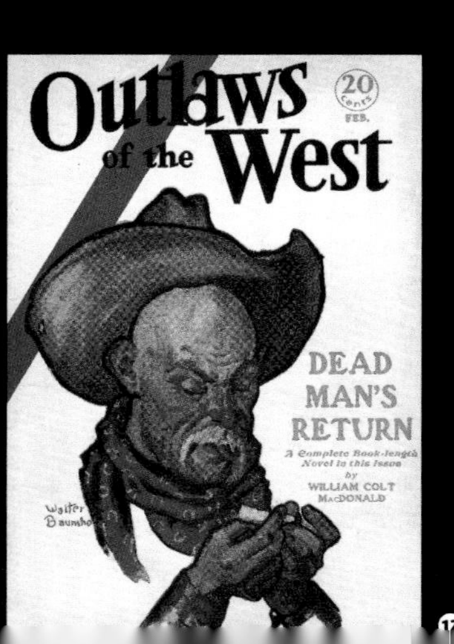

⑫ ••

Outlaws of the West

February 1932

Walter M. Baumhofer

A cover that was originally just a sketch by artist Baumhofer.

⓭ ••
Cowboy Stories
September 1926
Elliott Dold
Of all the pulps, only the Westerns had a sense of humor.

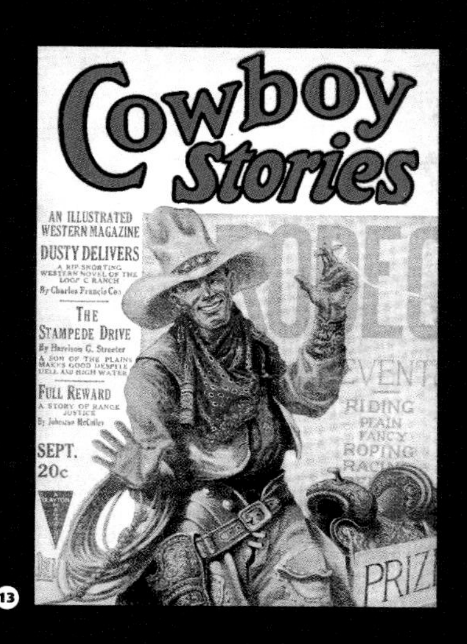

⓭

⓮ ••
Western Rangers
February 1931
Fred Craft
A man and his horse were inseparable.

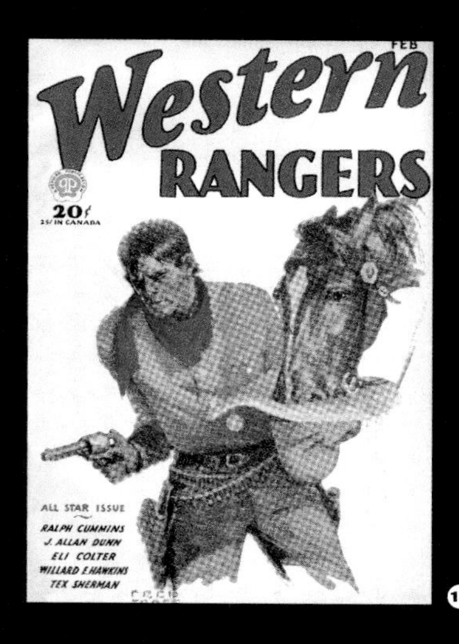

⓮

⓯ ••
Quick-Trigger Western Magazine
November 1929
Walter M. Baumhofer
The first issue of still another short-lived Western pulp.

⓯

⓰ •
Two Gun Western Stories
November 1928
Richard Lillis
The magazine was serious about "two guns."

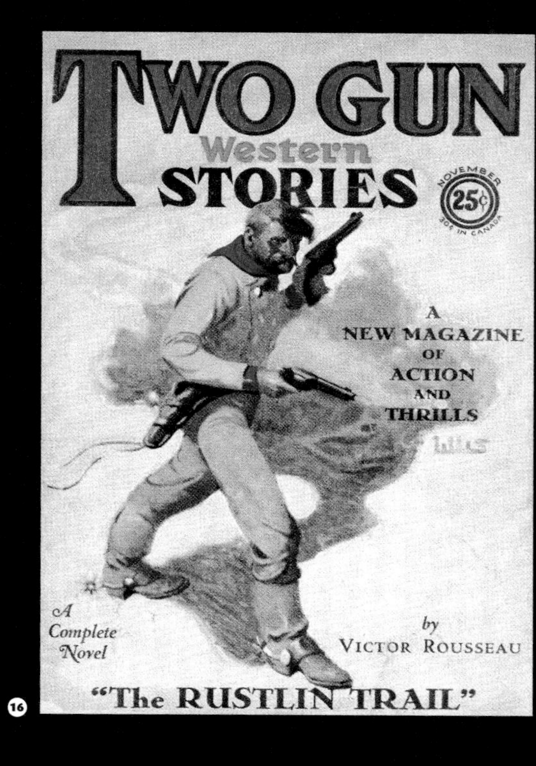

⓰

⓱ •
Western Trails
September–October 1929
Walter M. Baumhofer
Singing a Western ballad—with accompaniment.

⓱

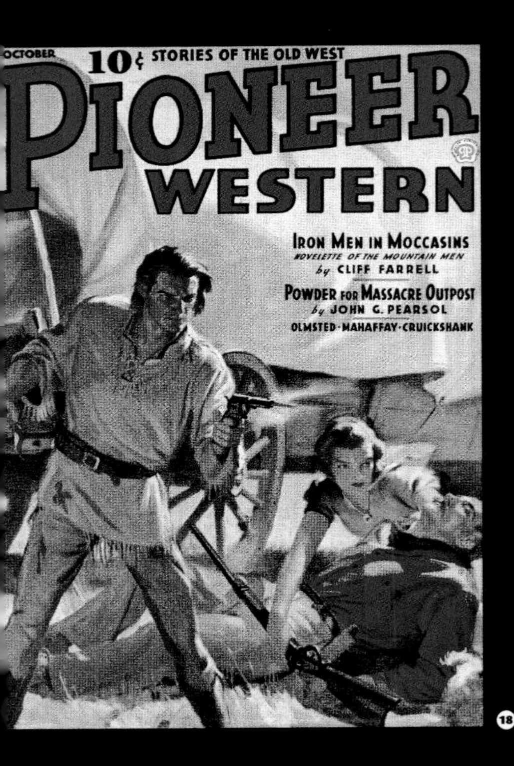

18

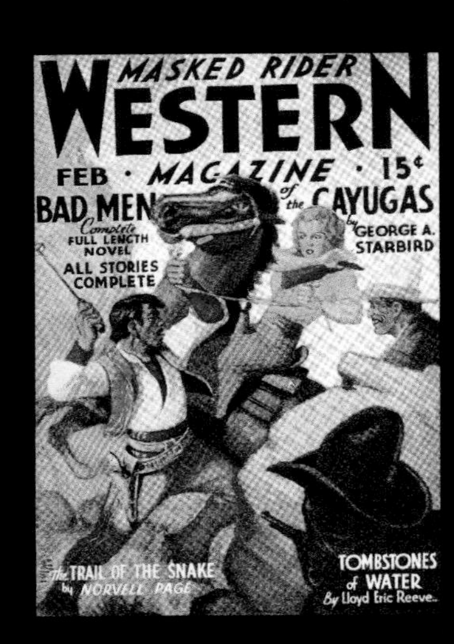

19

• ••
IONEER WESTERN
ctober 1937
m Lovell
nventing a new title
r the Western field was
ometimes difficult.

• ••
ASKED RIDER
ESTERN MAGAZINE
ebruary 1935
nknown
ho was that masked man?
robably inspired by the Lone
anger—before the Lone Ranger
nded up with his own magazine.

• •
ESTERN ROUND-UP
ctober 1935
arry F. Bjorklund
mong the lurid pulps, a black-
nd-white cover stood out.

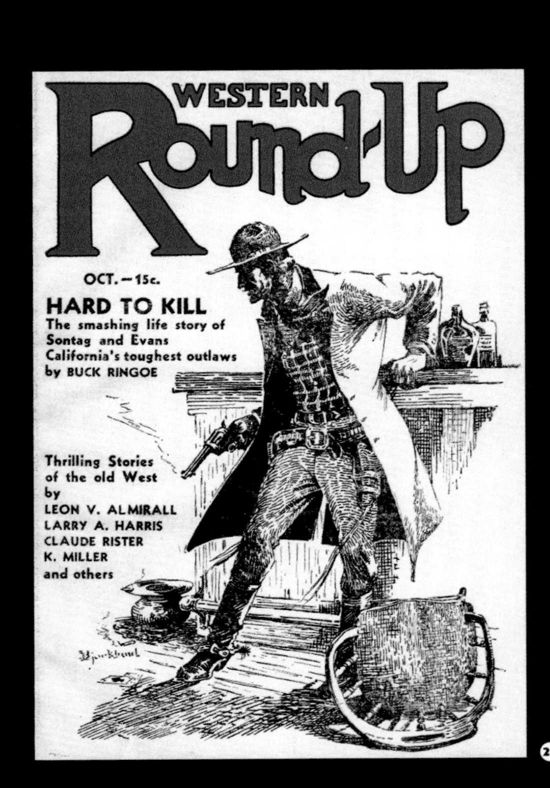

20

21 •••
THE LONE RANGER
July 1937
H.J. Ward
A magazine inspired by the popular radio show of the '30s.

22 •
FRONTIER STORIES
May 1928
H.C. Murphy
Dead man's hand coming up...

21

22

weren't nearly as discerning as the readers of *Adventure*, who usually demanded personal knowledge of geography and events in the stories they read.

The most famous writer of westerns was a man who wasn't particularly proud of them, who lived lavishly in a rented Italian villa overlooking the city of Florence, and whom readers and editors alike loved: readers, for his narrative flow and ability to handle plot and action; editors, for his ability to turn out a needed short story overnight or a novel in a week.

"Max Brand" was the best known pen name, out of the twenty-three he used, of Frederick Faust, a would-be classical poet and reluctant fiction factory. Faust was the true "King of the Pulps," a man who wrote for pulps and slicks alike but, all by himself, very nearly was *Western Story Magazine*. He appeared in 622 issues from 1920 through 1935 under eleven pen names. He wrote thirteen million words for this one magazine alone, at their top rate of five cents a word, for a total of nearly $15 million in 1998 dollars.

No other writer of westerns—or any other genre, for that matter—even came close.

23 •
Popular Western
September 1935
Unknown
Fifteen stories for fifteen cents—and every author was featured on the cover.

24 •
Red Seal Western
March 1936
Unknown
Note the *Hopalong Cassidy* novel by Clarence Mulford. Hopalong was popular in the pulps long before the TV series.

25

26

25 • • •
Pete Rice Magazine
May 1934
Walter M. Baumhofer
"Pete Rice" was the first Western hero pulp.

26 • •
Dime Western Magazine
December 1932
Walter M. Baumhofer
The first issue. *Dime Western* lasted from the early thirties to the mid-fifties.

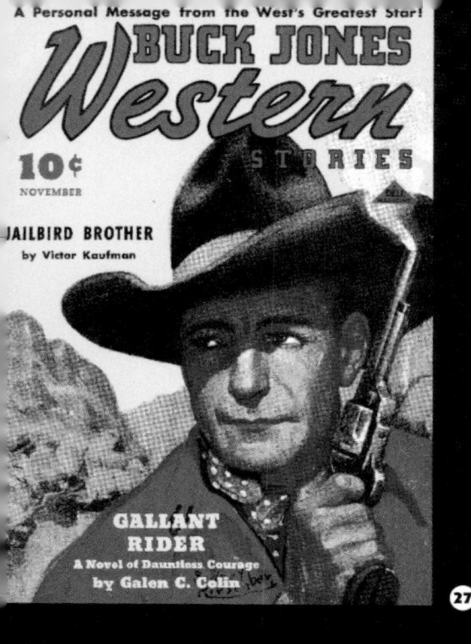

27

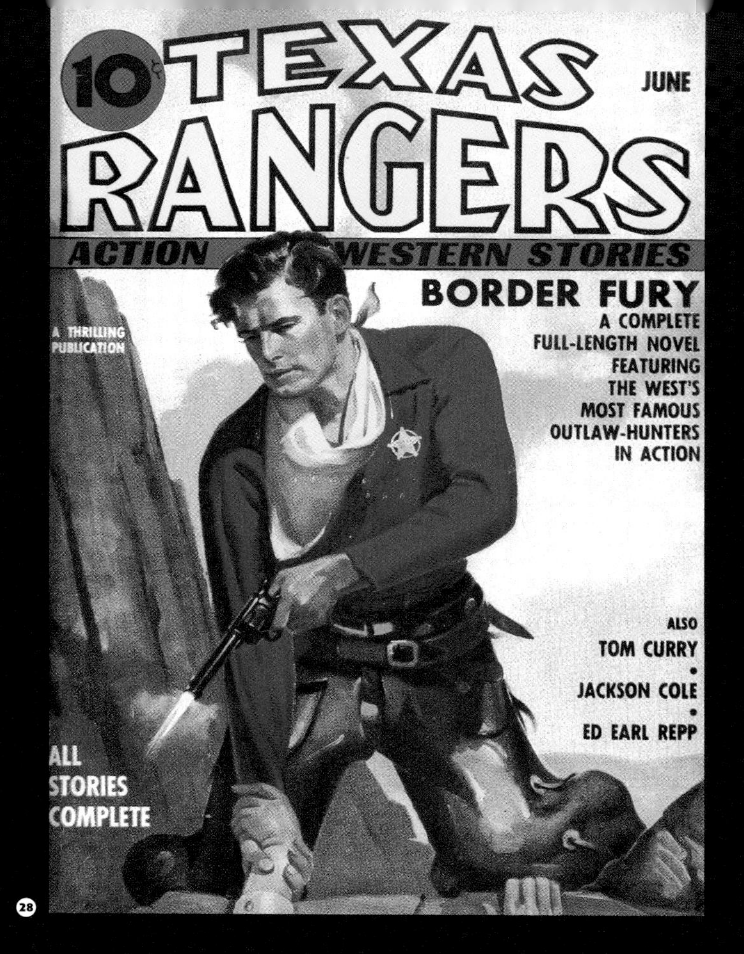

28

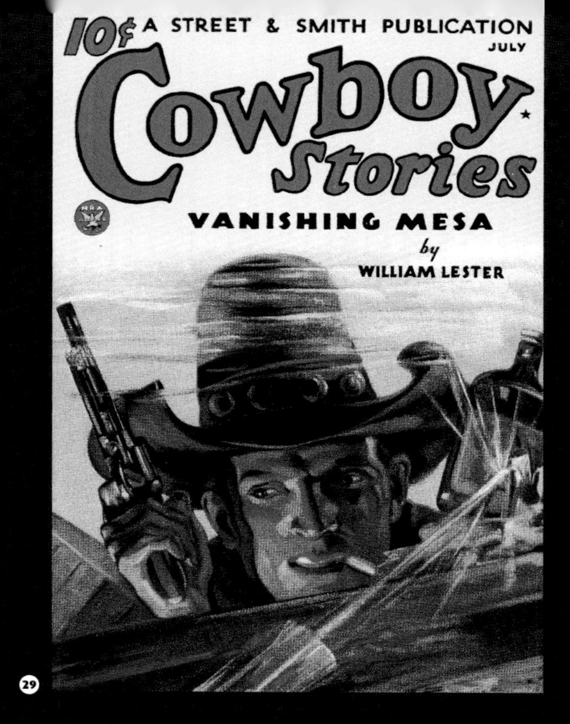

29

7 •••
3uck Jones Western Stories
November 1936
idney Riesenberg
3uck Jones was a lot
nore popular in films than
n magazines.

8 •
exas Rangers
une 1937
nknown
Of course there had to be a
nagazine about Texas Rangers.

9 ••
owboy Stories
uly 1934
.W. Scott
different publisher and
he covers suddenly were
ction-filled.

0 ••
3ull's-Eye Western Stories
ebruary 1935
. Clinton Shepherd
he first and only issue of
scarce pulp.

1 ••
Ace-High Western Magazine
ugust 1936
om Lovell
he first issue of *Ace-High*
nder a new publisher.

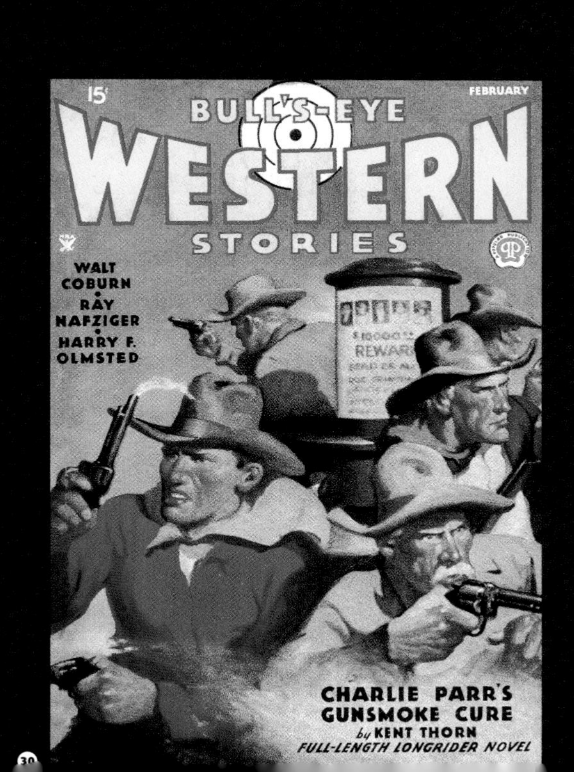

30

31

STREET & SMITH'S
WILD WEST
10¢
WEEKLY
ALL STORIES COMPLETE
MARCH 18
1939
A GUN LAWYER FOR CIRCLE J by Cleve Endicott

32 ••
WILD WEST WEEKLY
March 18, 1939
H.W. Scott
One of the great all-time poster covers for *Wild West Weekly*.

33 ••
10 STORY WESTERN MAGAZINE
January 1936
Don Hewitt
Another first issue.
Somehow Western wives always looked like Betty Crocker.

Frank Gruber, writer of both mysteries and westerns, claimed there were only seven basic western stories: the Union Pacific Story, the Ranch Story, the Empire Story (where the ranch is the size of the fabled King ranch), the Revenge Story, Custer's Last Stand (otherwise known as the Massacre Story), the Outlaw Story, and the Marshal Story.

Faust insisted that, while there may be seven basic stories, there was only one plot. In Faust's view, the basic plot was where "the good man becomes bad and the bad man becomes good." That way, he claimed, you always had conflict.

Faust should have known. At his peak he wrote more than a million words a year and sold every one of them.

The westerns faded in the '40s, and, unlike the science-fiction or mystery fields, never thrived in the digest format. Perhaps the reason was timing. From the turn of the century to the start of World War II, Los Angeles and San Francisco were mythical cities on a distant coast and in between was the West—the remains of the Frontier and the embodiment of the virtues of everything American. The Coast was five days away by car and three by train. Not many people made the trip, and the West remained wide open for any fantasy about cowboys and Indians, gunslingers and sheriffs, that you cared to imagine.

After the war, the distance to the Coast shrank to five hours by plane, and what had been remote and shrouded in myth became near and familiar. The barbed wire that cut across the wide-open spaces also cut across the imagination.

The Old West never recovered, and the New West suddenly was too close and prosaic, a place of grungy trailer parks, disintegrating desert towns, and posh gambling cities like Las Vegas and Reno. Reality had replaced fantasy, and when it came to western stories, who was interested in reality?

It took the popular novels of Louis L'Amour to revive the West for the average reader, and Larry McMurtry (*Lonesome Dove*) to people it with realistic heroes and villains far beyond the abilities of old-time pulp writers.

But the bestsellers of both were still far in the future.

34 ••
COWBOY STORIES
October 1925
Nick Eggenhofer
The first issue. When the pulps died, artist Eggenhofer, a German immigrant, went out West and turned his talents to "fine art."

34

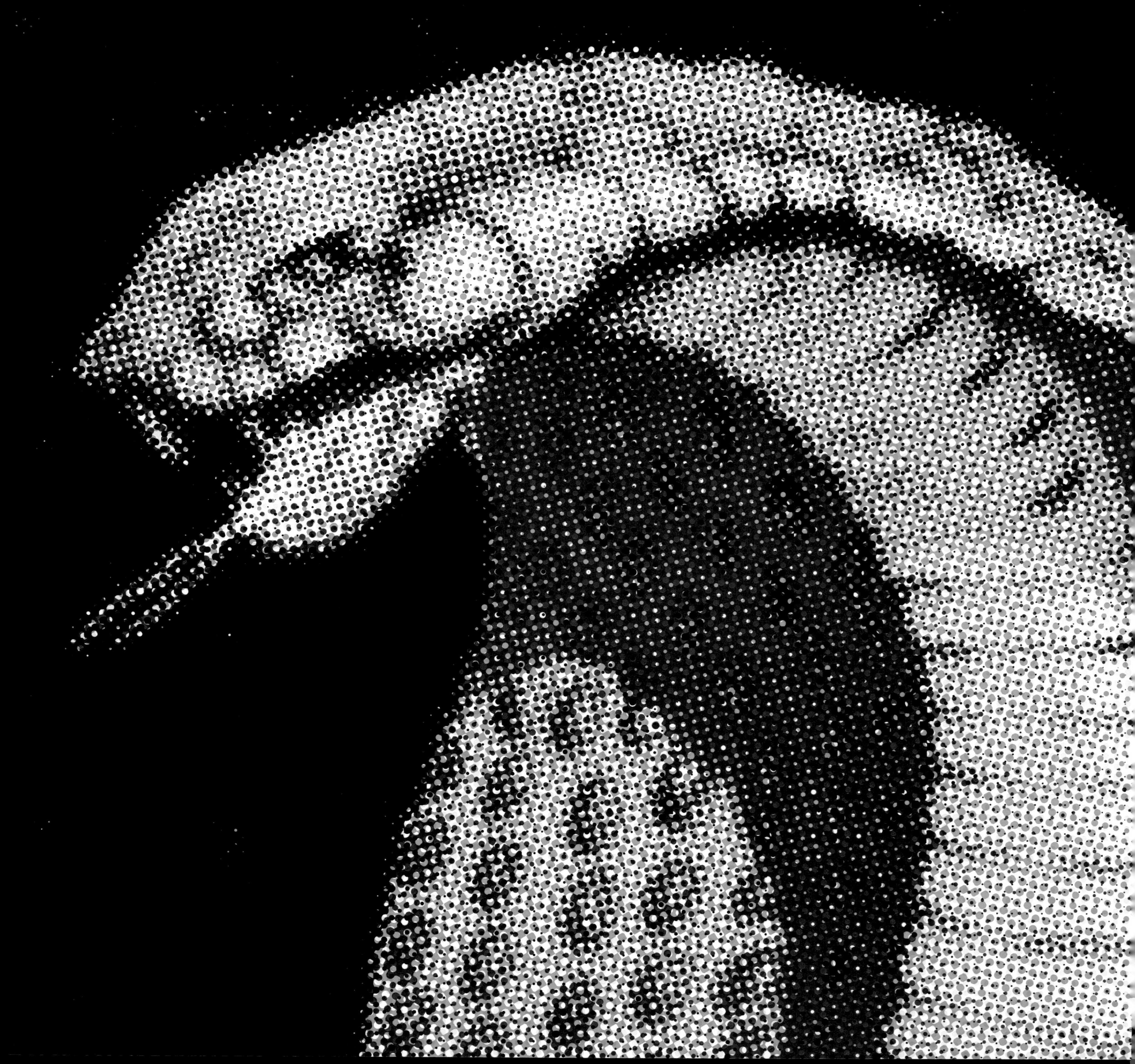

The Shadow Knows

Super Heroes and Super Villains

In 1930 Street & Smith sponsored a radio show called *The Detective Story Magazine Hour* to promote sales of its weekly *Detective Story Magazine*. A narrator introduced the show, and actors dramatized a story from the magazine. Later the narrator intoned the immortal words: "Who knows what evil lurks in the hearts of men? The Shadow knows...." The lines were delivered in a sepulchral voice by Orson Welles.

The narrator quickly became a character in his own right, and a magazine featuring "The Shadow" was a logical afterthought. Street & Smith wanted to protect its copyright of the character, and it was also anxious to test a pulp based on a series character, somewhat in the mold of its old Nick Carter and Buffalo Bill dime novels.

Originally *The Shadow* was scheduled as a quarterly, and the stories were provided by Walter B. Gibson (an amateur magician who had ghostwritten for Houdini) under the name of "Maxwell Grant."

The Shadow was a tremendous success. Gibson, with his magician's background, turned the plots into fascinating story structures featuring hidden staircases, two-way mirrors, robots, and all the usual paraphernalia familiar to a magician. The magazine soon was published twice a month and sold three hundred thousand copies.

❶ • • •
THE SHADOW
January 15, 1933
George Rozen
The Shadow was the first and most popular of the hero pulps.

❷ • • •
THE SHADOW
April 1, 1934
George Rozen
The cover artists for *The Shadow* excelled at painting posters.

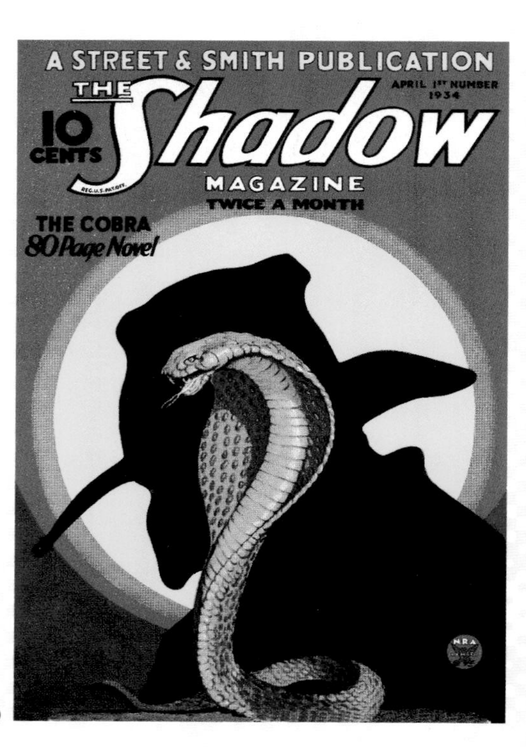

Imitators followed closely on the heels of such success. In 1933 Street & Smith launched its own entry, *Doc Savage*. Under the name of "Kenneth Robeson," Lester Dent wrote novels about the "Man of Bronze." It was high adventure on a global scale with enough planes, exotic enemies, faithful sidekicks, and unusual locales to offer the reader a *Raiders of the Lost Ark* on a monthly basis.

Basically *The Shadow* was a mystery magazine, with the Shadow frequently assuming the identity of millionaire playboy Lamont Cranston. Eventually the author revealed that Cranston, too, was an assumed personality, that the Shadow was really Kent Allard, a World War I aviator and allied spy. Who knows who the Shadow may have been revealed to *really* be if the magazine had continued a few more years?

Doc Savage was an adventure publication starring Clark Savage, Jr. Doc, who had an incredible physique (naturally), was a surgeon, scientist, and philanthropist all rolled into one—a perfect role model for teenagers of the Depression-ridden 1930s!

3 ••
THE SHADOW
May 1, 1936
George Rozen
An action cover. A departure from the usual poster.

4 •••
THE SHADOW
July 1, 1934
George Rozen
If the Shadow couldn't "cloud your mind" maybe a bullet would.

❺ • • •

Doc Savage Magazine

April 1934

Walter M. Baumhofer

Giant green hands on pulp covers were a genre by themselves.

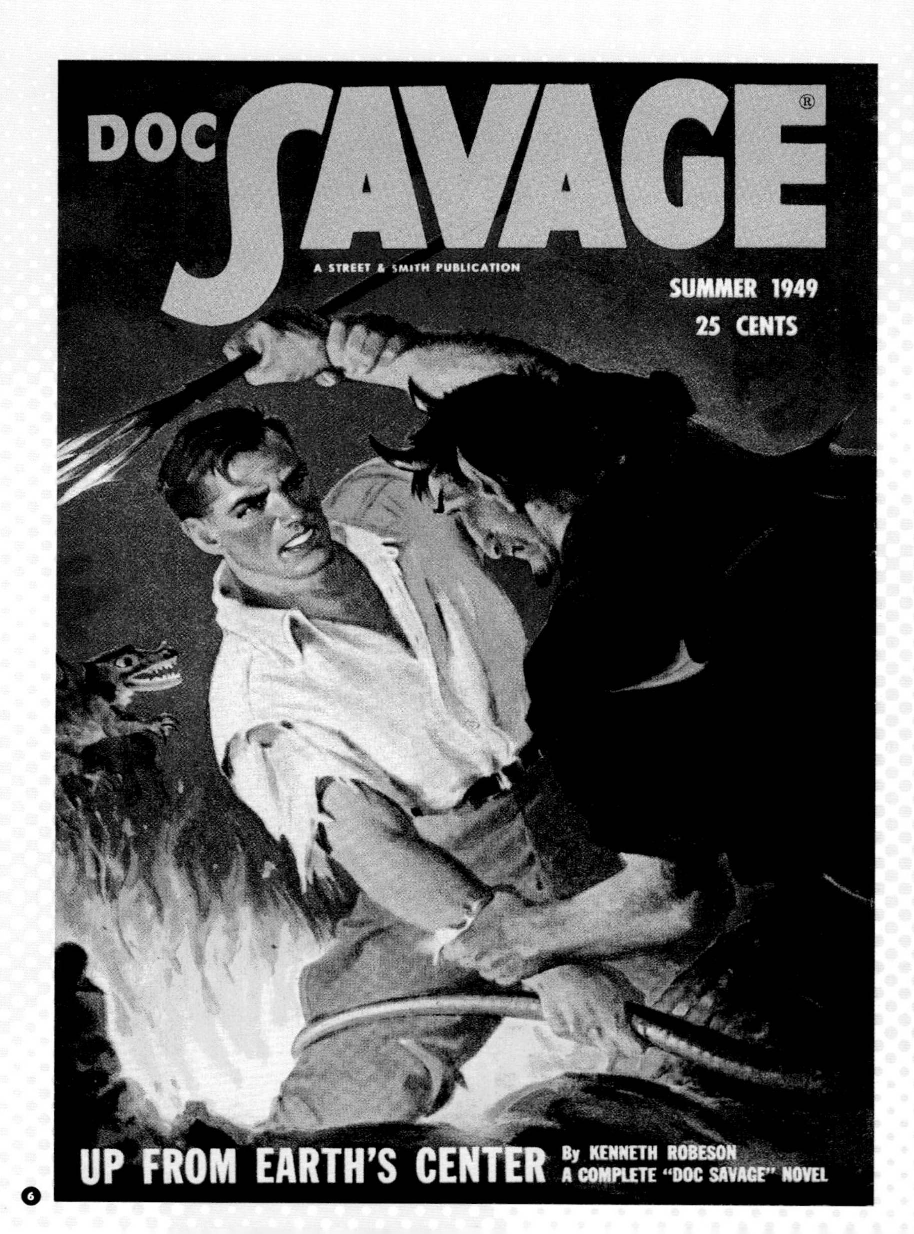

❻ • • • •

Doc Savage Magazine

Summer 1949

George Rozen

Some dealers consider this last issue almost as valuable as the first.

❼ • • •

Doc Savage Magazine

August 1933

Walter M. Baumhofer

Doc Savage was the third of the hero pulps, from the same publisher as *The Shadow* and almost as popular.

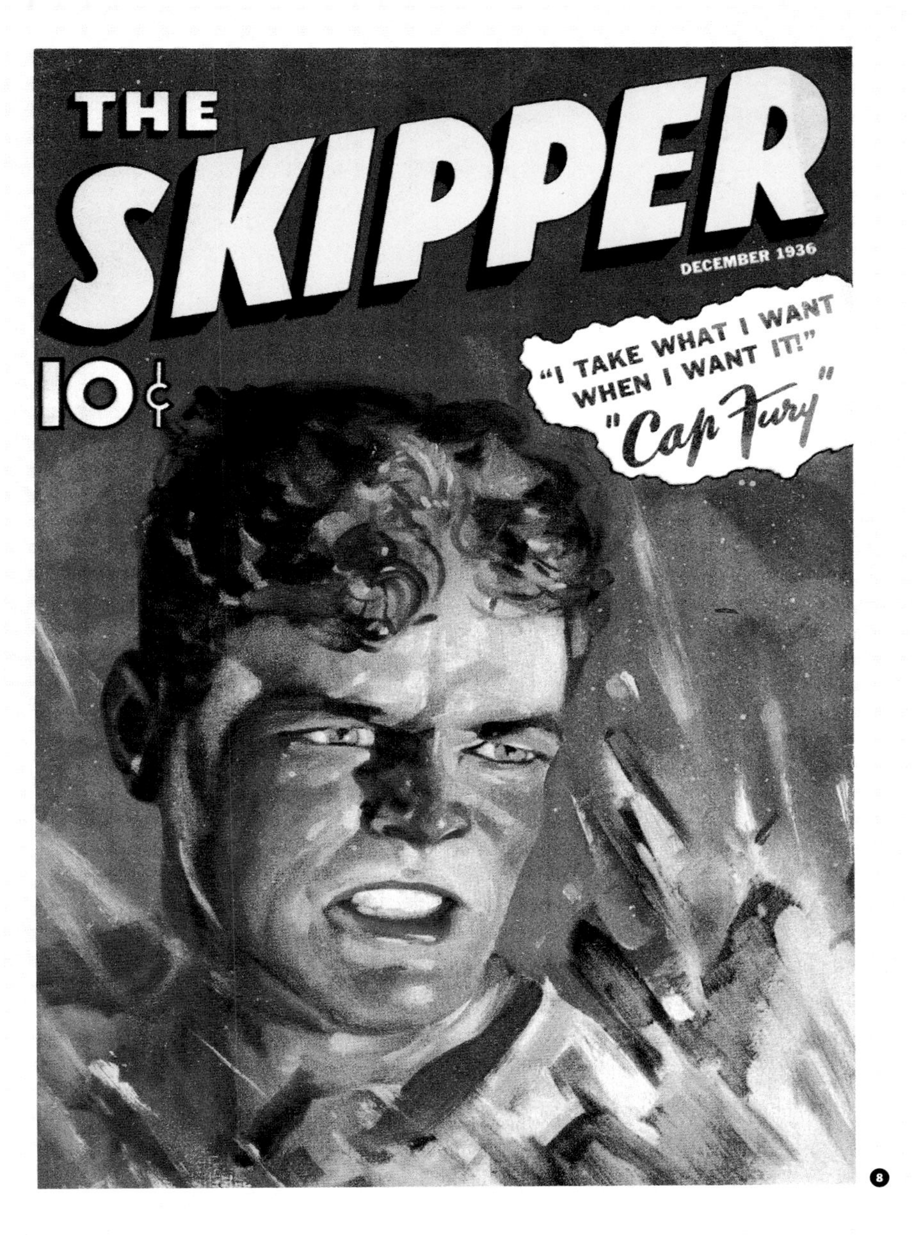

8 ••
THE SKIPPER
December 1936
Lawrence D. Toney
The Skipper was a sea-going hero pulp.

9 ••
THE WHISPERER
October 1936
John Newton Howitt
Still another hero pulp from the publishers of *The Shadow*.

10 ••
THE PHANTOM DETECTIVE
May 1936
Rudolph Belarski
The second—and longest-lived—of the hero pulps.

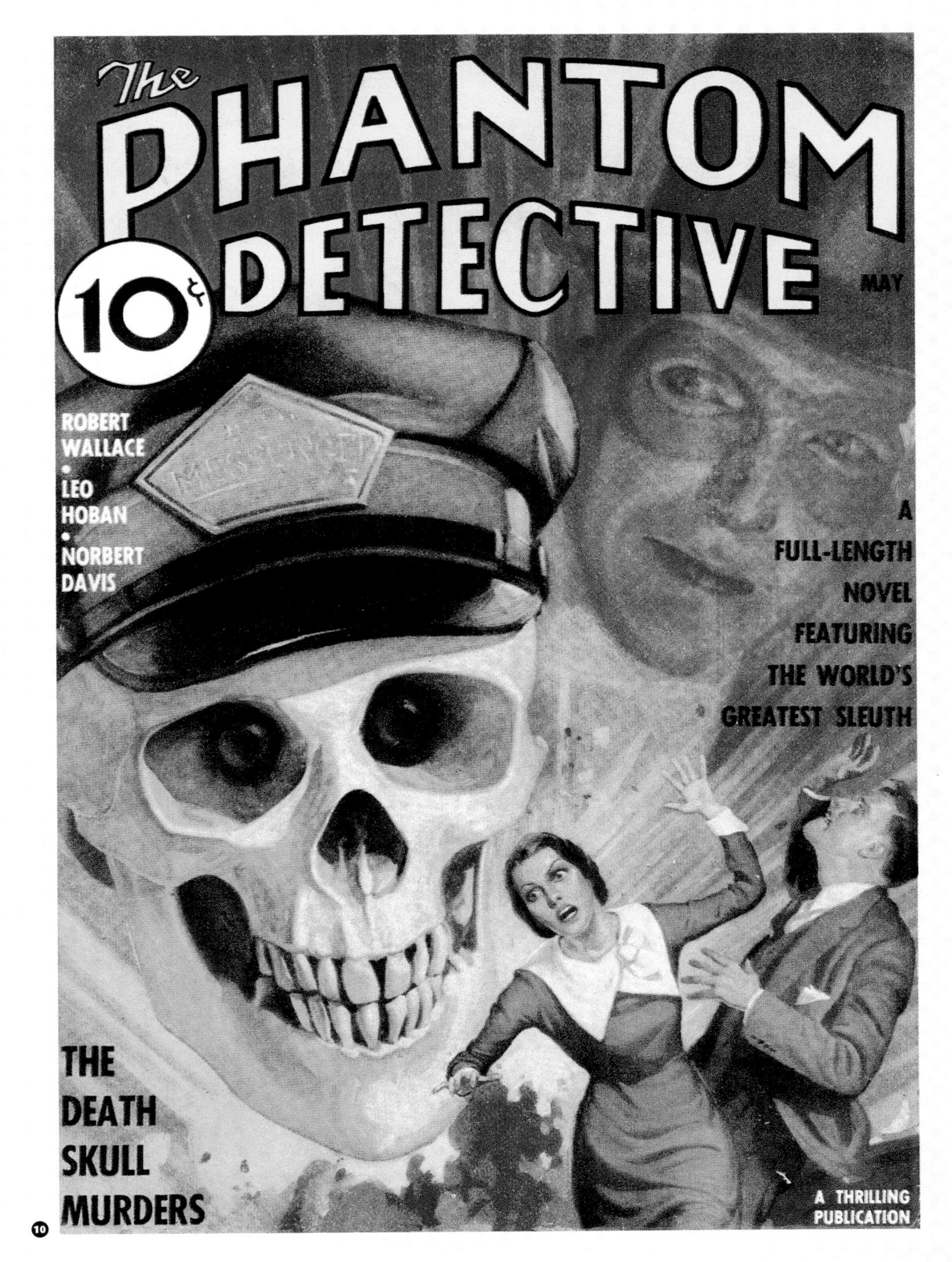

11 •••
ERENCE X. O'LEARY'S
WAR BIRDS
April 1935
Rudolph Belarski
O'Leary starred in pulps about
World War I and, when they
failed, switched to rocket ships.
That didn't help either.

12 •••
DUSTY AYRES
AND HIS BATTLE BIRDS
May-June 1935
Frederick Blakeslee
The magazine started as an
air pulp, then switched to a
science-fiction format to
attract more readers. It didn't...

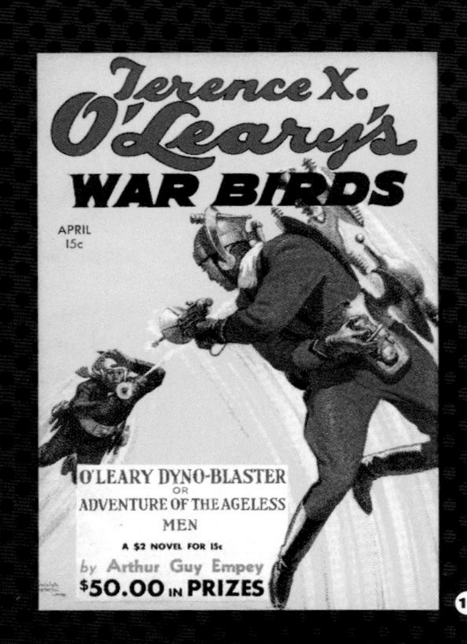

11

12

The second hero pulp actually was *The Phantom Detective* dated February 1933, one month ahead of *Doc Savage*. Following its success were *The Spider*, dated October 1933 and aimed directly at *The Shadow*'s audience; and *G-8 and His Battle Aces*. The Phantom, another millionaire playboy named Richard Curtis Van Loan, was a master of disguise. Created by ex-aviator Robert J. Hogan, G-8 was a flying ace and spy, much like Kent Allard, in World War I, which he refought for the 110-issue run of the magazine. The wildly improbable villains included one who had trained a tiger to leap from the cockpit of his plane onto an allied plane below. After it had finished off the pilot, the tiger leaped back into the villain's plane, now flying beneath. A variation had Chinese villains leaping from plane to plane.

The Spider, most of whose exploits were written by "Grant Stockbridge," was actually wealthy New Yorker Richard Wentworth. (During the Depression it was comforting for the poor to know the rich were on their side when it came to fighting crime.) Other writers occasionally wrote novels for *The Spider*, but the character was largely the brainchild of ex-newspaperman Norvell Page, who frequently dressed as the Spider, complete with cape and slouch hat.

Hoping to cash in on the prosperity of *The Spider* was *Operator #5*. According to the original author of the series, Frederick Davis, writing under the name of "Curtis Steele," the premise was simple: "Operator #5 must single-handedly, or almost, save the nation from complete destruction regularly every month."

The magazine was notable for its thirteen-issue "Purple Invasion" series, sometimes referred to as the *War and Peace* of the pulps. Much of the popularity of *Operator #5* undoubtedly could be traced to the prevailing paranoia of the times about hostile foreign nations—one of the reasons why the country was resolutely isolationist and wanted nothing to do with foreign wars. Fictional wars were something else again.

Kenneth Robeson, creator of *Doc Savage*, the "Man of Bronze," also created *The Avenger*, the "Man of Steel." The "Iron Man" was left for comic books years later. *The Avenger* ran for 24 issues but didn't have the staying power of its big brother.

The hero pulps, the most popular of all the genres during the 1930s, also included *Bill Barnes*, about an air adventurer; *Captain Future*, a hero science-fiction pulp; *Dusty Ayres and His Battle Birds*, an air war/science-fiction pulp; *Secret Agent X*; *The Secret 6*; *The Skipper*; *The Whisperer*; and many others.

There were western-hero pulps as well, including *Pete Rice Magazine*; *The Lone Ranger*, inspired by the radio show; and *Hopalong Cassidy's Western Magazine*, a latecomer that rode the coattails of the popular television series (based, in turn, on earlier Hopalong Cassidy stories in the western magazines).

Some pulp critics claim the very first hero pulp actually was *Wild West Weekly*, since the first issues detailed the adventures of young Billy West, nicknamed "Wild" in the original dime novel. But after a few issues, the magazine became largely devoted to stories about other series characters.

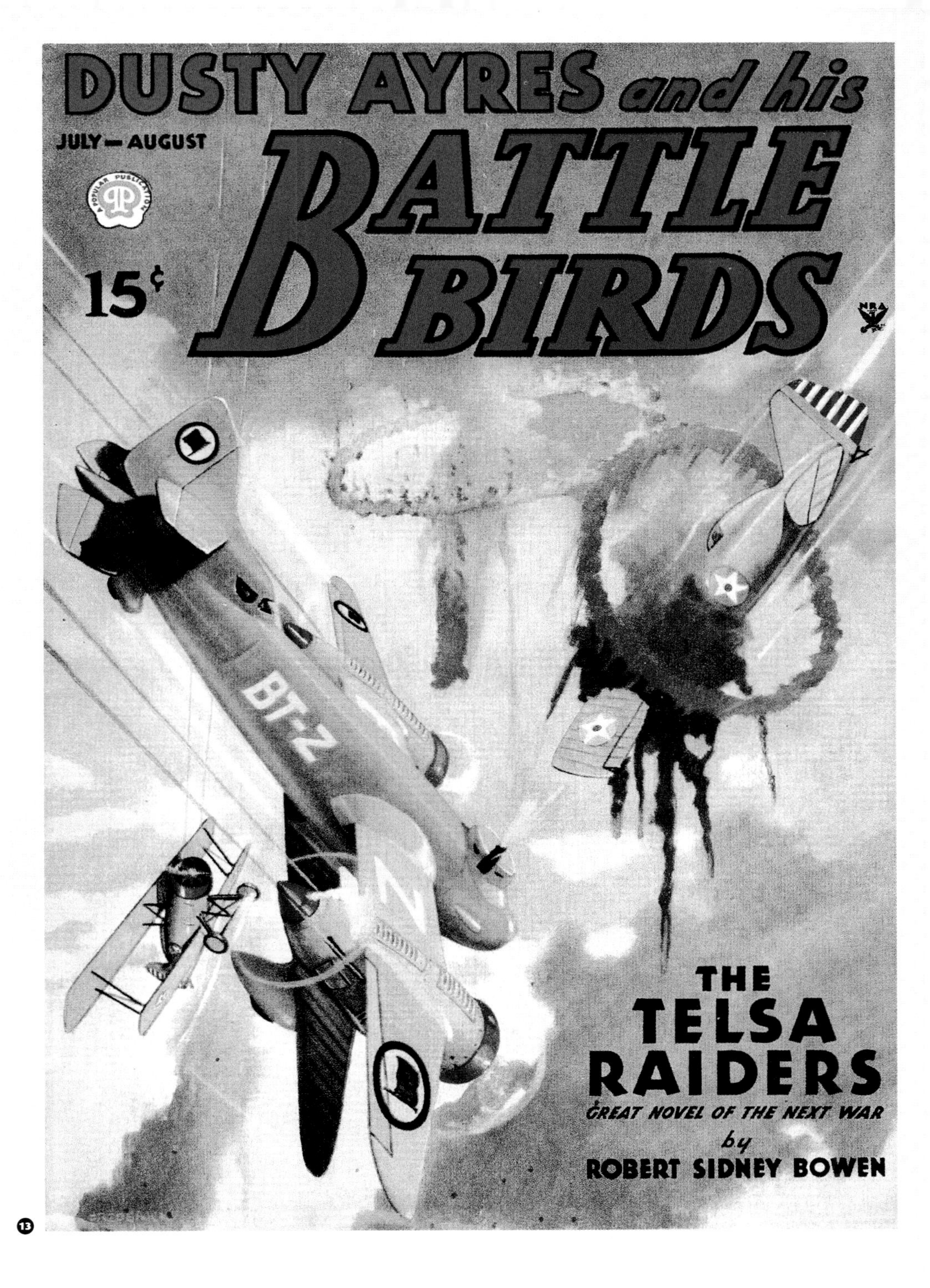

13 •••
Dusty Ayres and His Battle Birds
July-August 1935
Frederick Blakeslee
Sales were low despite the sensational covers.

14 •••
Bill Barnes Air Adventurer
February 1934
Frank Tinsley
The first issue of an air hero pulp.

15 ••
G-8 and His Battle Aces
May 1938
Frederick Blakeslee
The stories were wildly improbable—and the readers loved them.

16 ••
G-8 and His Battle Aces
January 1938
Frederick Blakeslee
The covers were absurd but gripping for a teenager in the '30s.

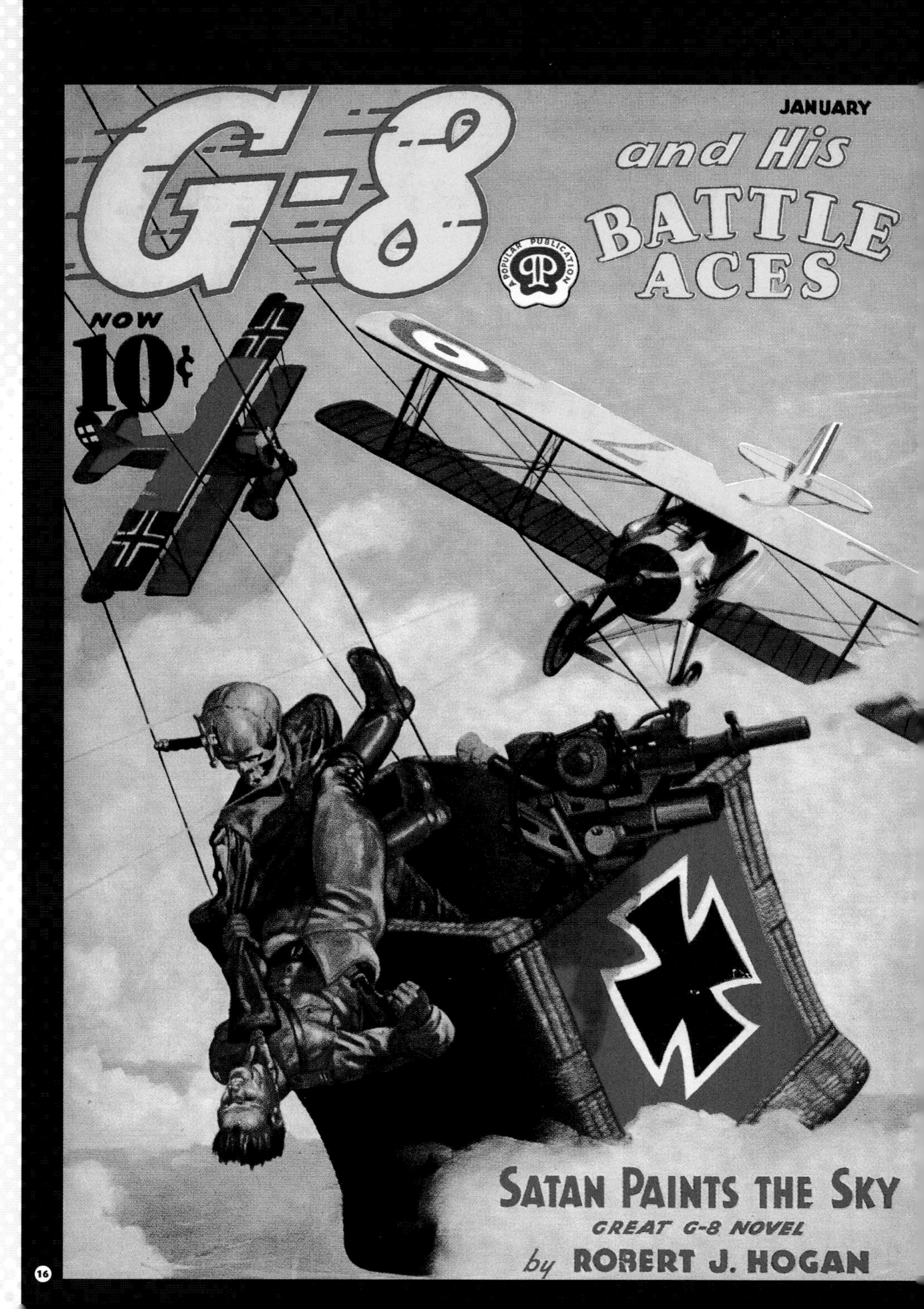

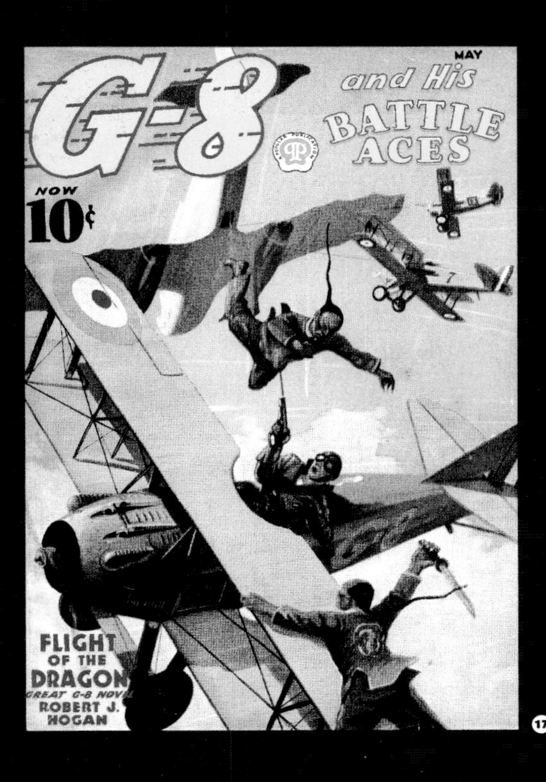

17 ••
G-8 and His Battle Aces
May 1937
Frederick Blakeslee
In *G-8* you could never tell who might drop in.

18 ••
Bill Barnes Air Adventurer
September 1934
Frank Tinsley
Biplane dive bombers? Anything was possible in the pulps.

The hero pulps even had a sub-genre—the villain pulp—though all its members were short-lived. The first was *Doctor Death*, a character who originally appeared in *All Detective Magazine*. Along with the ongoing hero, you also had an ongoing villain, though not quite villainous enough to justify publication beyond three issues. The next title, only slightly more successful, was *The Mysterious Wu Fang*, patterned after Sax Rohmer's "Fu Manchu" stories in *Collier's*. Henry Steeger, president of Popular Publications, even hired Richard Flanagan, illustrator of Rohmer's *Collier's* tales, to do the inside drawings. The author was Robert J. Hogan of *G-8* fame.

Wu Fang ran for seven monthly issues, then was abruptly dropped in favor of the bi-monthly *Dr. Yen Sin*, with stories by Donald E. Keyhoe. Moralists of the period reportedly objected to "yen" and "sin" in the title and after three issues, *Dr. Yen Sin* also was dropped.

The use of an Asian as the villain in *Wu Fang* and *Dr. Yen Sin* (or for that matter, "Fu Manchu") was common in the pulps, with Asian villains showing up with dismaying frequency on the covers of adventure and mystery magazines. For the authors, publishers, and readers, regrettably, it reflected common prejudices of the times. There were Asian heroes in the movies and on the radio—Charlie Chan and the Green Hornet with his faithful sidekick, Kato, come to mind—but beyond them, the pickings were slim. One wonders what the stories and covers might have been like if Bruce Lee movies had been popular at the time.

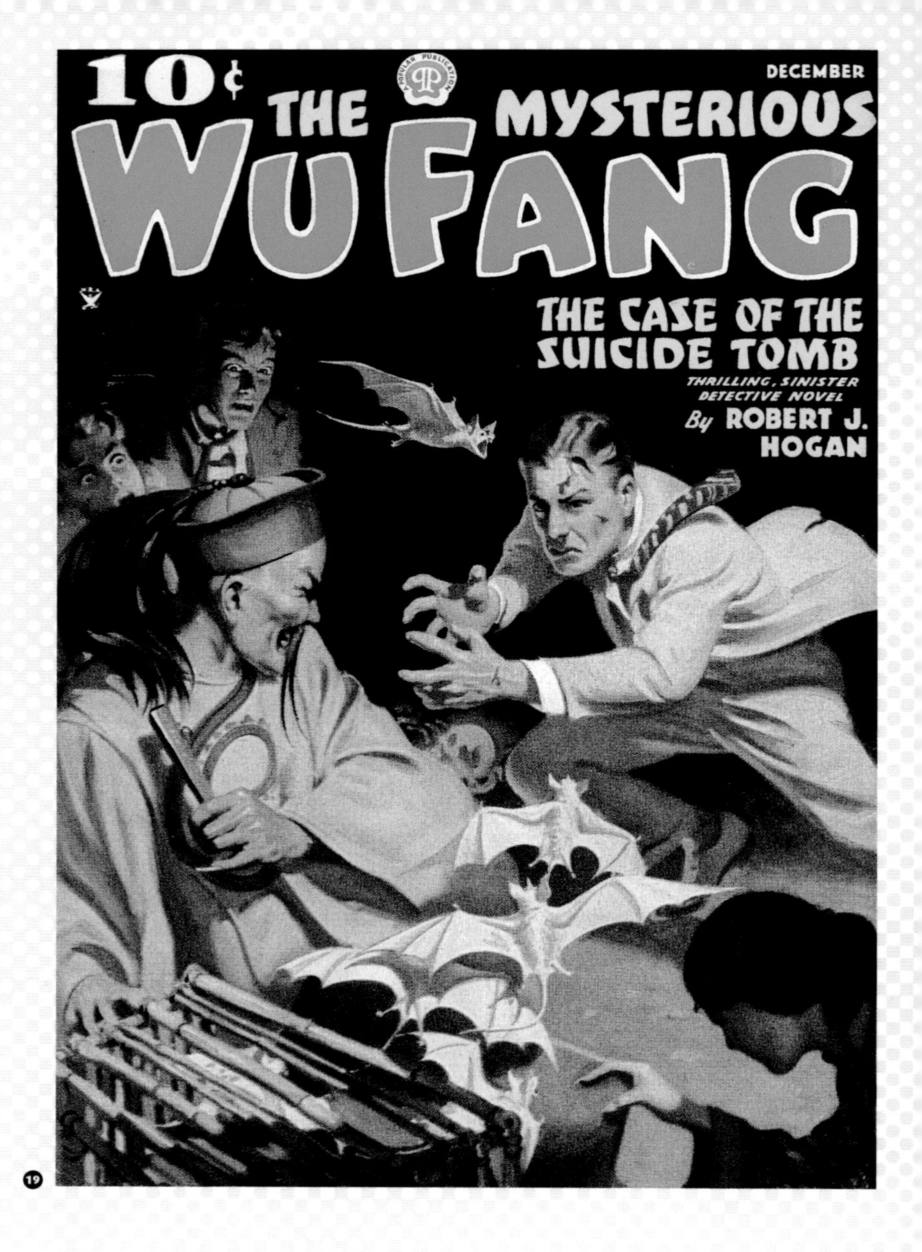

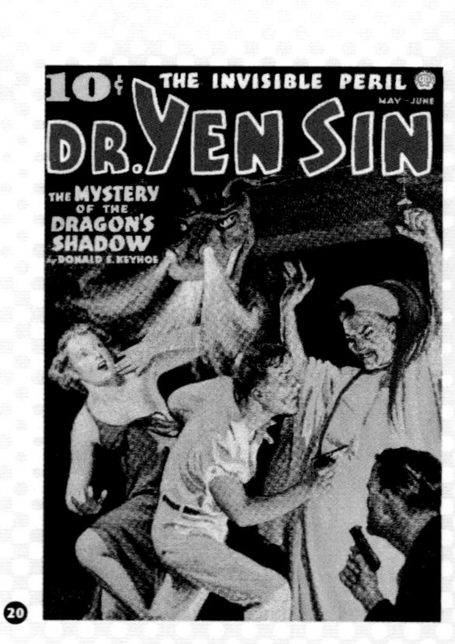

19 •••
The Mysterious Wu Fang
December 1935
Jerome Rozen
Wu Fang was a pulp imitation of Sax Rohmer's *Fu Manchu*.

20 •••
Dr. Yen Sin
May-June 1936
Jerome Rozen
This successor to *Wu Fang* was just as unsuccessful.

21 •••
OPERATOR #5
November 1934
John Newton Howitt
The magazine once published thirteen consecutive "novels" in the "Purple Invasion" series, nicknamed the *War and Peace* of the pulps.

22 ••
NICK CARTER MAGAZINE
July 1935
Jerome Rozen
With the popularity of hero pulps, *Nick Carter*, originally a dime novel, was bound to return.

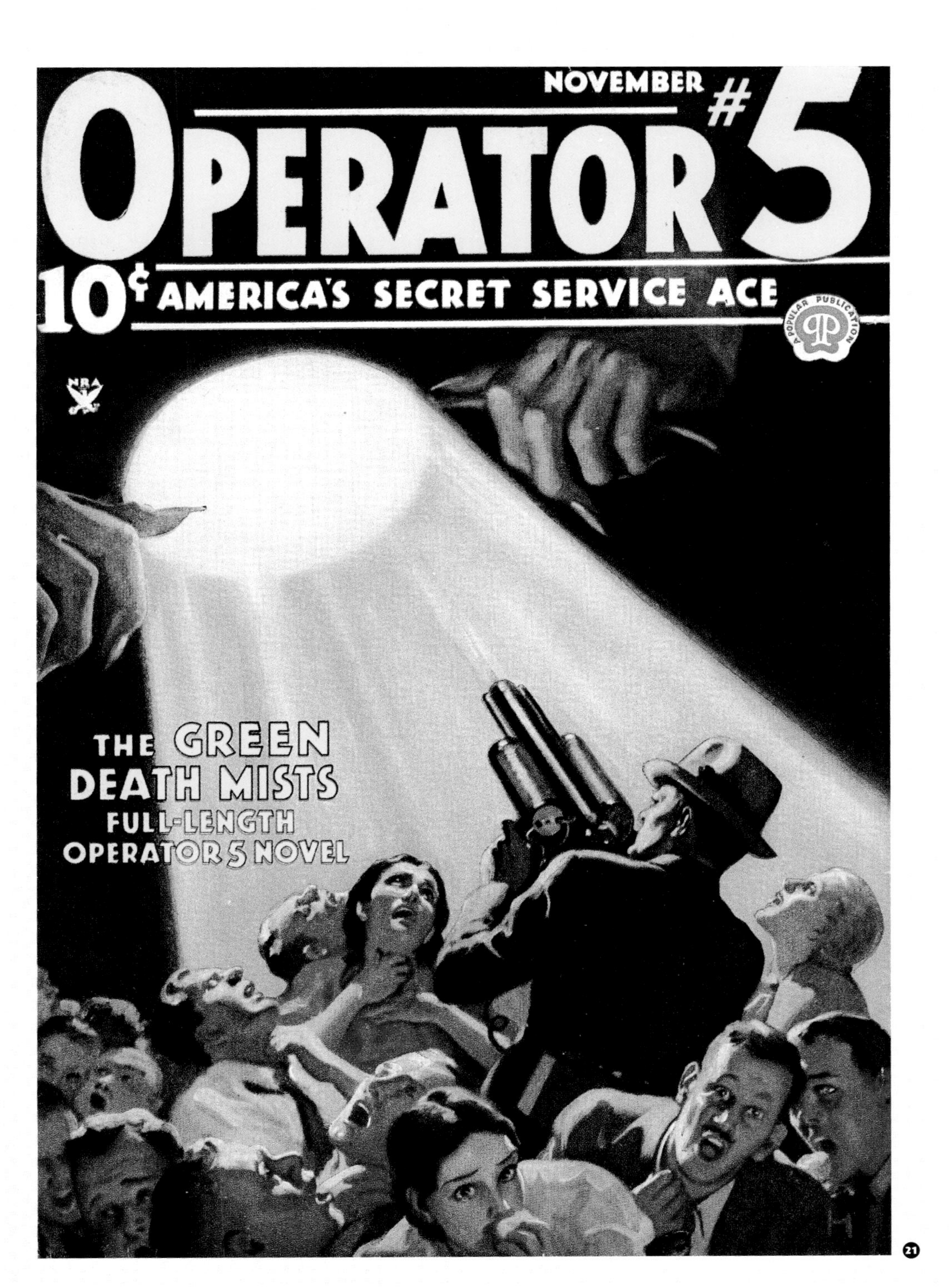

21

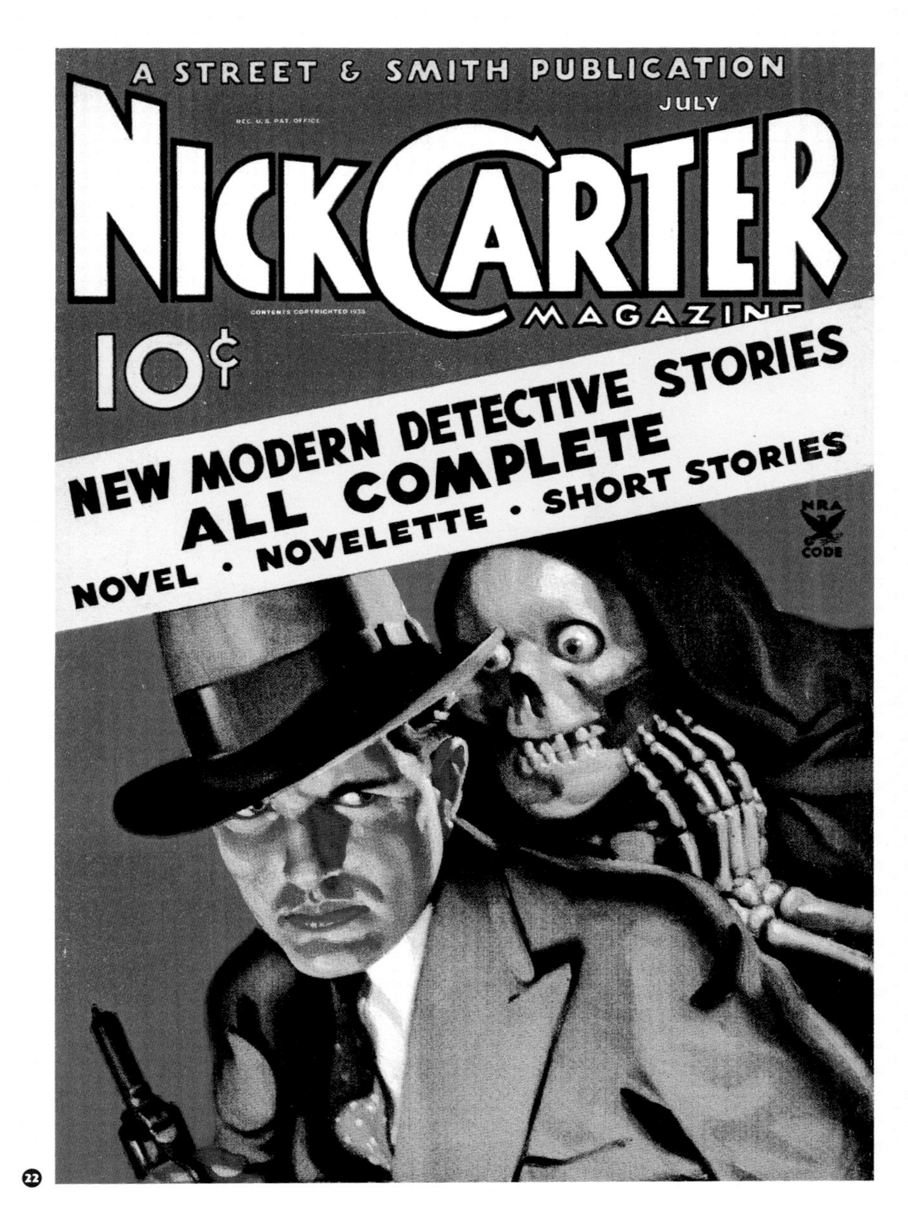

22

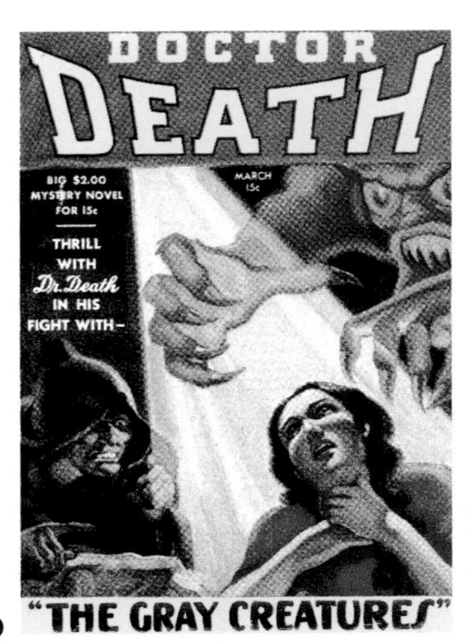

23

23 •••
DOCTOR DEATH
March 1935
Rudolph Zirn
Those clutching green hands again...

The same could be said for Blacks, who were almost always pictured as African savages rather than African Americans. Joe Louis was a famous and popular boxer, but that didn't seem to dent the prevalent attitude toward race. Matinee idols who might have crossed the color line, like Sidney Poitier, Denzel Washington, Lou Gossett Jr., Billy Dee Williams, and James Earl Jones hadn't yet appeared on the scene.

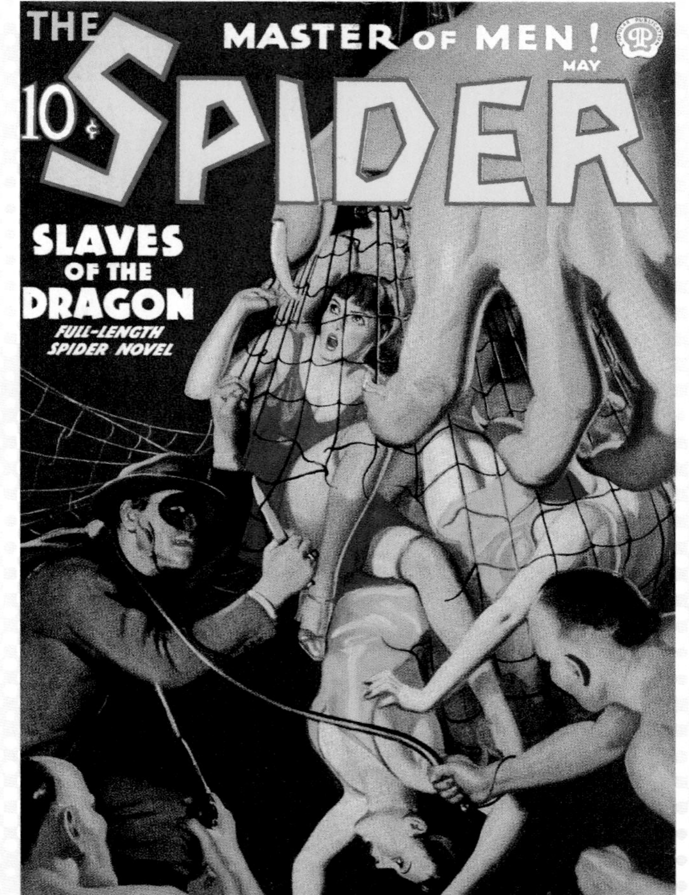

24 • • •
THE SPIDER
December 1934
John Newton Howitt
The Spider was Popular Publication's answer to *The Shadow*.

25 • • •
THE SPIDER
May 1936
John Newton Howitt
Huge green hands were all over the pulps.

26 •••
Captain Satan
March 1938
Malvin Singer
Another hero pulp that just didn't have the spark...

27 •••
Double Detective
February 1941
Unknown
The Green Lama was a hit and featured above the title.

29

29 ••
Secret Agent "X"
November 1934
J. George Janes
This was 1934's version of *Halloween*...

26

28 ••••
The Octopus
February-March 1939
John Newton Howitt
A rare one-shot, retitled the following issue as *The Scorpion*.

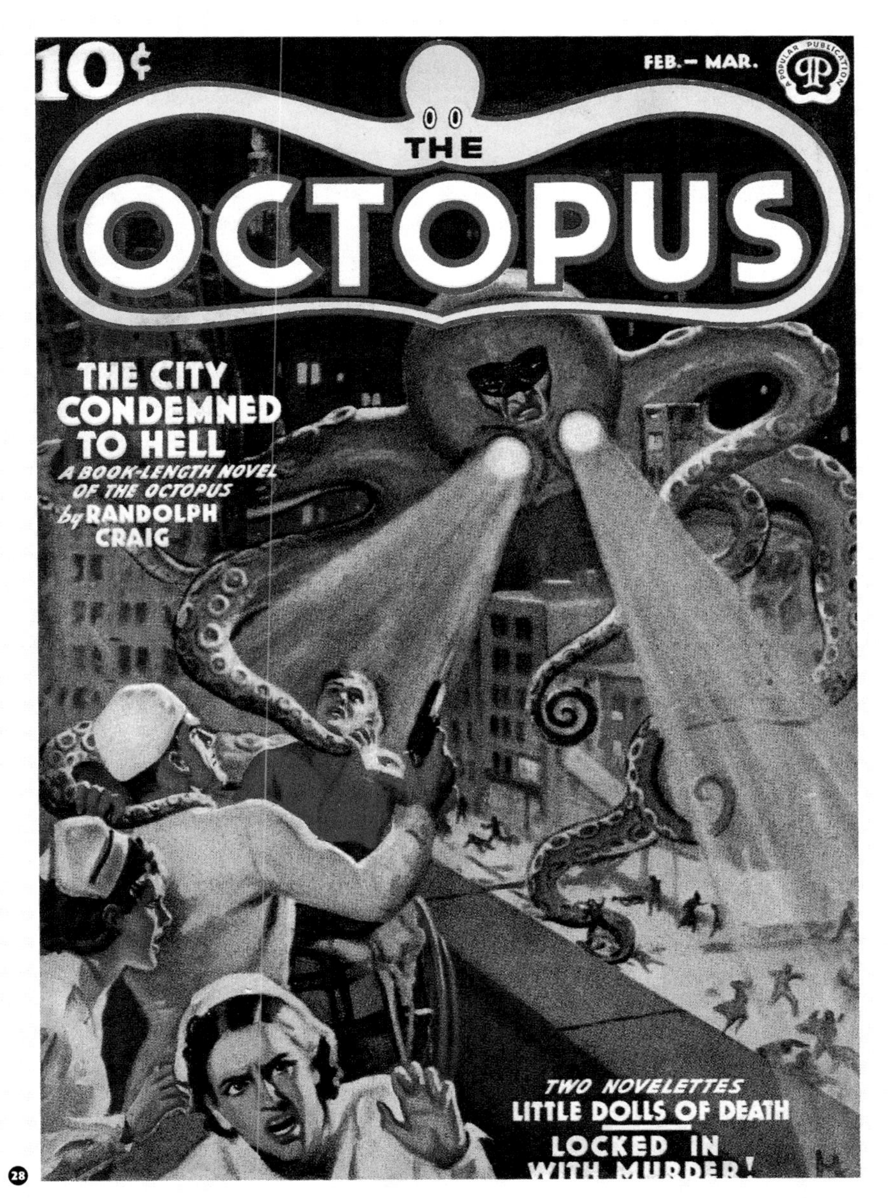

28

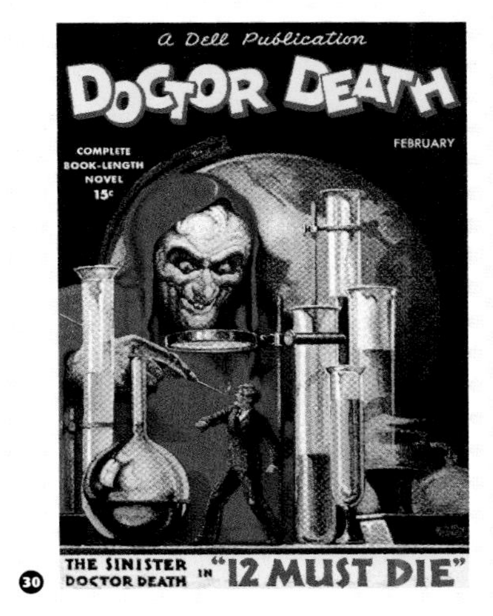

30

27

30 •••
Doctor Death
February 1935
Rudolph Zirn
This was nightmare stuff for the teenagers of the '30s.

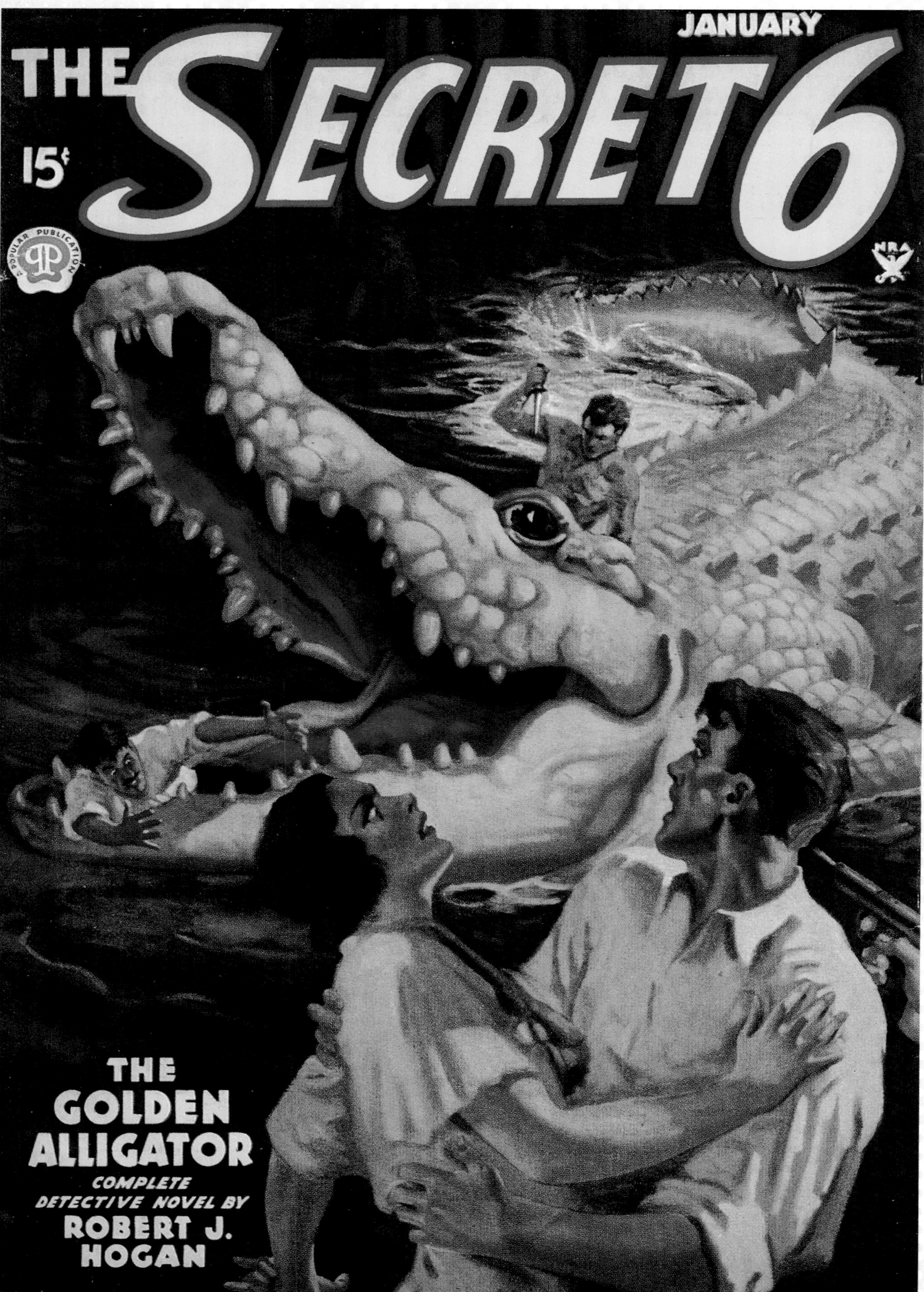

31 •••
The Secret 6
January 1935
Henry Alan
No doubt one of the alligators lost in New York's sewer system.

32 ••
Captain Zero
March 1950
Raphael de Soto
The last of the hero pulps. No pizzazz and no sales.

The hero pulps lasted almost as long as the pulps themselves. After the pulps died many characters continued in the comic books, which had begun to feature them in the '40s, including the Shadow, Doc Savage, Bill Barnes, and even Sheena, Queen of the Jungle.

Years later many of the characters returned in paperback reprints. Doc Savage enjoyed an enormously profitable resurrection by Bantam Books. Film producer George Pal, producer of *The Wonderful World of the Brothers Grimm*, and the underrated science-fiction thriller, *The Power*, even made a film about Doc—*Doc Savage: The Man of Bronze*.

Five publishers (Bantam, Belmont, Pyramid, Jove, and Tempo) split *The Shadow* reprints, and Alec Baldwin starred in the 1994 film *The Shadow*. Pocket Books printed some of the old novels about the Spider, and even the Avenger saw new life as a paperback series.

Perhaps the oddest pairing of all was the publication of some of the Phantom novels; several novels of Operator #5; and Dr. Death, (in four books, all bearing a cover portrait of editor Earl Kemp as Dr. Death himself). All were published by the Greenleaf Publishing Company, better known for its "Nightstand" and "Midnight Reader" lines of erotic novels. Of all the paperback reprints, those by Greenleaf are the hardest to find and the most valuable.

Years after the titles had vanished, mention "pulp magazines" and those who remember the originals will think fondly of *The Shadow* or *Doc Savage* or *G-8*—or perhaps even *Dr. Death*.

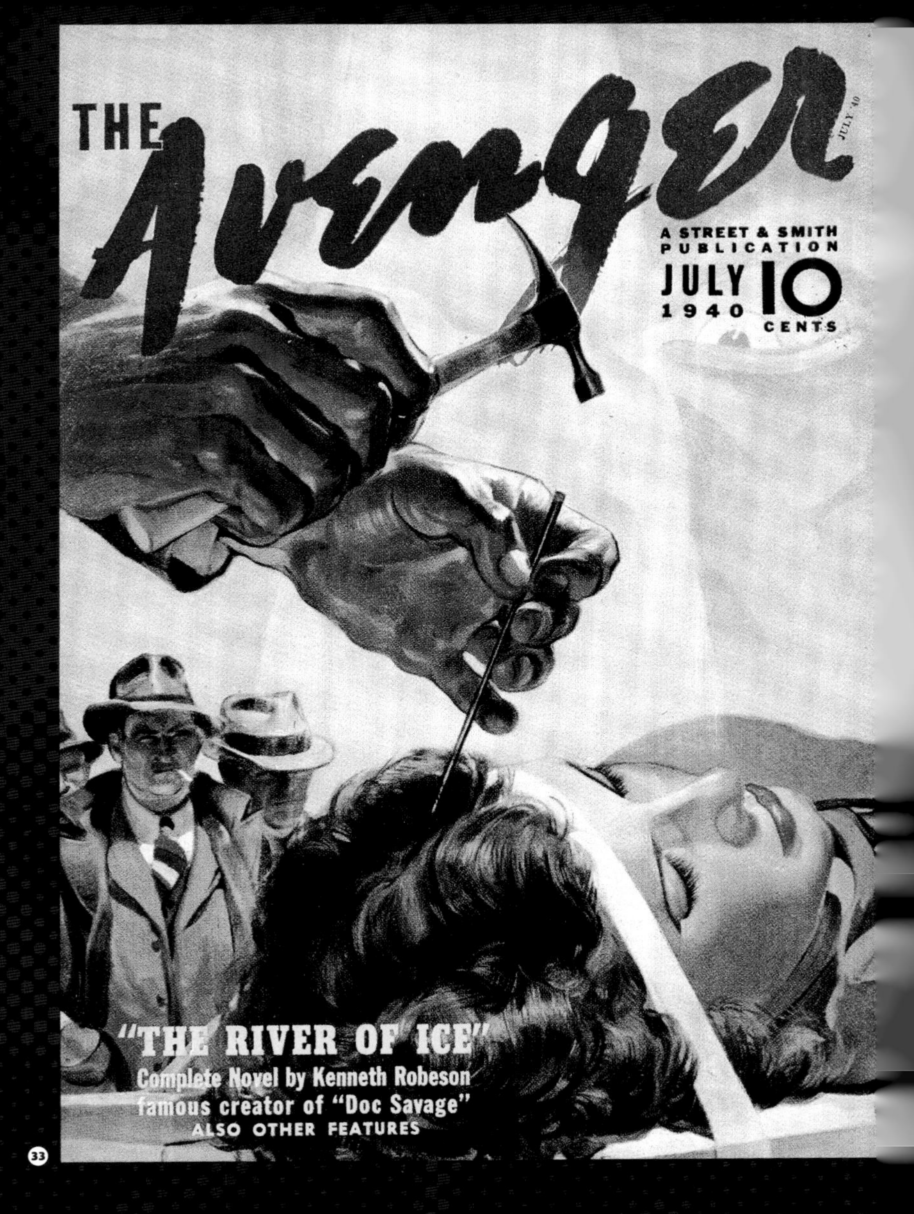

33 ••
THE AVENGER
H.W. Scott
July 1940
Some pulp covers were grisly, but this took the prize for sadism.

34 ••
THE WIZARD
February 1941
Hubert Rogers
Few readers got excited about *Adventures in Money Making* when a war was raging in Europe.

Nightmares on Main Street

The Mad-Slasher Pulps

By the early 1930s the pulps were testing the limits of sensationalism in the mystery and detective magazines, some of which were quite sensational enough as it was. But Henry Steeger of Popular Publications decided to take the sensational a step further. He had just returned from Paris with visions of the Grand Guignol Theater and its graphic depictions of torture and murder dancing in his head.

At the time Popular's *Dime Mystery Book*, a companion to *Dime Detective*, was doing badly. The publisher responded quickly with changes. He shortened the title to simply *Dime Mystery*, and shrank the "book-length" novel to make room for short stories, which were a combination of gothic mystery, terror, and sadism of a "heart-quickening" type.

Popular changed the covers as well. The new formula was to show a woman about to be butchered or in the process of being tortured or whipped. Sometimes her boyfriend was at hand, tied up and unable to help. The formula was unique, eyebrow-raising—and successful.

Dime Mystery enjoyed an immediate spurt in circulation and soon was joined by Popular's *Terror Tales* and *Horror Stories*. The difference between the latter two was not always obvious to the reader (or author), but editor Rogers Terrill summed it

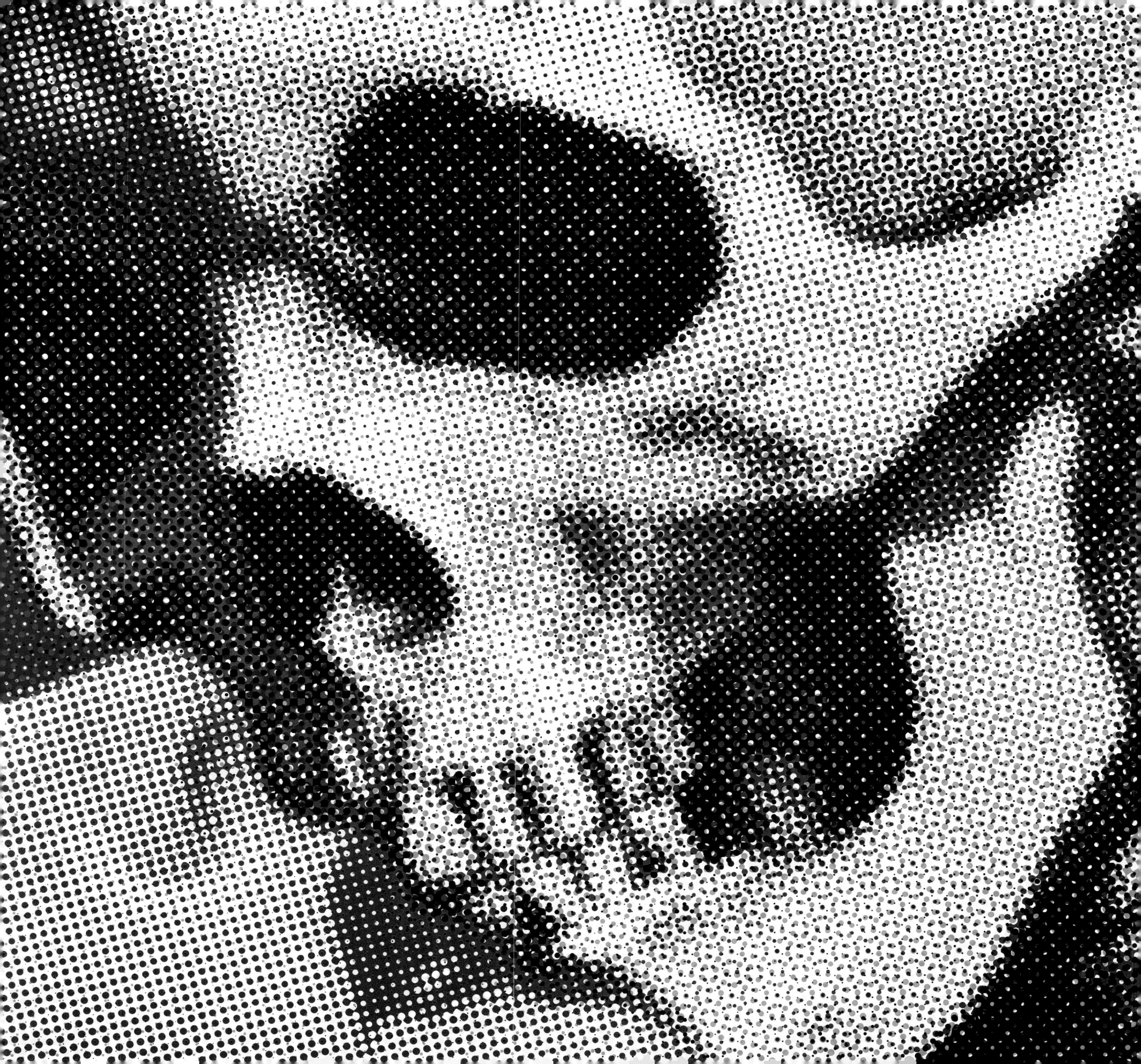

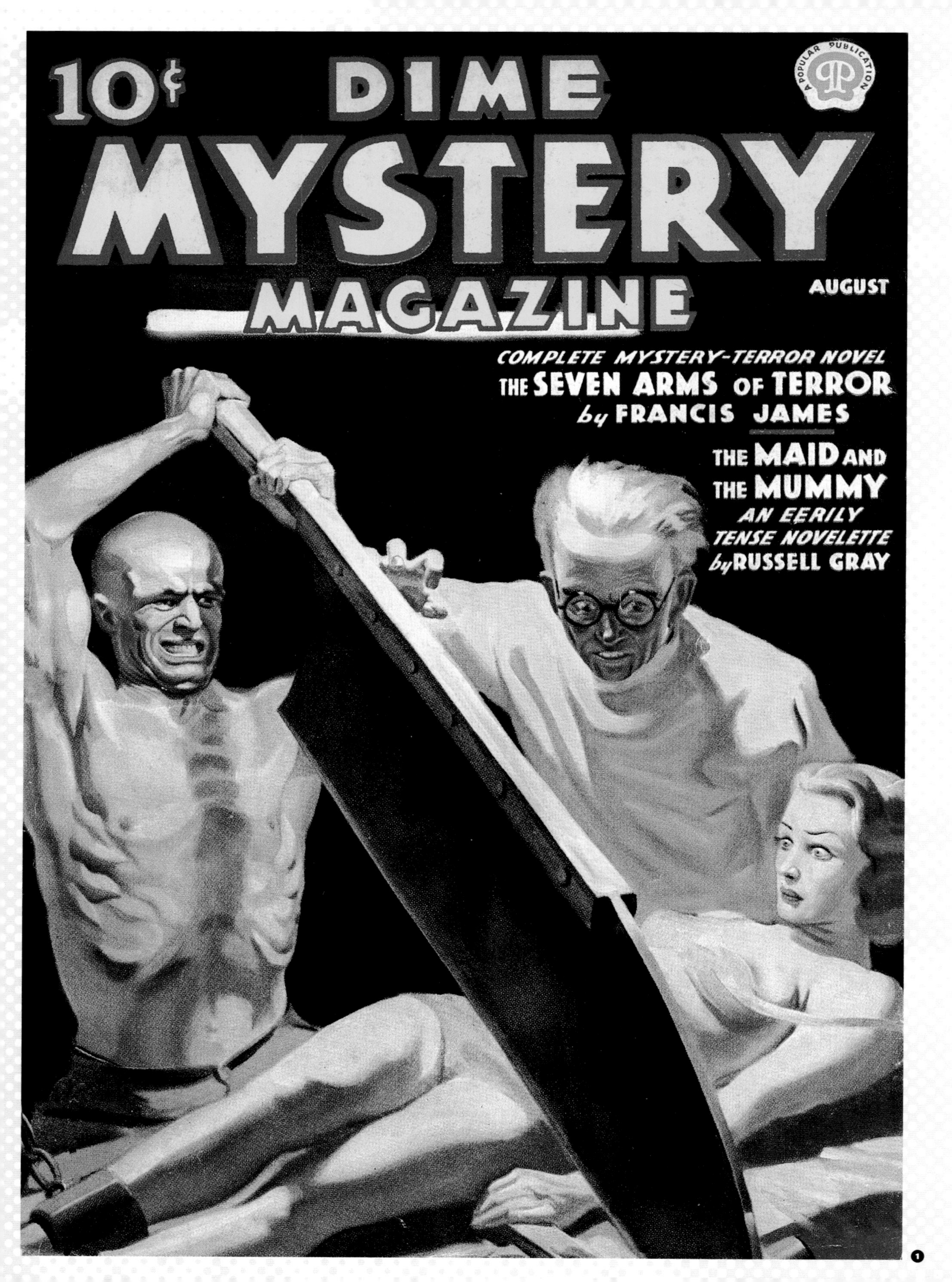

❶ ••
DIME MYSTERY MAGAZINE
August 1937
Graves Gladney
The unkindest cut of all.
The magazine could never be
published today.

❷ ••
DIME MYSTERY MAGAZINE
December 1934
Walter M. Baumhofer
The first appearance anywhere
of a creature from a black lagoon.

❸ ••
DIME MYSTERY MAGAZINE
July 1938
Unknown
Wall Street had its bears and
bulls and now its werewolves.

up neatly: "Horror is what a girl would feel while watching a ghoul practice diabolical rites from a safe distance; terror is what she would feel if she knew she were going to be the next victim."

As usual with any successful genre, competition wasn't slow in developing. There was *Ace Mystery* ("Princess of Pain"); *Mystery Novels and short stories* ("Maidens of Bondage"); *Strange Detective Mysteries* ("Coming of the Boneless Men"); *Thrilling Mystery* ("Slaves of the Dancing Death"); and *Marvel Tales* ("Lust Rides the Roller Coaster"). Among the genre's aficionados, "mystery" now had become a code word for stories of torture.

With time the girls on the front cover wore increasingly less, and the scenes of torture became more graphic. Inside the stories usually hewed to a consistent formula: no matter how outlandish and weird the circumstances, in the end everything had to have a natural, if not plausible, ending—frequently, though not always, involving a mad scientist. This distinguished the magazines from the more literate *Weird Tales* and *Strange Stories*, which tended to the supernatural in a story's resolution.

It's interesting to note that the formula for the 1930s terror tale, in its entirety, seemed to be the template for E.L. Doctorow's recent bestseller, *The Waterworks*.

Not all the magazines hewed to the relatively innocuous story formula of *Terror Tales* and *Horror Stories*. The Red Circle line of *Mystery Tales*, *Uncanny Tales*, and *Real Mystery* were heavy on sexual sadism and eroticism, with intriguing story titles such as "Debutantes for the Damned," "Dead Mates for the Devil's Devotees," and the all-time winner, appearing in Red Circle's *Marvel Tales*, "Fresh Fiancés for the Devil's Daughters" by "Russell Gray" (Bruno Fischer). The story concerns a beautiful woman who traps and tortures the men who spurned her, along with their wives. She then selects a lover from among her victims to bed down with before continuing the various tortures.

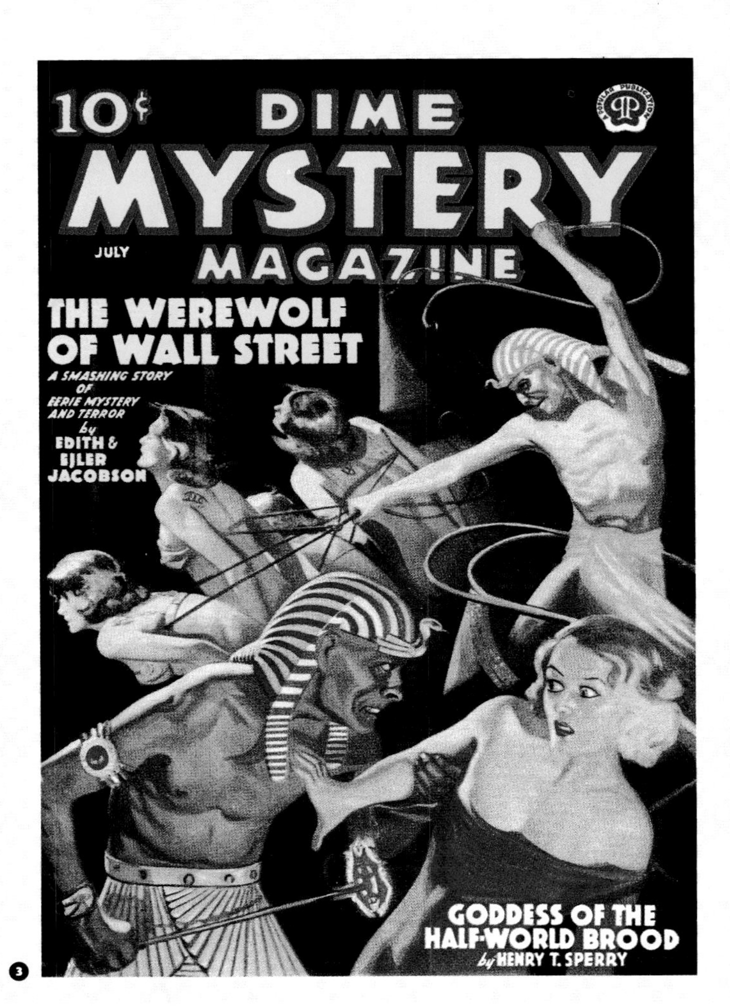

3

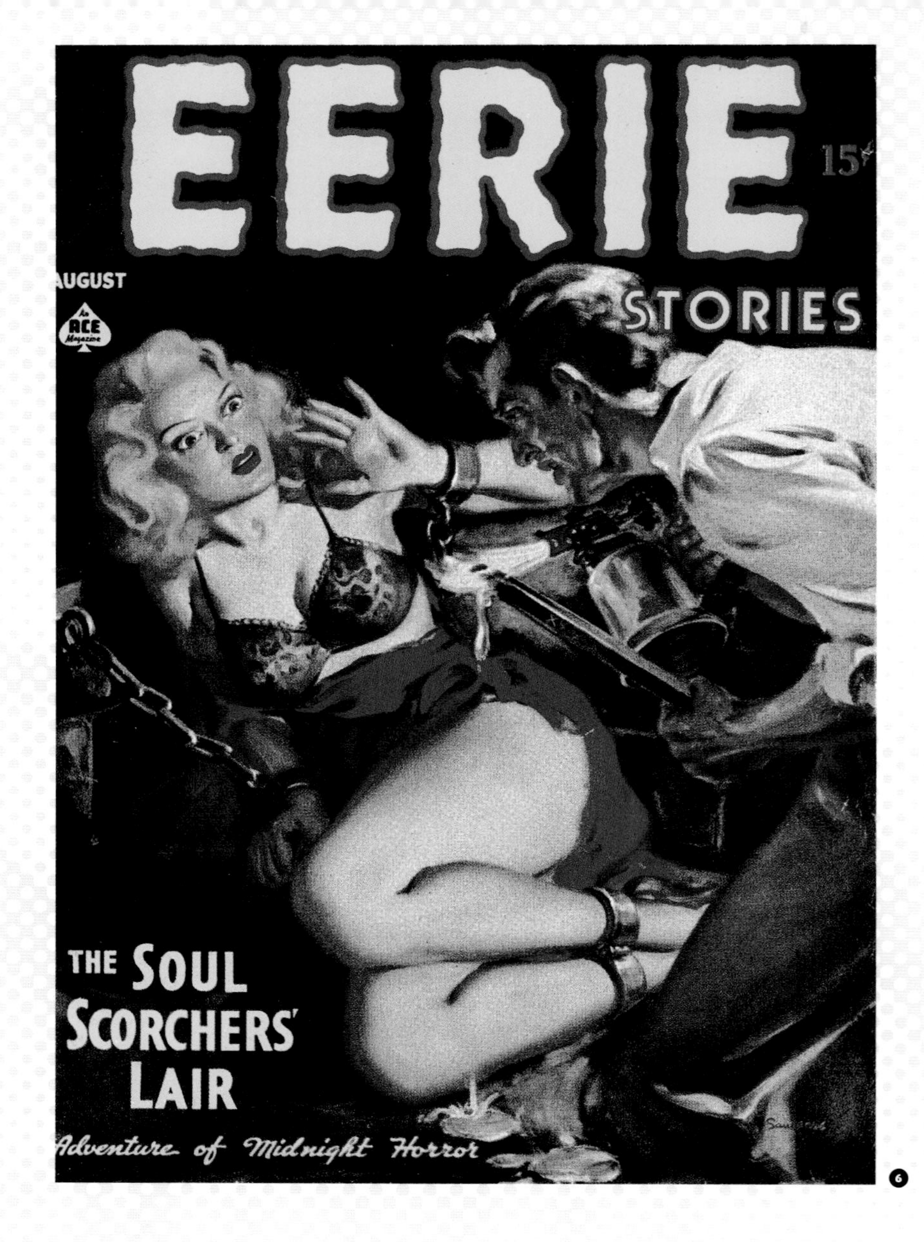

6 •• **EERIE STORIES**
August 1937
Norman Saunders
A competitor to *Terror Tales* and *Horror Stories*.

7 •• **EERIE MYSTERIES**
August 1938
Norman Saunders
Another "eerie" girl—with more clothes.

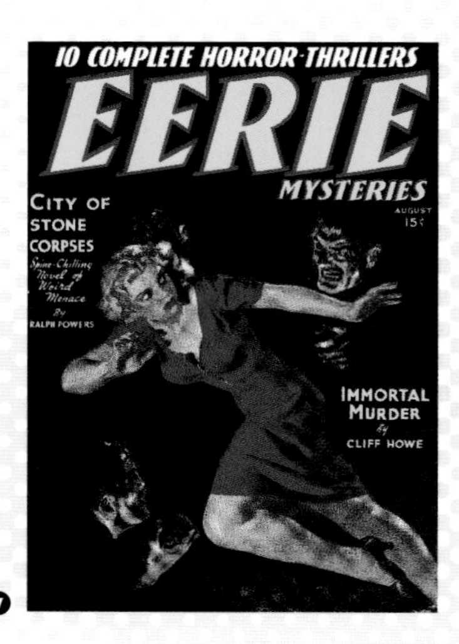

8 ••• **TERROR TALES**
August 1935
John Newton Howitt
Every cover featured women in peril.

4 ••• **TERROR TALES**
October 1934
John Newton Howitt
The magazine specialized in cold hearts and bony hands.

5 ••• **HORROR STORIES**
September 1935
John Newton Howitt
Today feminist groups would be up in arms about this cover—justifiably.

9 • • •

Horror Stories

February 1935

Rudolph Zirn

The Grand Guignol Theatre in Paris inspired the publisher.

10 • • •

Horror Stories

October 1935

John Newton Howitt

The nightmare of some brides before the wedding.

11 • • •

Terror Tales

September 1934

Rudolph Zirn

The first issue of the first "shudder pulp." Note again the "clutching green hands."

Hot stuff for the pulps back then—too hot. There were no feminist groups to urge the newsstands be cleaned up of publications that were obviously denigrating and insulting to women. But Mayor Fiorello LaGuardia of New York made all the appropriate noises, and the torture scenes disappeared from the covers; the women suddenly acquired more clothing; and some of the magazines switched to a less controversial mystery and detective format.

The "shudder pulps" featured some bylines that appeared in no other magazines. But there also were familiar names such as Arthur J. Burks, Frederick C.

⓬ ••
Marvel Tales
May 1940
J.W. Scott
Marvel was a science-fiction magazine that switched to horror.

⓭ •••
Mystery Novels and Short Stories
December 1939
Unknown
Add bondage and torture to the cover appeal.

Davis, Wayne Rogers, Hugh B. Cave, Henry Kuttner, the ever-popular Robert Leslie Bellem, and Donald Dale. Nor were the shudder pulps strictly a male preserve; "Donald Dale" was in actuality one Mary Dale Buckner.

By the early '40s the shudder pulps had reformed or disappeared from the newsstands. Martin Goodman, owner of the Red Circle group, ran afoul of the Federal Trade Commission with *Real Mystery*, but it wasn't in regard to the salacious and sadistic content of the magazine. It seems *Real Mystery* used reprints from *Uncanny Tales* and *Mystery Tales*, retitled them, and neglected to tell the readers of the deception.

Goodman now largely retired from the pulp-magazine business and spent his time developing a line of slick men's magazines and building his other business, Marvel comic books.

Grace note: Years after the demise of the pulps, Hugh B. Cave, one of the major contributors to the "weird menace" magazines, moved to Haiti. He wrote a number of fine horror novels based on the voodoo culture of the island. *Legion of the Dead* and *The Cross and the Drum* are two of his best novels from this period.

With the advantage of moral hindsight, it's easy to criticize the shudder pulps and reflect that the sadism and denigration of women depicted on their covers couldn't possibly happen now.

Those who rush to judgment must never have seen *Halloween*, *Nightmare on Elm Street*, *Friday the 13th*, or any of the other "slasher" movies so popular today.

14 ••
THRILLING MYSTERY
February 1937
Unknown
Dancing with the dead was a common theme for the "shudder pulps."

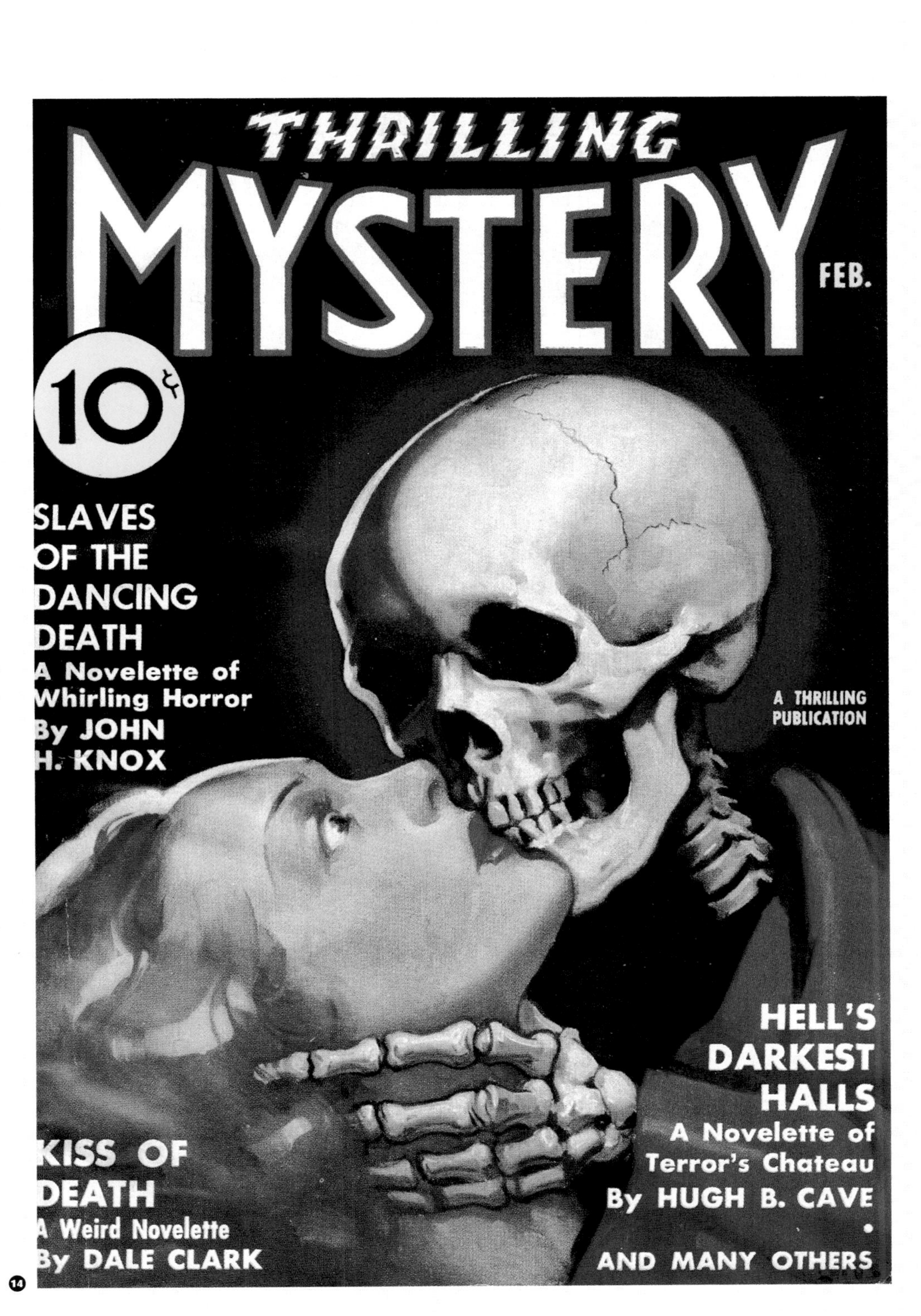

14

15 •••
THRILLING MYSTERIES
April 1935
Emery Clarke
The only issue.
The *Thrilling* line sued for using *Thrilling* in the title, then published *Thrilling Mystery* themselves six months later.

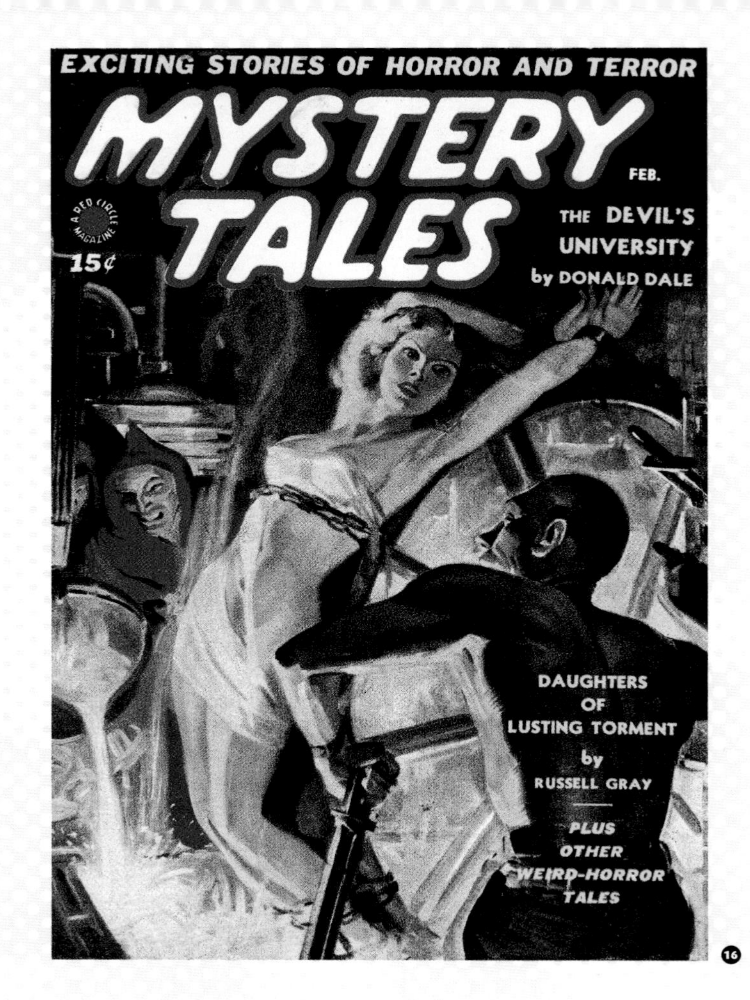

16 •••
MYSTERY TALES
February 1939
J.W. Scott
Anything went on the newsstands of the '30s.

17 •••
ACE MYSTERY MAGAZINE
May 1936
Sherman
A 1936 version of *Indiana Jones and the Temple of Doom*.

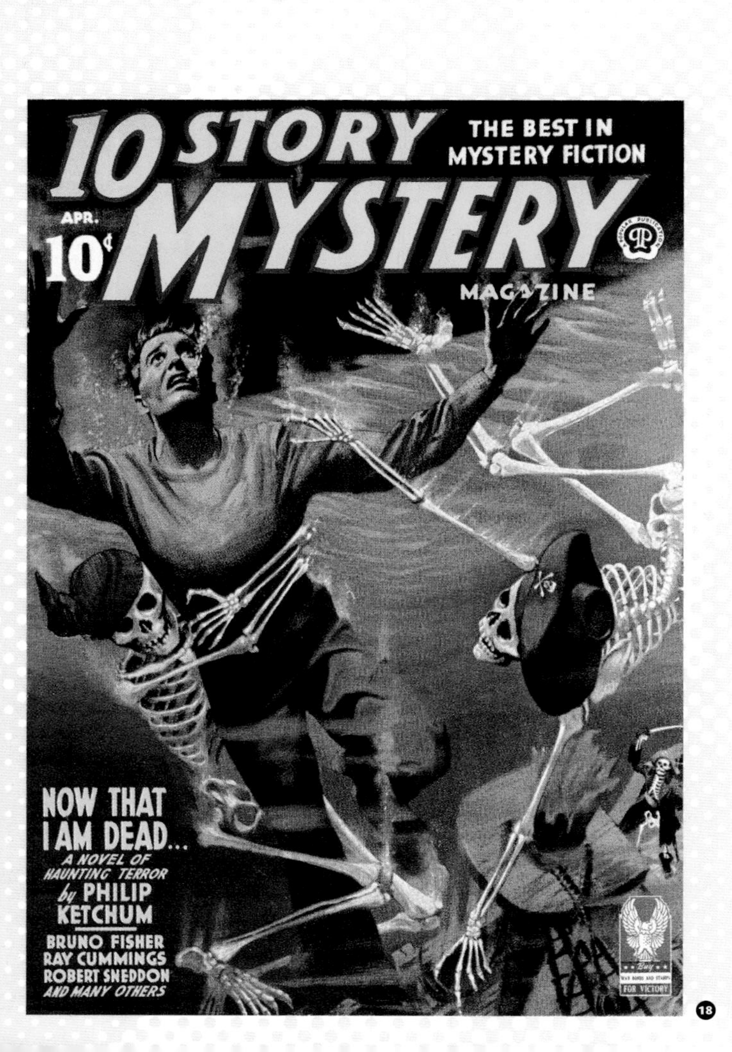

18 •
10-STORY MYSTERY
April 1943
Unknown
The last issue—and the shudder pulps were down among the dead men.

19 ••
THRILLING DETECTIVE
August 1940
Rudolph Belarski
Heads you lose.

21 • •

STRANGE DETECTIVE MYSTERIES

March 1943

Unknown

By 1943 the publisher had turned away from gore and came up with one of the cleverest covers ever published.

20 • •

STRANGE DETECTIVE MYSTERIES

November 1940

Unknown

Another cover that was horrifying and sadistic in the extreme.

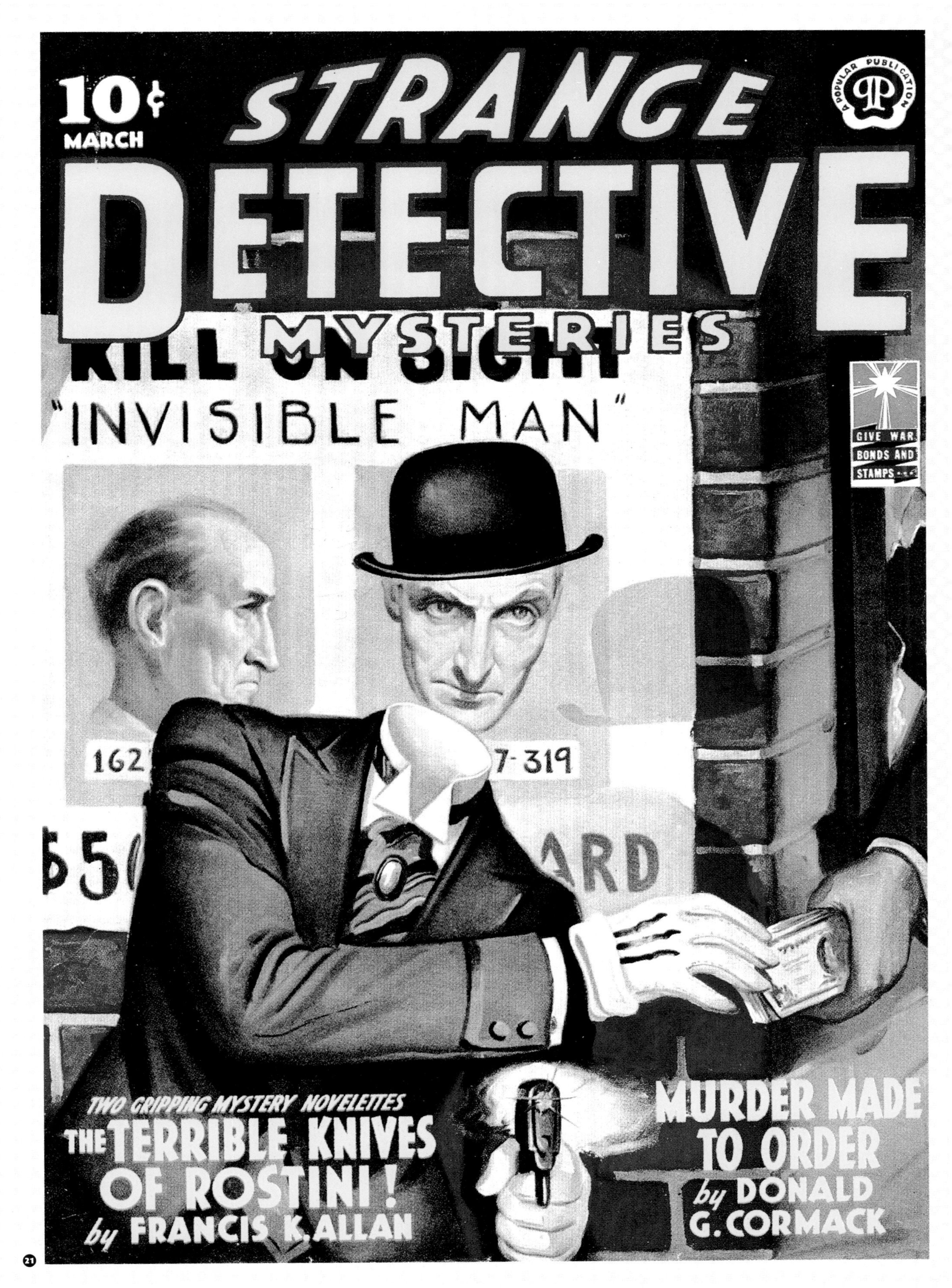

Come Up and See Me Sometime

Love, Sin, and Sex

Love stories and their erotic counterparts have probably been in print ever since Gutenberg invented moveable type, and some printer's devil composed a tale about a randy king and a peasant's daughter.

Women's magazines as such, with their collections of recipes, poems, fiction, essays, and dress patterns, date from the last century. Street & Smith was the first to publish an all-fiction version with *Women's Stories* back in 1913. Despite quality paper (at least initially—it turned to pulp paper with later issues) and attractive layout with many interior illustrations, it failed.

A more successful effort was its *Love Story Magazine*, launched in 1921, which, along with *Argosy*, was to claim the highest circulation of any pulp.

The difference between the failure of the first and the success of the second probably was in the timing. Romance, the staple of *Love Story*, was handled delicately, if at all, in women's magazines prior to World War I. But eight years had seen a seismic shift in the status and interests of women. Women's suffrage had become the law of the land in 1920; women had worked in defense plants and as nurses during the Great War; the Jazz Age was in full gear; and the "flapper" with her bobbed hair, stockings rolled below the knee, and frank interest in sex, had become a common sight in the big cities.

To women of that period, *Women's Stories* wouldn't even have rated as "quaint." But *Love Story* was a natural and a success almost overnight. Substantial competition, oddly enough, didn't develop until the late '20s and early '30s, when new titles flooded the market.

Despite being one of the most popular of the pulp genres, if not the most popular, few readers saved or collected the love pulps. Most of the authors were women, at least according to the contents page, though Cornell Woolrich showed up in *Sweetheart Stories* and L. Ron Hubbard in an issue of *Western Romances*. Rumors persisted that many male authors with excellent credentials in the mystery and adventure fields supplemented their incomes by adopting a feminine nom de plume and trying their hand at romance.

When the magazines were discontinued, the bylines vanished, and to the best of our knowledge no female writers have surfaced with credible claims to having toiled in the love-magazine vineyards. Neither did many male writers admit to having written for them. An exception might be made for the true-confessions field, for which a number of males wrote, including, of all people, Ray Palmer, who later became the editor of the Ziff-Davis *Amazing Stories*.

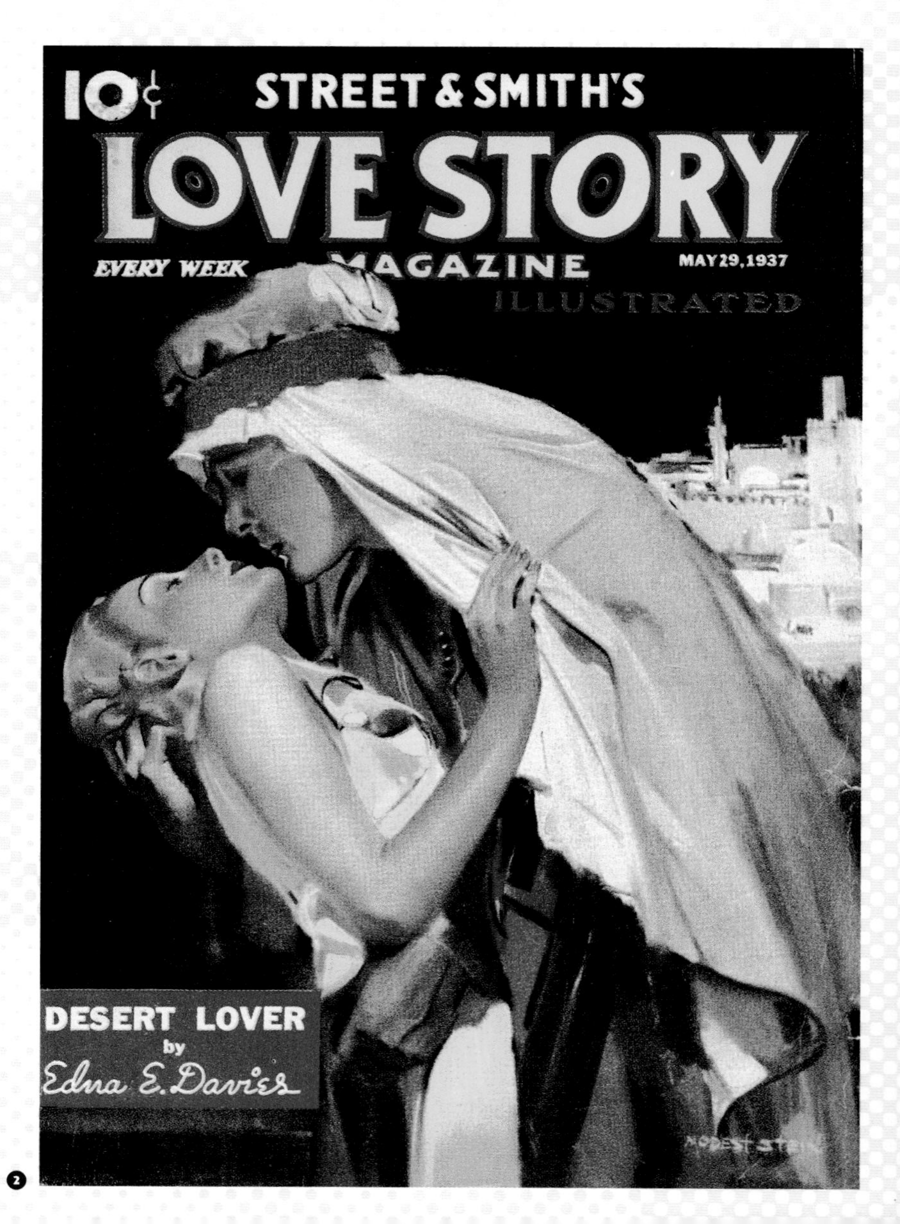

❶ •
LOVE STORY MAGAZINE
February 8, 1930
Unknown
Striking color and design for a love pulp.

❷ •
LOVE STORY MAGAZINE
May 29, 1937
Modest Stein
By the '30s the "story" covers had given way to idealized portraits.

LOVE STORY MAGAZINE
September 29, 1928
Modest Stein
The gossips.

4 •
LOVE STORY MAGAZINE
March 9, 1929
Modest Stein
The ace of spades definitely meant unlucky in love.

5 •
Breezy Stories
March 1937
Enoch Bolles
The sexy cover was deceptive. Inside was the standard love pulp.

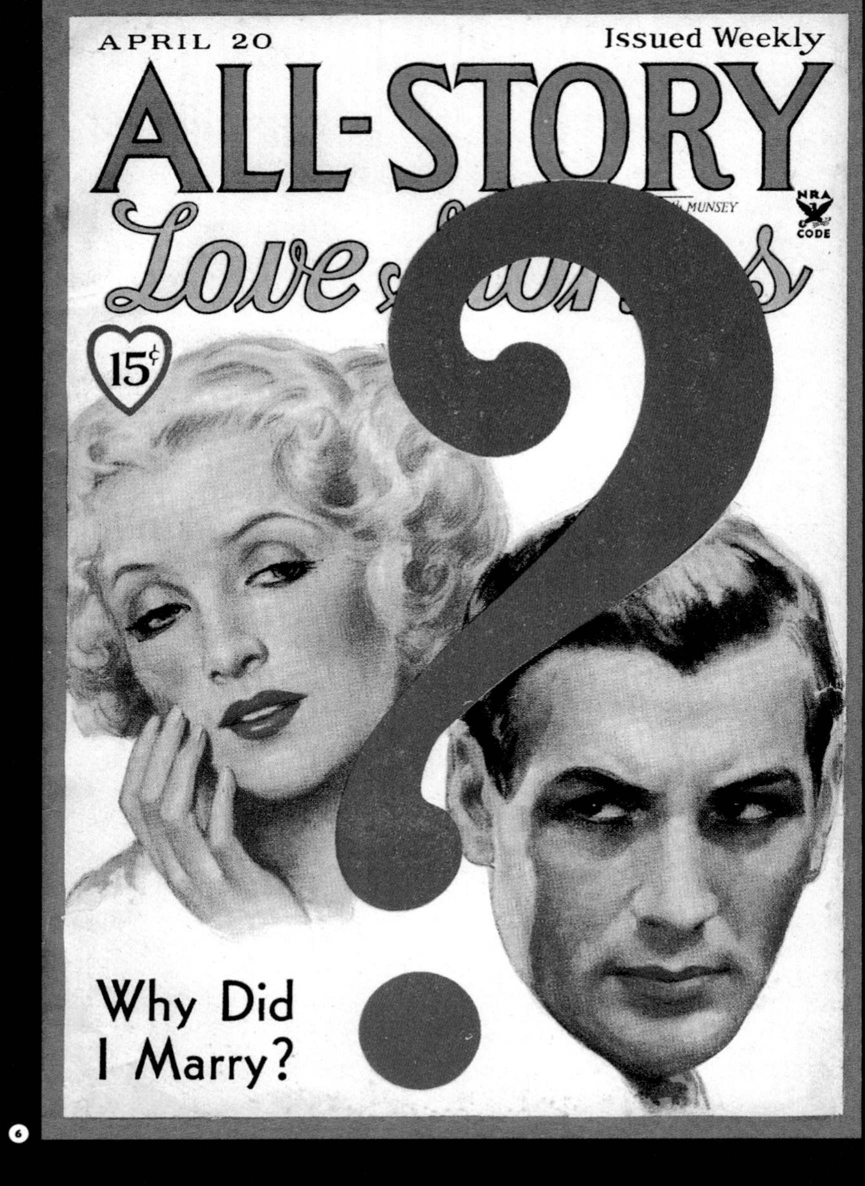

6 •
All-Story Love Stories
April 20, 1935
Unknown
To marry or not to marry: that was always the question in love pulps.

7 •
Love Short Stories
February 1940
Unknown
The "clinch" was always a big deal for the readers of love pulps.

eetheart Stories
vember 4, 1930
known
obably where the phrase
etty boy" came from.

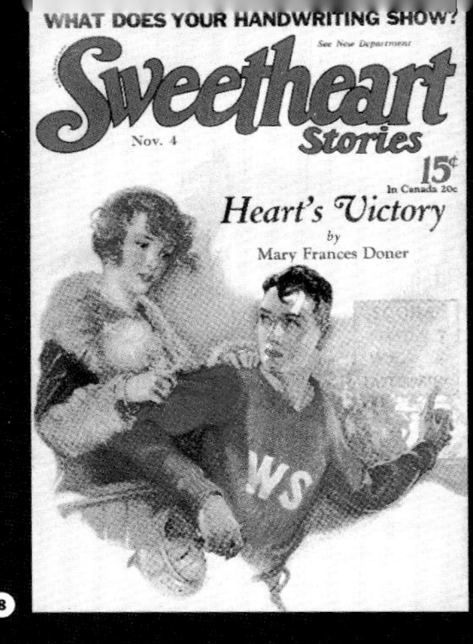

9 •
All-Story Love Tales
June 4, 1938
Unknown
She wasn't going to play second fiddle to a dummy.

10 •
Pep Stories
February 1930
Unknown
By the early '30s the cover girls of the sexier magazines looked like calendar pin-ups.

⓫ •
Rangeland Romances
August 1937
William Luberoff
He may be holding the girl, but she's holding the gun.

⓬ •
Rangeland Romances
June 1947
Unknown
By the '40s the covers for Western romance pulps had lightened up.

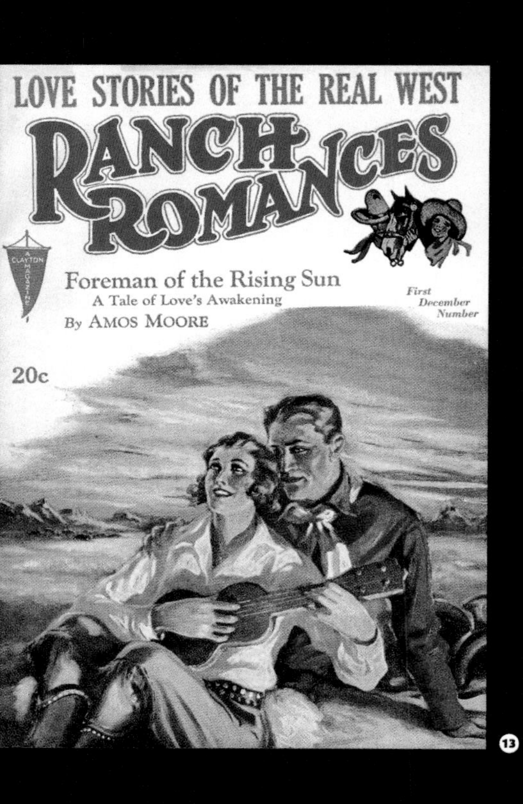

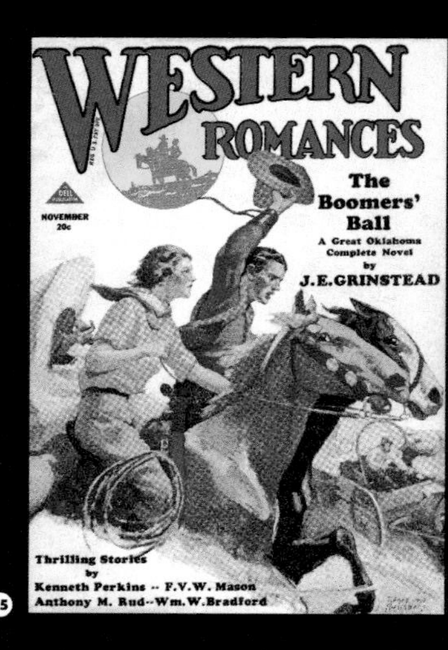

⓭ •
Ranch Romances
December 4, 1931
Unknown
The first romance Western was fantastically successful. It was still in publication in the '60s.

⓮ •
Romantic Range
September 1938
Unknown
The romance Western was so successful almost every publisher printed one.

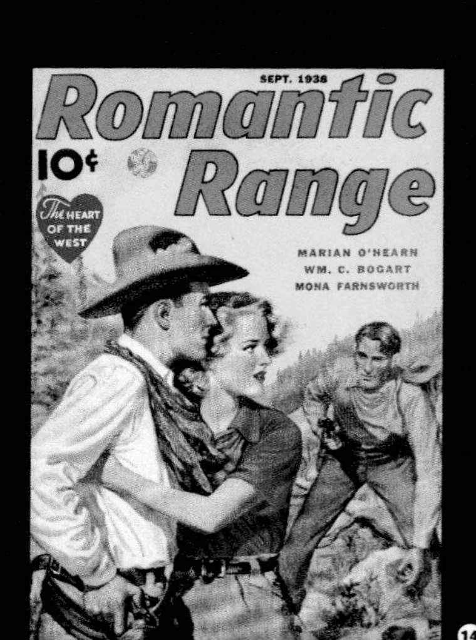

⓯ •
Western Romances
November 1931
Sidney Riesenberg
An early competitor to *Ranch Romances* but not nearly as popular.

The love magazine format usually was the same—a half-dozen novelettes and short stories, plus an advice column considerably less sophisticated than today's "Dear Abby." And, of course, a pen-pal column. Most readers reportedly were in their early and middle teens with a heavy sprinkling of high-school girls, young sales clerks, and secretaries, a natural market for the magazine *Seventeen*, a slick which came on the scene years later.

Content-wise the magazines published simple romances with a happy ending, usually including marriage or an offer of one. The love pulps dealt in wishful thinking and fantasy, thus distinguishing them from the true-confessions magazines, which co-existed with them and specialized in sin and redemption.

The "shelter" magazines, the famed "Seven Sisters" of publishing (*Ladies' Home Journal*, *McCall's Magazine*, *Good Housekeeping*, and so on) printed little fiction that would appeal to the same audience, instead specializing in articles about the happy home for those already married or about to be.

Cosmopolitan had been around for years but had yet to see the editorship of Helen Gurley Brown, who would advocate full-speed-ahead-and-damn-the-torpedoes when it came to catching a man. There was no room for the romantic wimp or wishful thinker; it was strictly nitty-gritty time and don't-forget-your-diaphragm. Ms. Brown's *Cosmo* would have been a natural for the *Love Story* audience.

16 ••
Spicy Western Stories
November 1936
H.J. Ward
Spicy Western was never as popular as the other *Spicy* titles.

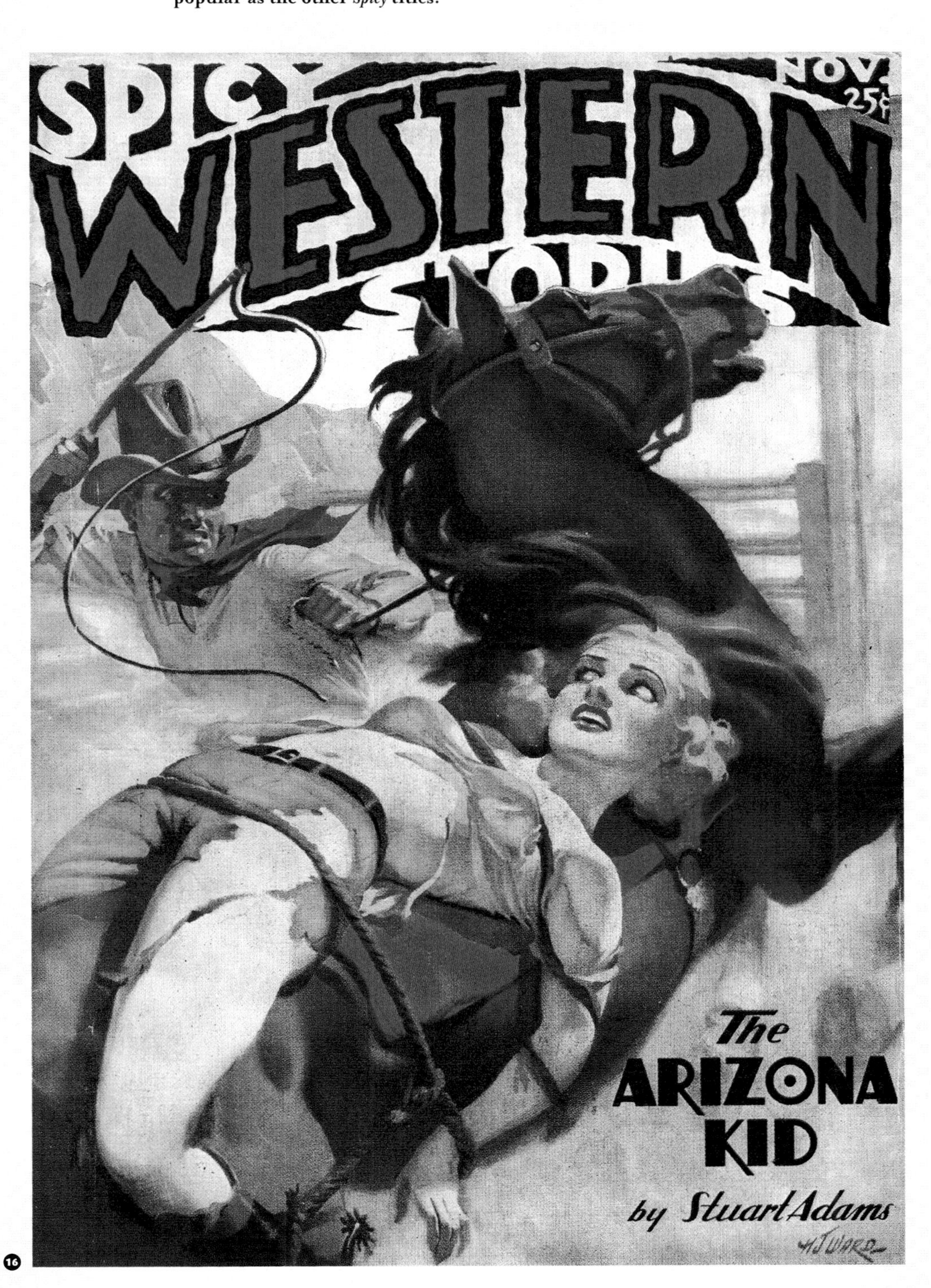

16

17 •••
SPICY-ADVENTURE STORIES
August 1937
H.J. Ward
She earned her medals the hard way.

18 •••
NEW MYSTERY ADVENTURES
December 1935
Norman Saunders
Artist Saunders used the pen name of "Blaine." For good reason.

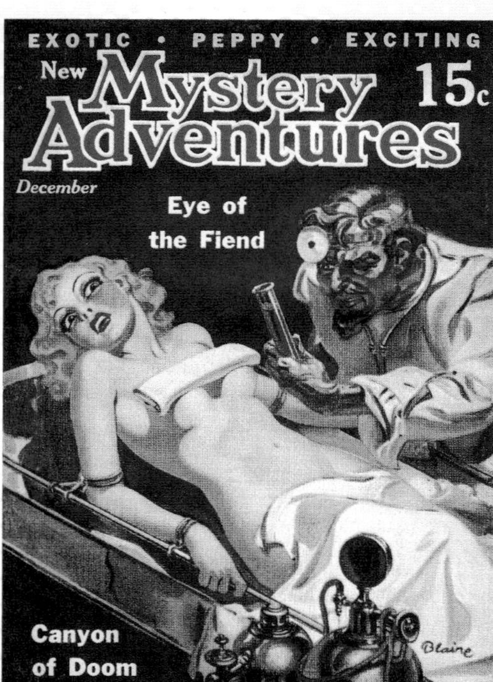

When the pulps died, the love pulps died with them, some of the audience drifting to the younger oriented women's slicks (*Charm*, *Mademoiselle*, *Glamour*); of course, *Seventeen*; and eventually Helen Gurley Brown's *Cosmopolitan*. Former readers might have missed the lightweight romantic fiction of the love pulps, but later there would be Jacqueline Susann and Danielle Steele to satisfy the demand with a decidedly racier product.

The more erotic magazines, designed strictly with men in mind, were usually slim affairs with oversize pages and had been around even longer than the love pulps. They were under-the-counter products with rotogravure inserts of slightly overweight nudes, semi-pornographic fiction, and off-color jokes. (The same literate duo who had launched *The Black Mask* started two of the milder ones, *Parisienne* and *Saucy Stories*.) *Pep Stories* and *Snappy* adopted the pulp format early on, but their stories were little more than tales about flappers.

20

19

19 •••
Spicy-Adventure Stories
November 1934
H.J. Ward
The first issue of a rare *Spicy* title.

20 •••
Mystery Adventure Magazine
November 1936
Norman Saunders
The magazine was a strange mix of mystery and adventure with frequent sexy covers. The "Domino Lady" starred in several different magazines.

21 •••
Spicy Mystery Stories
February 1936
H.J. Ward
The only resemblance to the film or the comic book was the title.

22 •••
Spicy Mystery Stories
June 1935
H.J. Ward
The most famous *Spicy* title of all, mixing sex and fantasy.

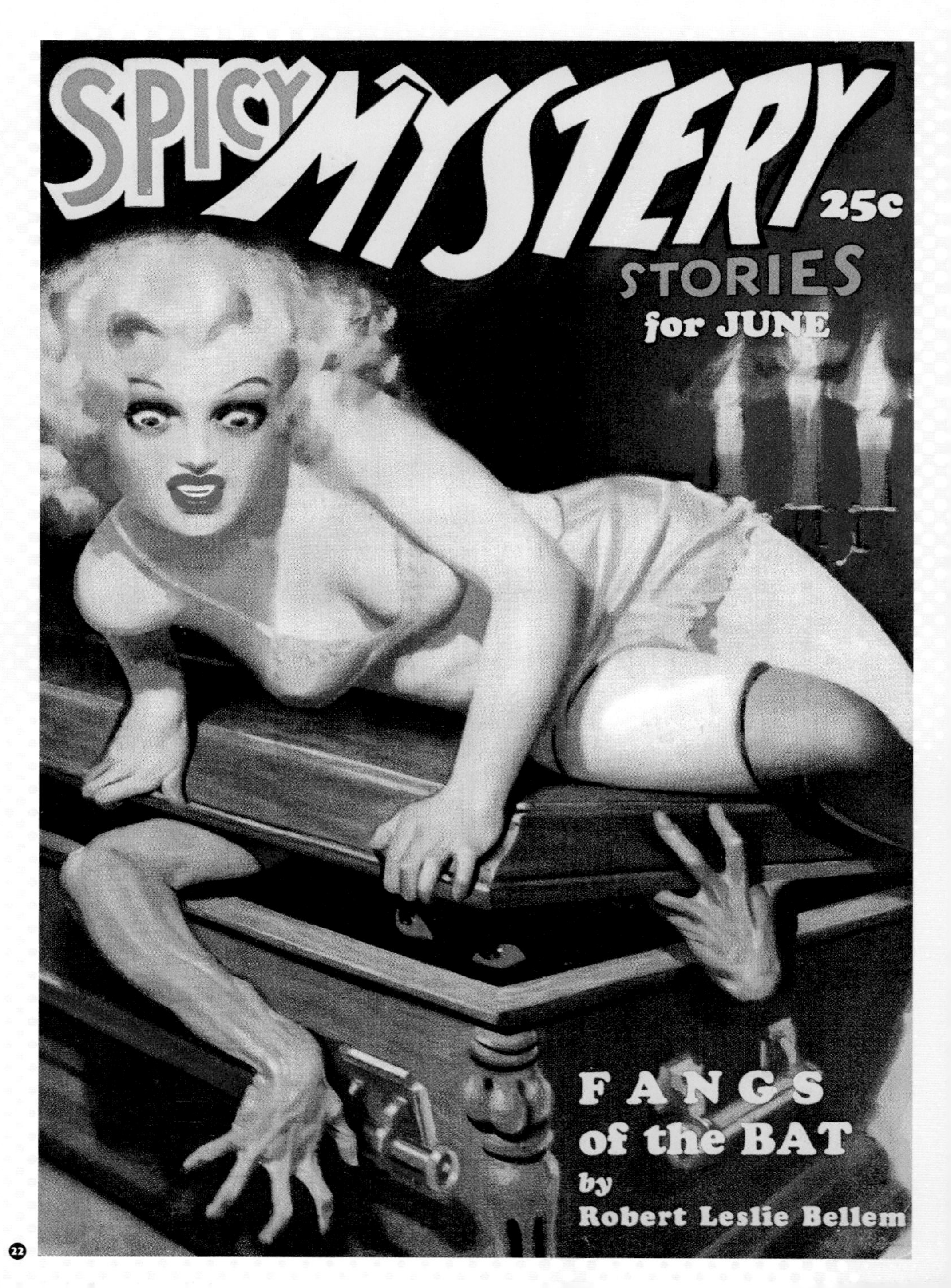

23 •••
Spicy Detective Stories
December 1934
H.J. Ward
With artist Ward the emphasis definitely shifted to the girl.

24 • • •
Spicy Detective Stories
October 1936
H.J. Ward
Gats, gals, and gunsels. But mostly gals.

25 • • •
Spicy Detective Stories
August 1934
Howard Parkhurst
In an early *Spicy* the emphasis was as much on the menace as on the girl.

26 • • •
Spicy Mystery Stories
November 1936
H.J. Ward
The title of the story was hard to beat.

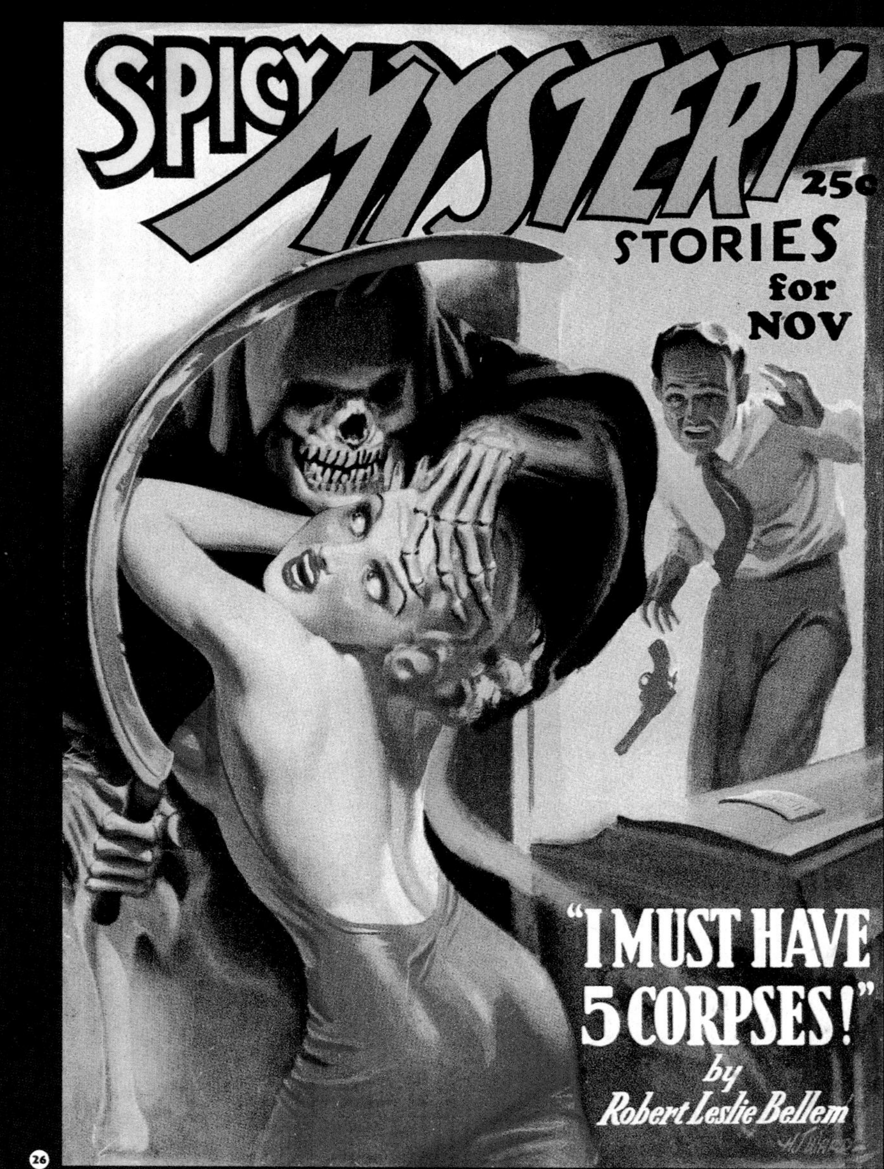

It remained for magazines like *Spicy Detective* and *Spicy Mystery* to promote heaving bosoms, fleshy thighs—and heavy breathing among their male readers. Unlike most pulps the *Spicys* were extensively illustrated, the girls in the drawings wearing transparent wisps of clothing to emphasize their allure. *Spicy Detective* even ran a comic strip, "Sally the Sleuth," which was more than a little reminiscent of the old pulp ads for "comic booklets—the kind men like."

Covers depicted the handsomely endowed Spicy girl in a detective, western, adventure, or even a science-fiction or weird-romance setting. If there was a villain in sight, it was unlikely he had murder on his mind. Today the *Spicys* are collectors' items, due largely to the dazzling covers by artist H.J. Ward.

27 ····

VICE SQUAD DETECTIVE

1934

Unknown

The magazine was reportedly seized at the printing plant by the police with only a few copies reaching big-city distributors.

28 ····

SAUCY ROMANTIC ADVENTURES

May 1936

Norman Saunders

The first issue.
The "Domino Lady" was a female crime fighter.

Many of the pulp regulars wrote for them, usually adding a little sex to their rejects before recycling them under various pen names. Robert E. Howard wrote for the *Spicys* under the name of "Sam Walser." But it remained for Hugh B. Cave to come up with the classic pseudonym of "Justin Case." Two writers with less shame were E. Hoffman Price and the ubiquitous Robert Leslie Bellem, who published under their own names and managed to hit most of the *Spicys* from their first issue on.

Society can stand sin and sex only in small doses, and by late 1941 the *Spicy* publishers were forced to take the veil. Overnight *Spicy* became *Speed*, existing titles were cleaned up, and new magazines introduced with innocuous titles such as *Magic Love* and *Amour*. The *Speed* titles and the others quickly died from an overdose of purity. However, one of the silent partners in the *Spicys* managed to get by quite comfortably on his other publishing venture—DC Comics, publishers of *Action Comics*, *Superman*, and *Batman*.

The longest lived of the love pulps were the western love magazines, in which many authors were recognizable names in the western field. Love in the open air and under western skies was somehow more acceptable than in the cramped apartments and railroad flats of the cities.

The first and most successful of the western-romance pulps, *Ranch Romances*, lasted until the early '70s, nearly two decades after the rest of the pulps had turned up their toes. Rumors were that while its circulation in the East had nearly vanished, it still sold quite well in the Northwest.

29 • • •
SAUCY MOVIE TALES
January 1937
Norman Saunders ("C. Blaine")
An enthusiastic high-kicker at a tinsel-town party.

29

Winning One For the Gipper

Teenage Dreams of Glory

The sports pulps were never as popular as westerns or mysteries, but we can trace their lineage just as far back to the most famous dime-novel hero of all—Frank Merriwell.

Writing under the house name of "Burt L. Standish," William Gilbert Patten was Merriwell's creator. Patten, fascinated by dime novels, wrote two short stories at the age of fifteen and sold both—for six dollars. His parents had wanted him to be a preacher, but young Patten promptly turned his back on the Bible and the collection plate to concentrate on writing.

"Frank Merriwell," written at the suggestion of Street & Smith, first appeared in *Tip-Top Weekly*, published in 1896. Readers avidly followed his various adventures, but his peak of popularity was as a star athlete at Yale, where he won almost every game he played or event he entered.

Years after the dime novels had died, Merriwell surfaced again in *Tip-Top Semi-Monthly* edited by "Burt L. Standish." The magazine had become a ten-cent pulp heavy on sport stories and the adventures of the various Merriwells (one had never proved quite enough; there was also Dick Merriwell, younger brother of Frank) in college and out.

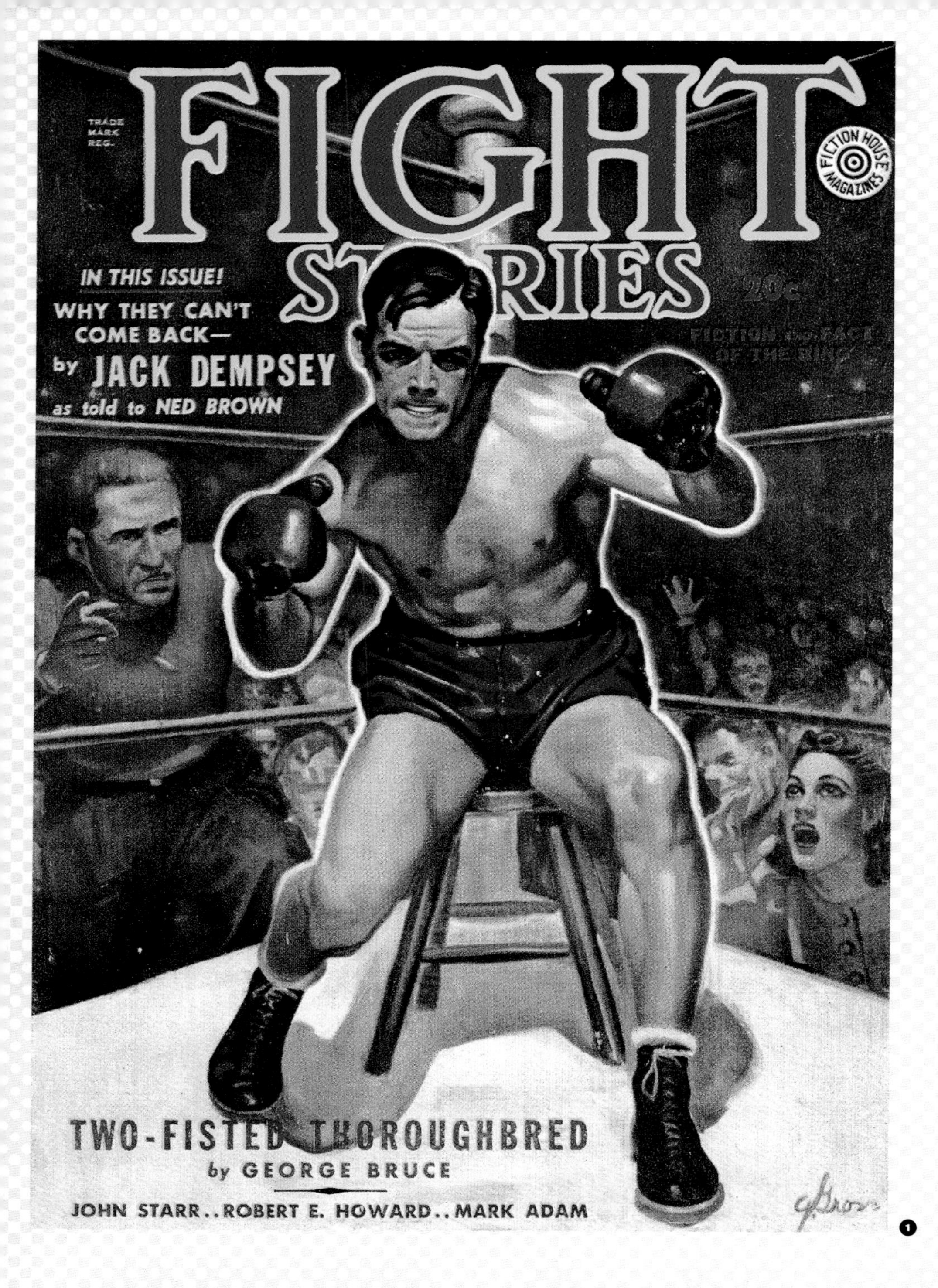

❶ ••
Fight Stories
Summer 1940
George Gross
Authors on the inside included Robert E. Howard of "Conan" fame.

Frank was to be revived still again when Street & Smith launched *Sport Story Magazine* in the early '20s during what was known as "the golden age of sport," with athletes such as Jack Dempsey, boxing; Bill Tilden, tennis; Babe Ruth, baseball; and Paavo Nurmi, Finnish long-distance runner, winner at the 1920 Antwerp Olympic Games, dominating the sports scene. The magazine did exceedingly well, building up to a circulation of 150,000 within a year or two from introduction.

Merriwell was more than welcome as a fictional hero, though he was gradually phased out of future issues as an attempt was made to tie the magazine closer to the real sports heroes of the day.

In the '30s *Sport Story* was joined by *All-America Sports*, 1933; *Thrilling Sports*, 1936; *Popular Sports*, 1937; *Dime Sports*, 1935; and so on, and magazines devoted to a single sport such as *Fight Stories*, 1928; *Basketball Stories*, 1937; *All-American Football*, 1938; *Baseball Stories*, 1938; etc. Jack Dempsey was popular enough to have a magazine named after him, though it didn't last for many issues.

Later many of the magazines became cyclical. Football magazines appeared in the fall and winter, while baseball titles were spring and summer publications.

World War II and the paper shortage hit the sports pulps hard, but there were contributing reasons for their decline. Sports titles had a split personality, carrying fact articles as well as fiction, recognizing their readers' interest in the reality of sports as well as the fantasy. Street & Smith's slick sports annuals were

2 •
Jack Dempsey's Fight Magazine
May 1934
Earle K. Bergey
The first issue of the only pulp to be named after an athlete. There was no *Babe Ruth Stories* or a *Jim Thorpe Magazine*.

3 •
Sport Story Magazine
November 1, 1938
H.W. Scott
A touch of humor was rare in a sports pulp cover.

4 •
Sport Story Magazine
June 25, 1935
Earle K. Bergey
A rare sports pulp cover featuring a swimmer.

5

5 •
Fifteen Sports Stories
March 1948
Unknown
It cost a penny-and-a-half per story, a bargain for the teenage reader.

6 •
Football Stories
Fall 1944
George Gross
Baseball, football, boxing, and basketball had their own magazines, but hockey didn't, and neither did soccer, swimming, or tennis.

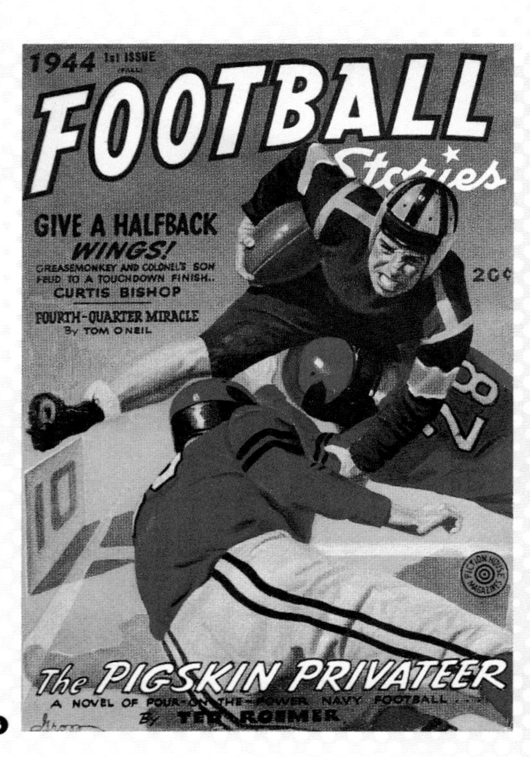

6

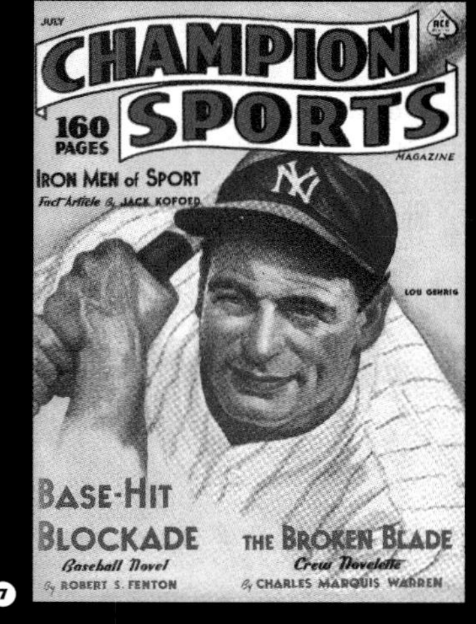

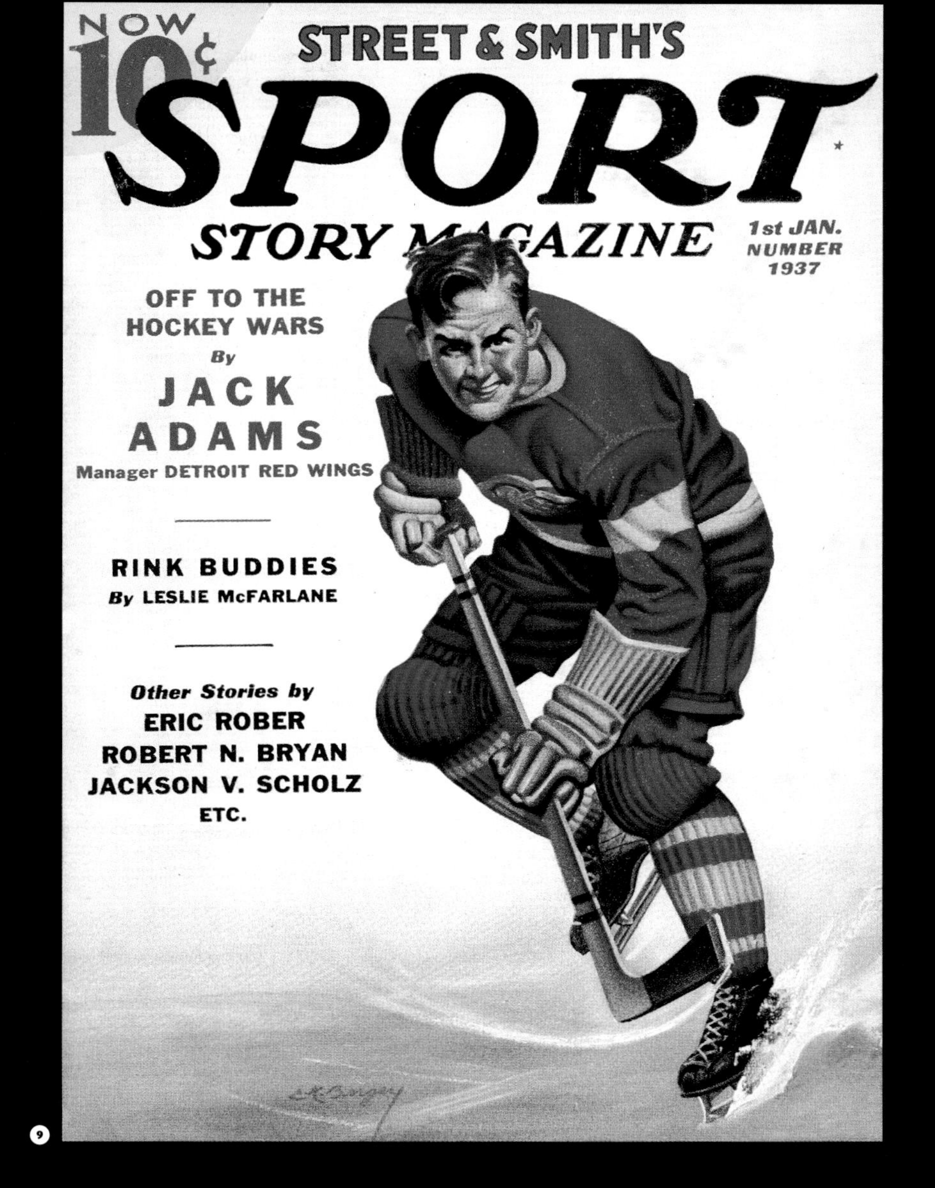

9 •
Sport Story Magazine
January 1, 1937
Earle K. Bergey
Sports pulps are relatively rare. Many read them but few readers bothered saving them.

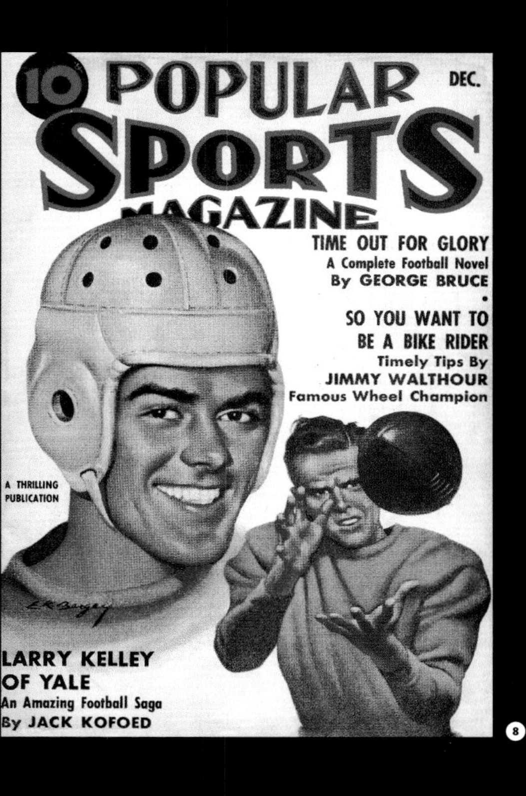

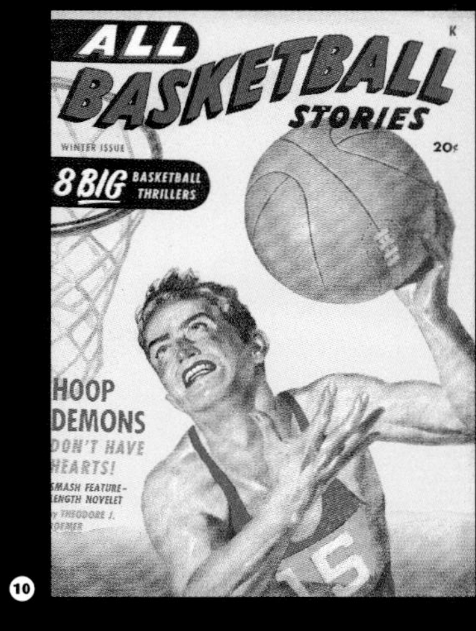

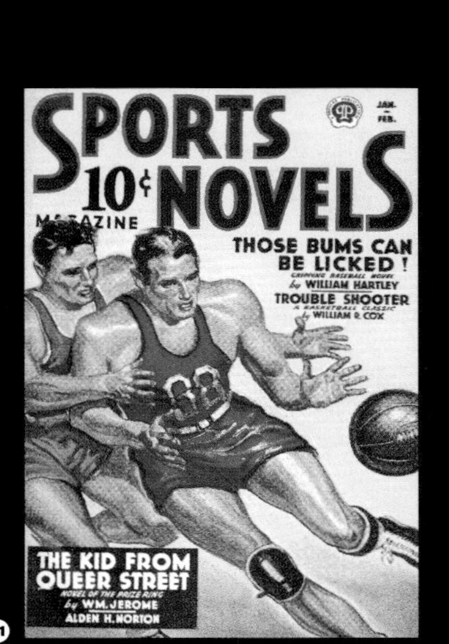

10 •
All Basketball Stories
Winter 1947-48
Allen Anderson
Sports were seasonal, and so were the pulps covering them.

7 •
Champion Sports
July 1937
Rafael de Soto
Sports pulps sometimes featured portraits of champions like Lou Gehrig.

8 •
Popular Sports
December 1937
Earle K. Bergey
Another sports celebrity cover: a football hero for the fall.

11 •
Sports Novels
January-February 1940
Unknown
The story titles were innocent in the '40s, but not in the '90s.

especially popular. *Football Year Book* and *Baseball Year Book* sold more than three hundred thousand copies each, and no doubt pulled some circulation from the pulp sports titles. Eventually, of course, *Sports Illustrated*, a weekly magazine devoted to sports, appeared on the scene, though the pulps were gone by then.

Sports titles labored under another handicap, especially during the '30s. *Sport Story* and other titles were magazines to be read on rainy afternoons. During sunny days the target audience hardly was curled up on the sofa reading about fictional sports heroes. They were outdoors trying to sink a basketball through the hoop hung over the garage doors, or at the lot on the corner playing a pick-up game of baseball, or maybe out in a nearly empty street (there were such things in the '30s) playing touch football.

The magazines also limited their potential audience by restricting their coverage of sports pretty much to boxing, baseball, football, and basketball. Few covered swimming or diving, tennis or soccer, archery or marksmanship. Certainly none covered figure skating or bobsledding. Of all the titles *Sport Story* was the most varied and, in the long run, the most successful. But even it failed in competition against the real thing: the slick annuals, the growing coverage of sports in the daily paper, and eventually the paper shortage. Even the one thing the sports pulps could offer—the frequently dramatic full-color covers by George Gross and other artists—was not enough.

Like the writers for *Adventure*, the writers of sports stories were usually familiar with the sports they wrote about. Many were sports reporters for the daily papers who moonlighted in fiction. And some were former stars of various sports. Jackson V. Scholz, while he wrote about a variety of sports, was most at home with track and field, in which he had competed as a sprinter in the 1924 Olympics.

Scholz went on to write many books for teenage sports enthusiasts, but moviegoers may remember him from the film *Chariots of Fire*, in which he was played by actor Brad Davis.

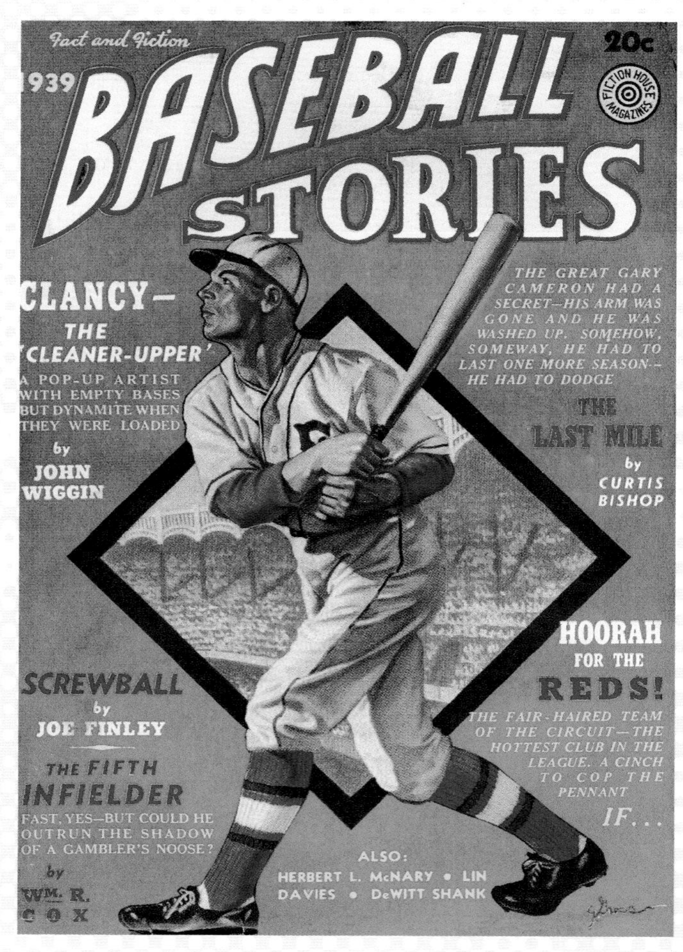

12

⓬ •
BASEBALL STORIES
Summer 1939
George Gross
A summer issue devoted to baseball, fiction and fact.

⓭ •
THRILLING SPORTS
Summer 1946
Earle K. Bergey
Summer was the perfect time for a baseball cover.

⓮ •
ALL-AMERICAN FOOTBALL MAGAZINE
Fall 1943
George Gross
A stunning cover for a sports pulp covering football.

FROM BAYONETS TO BIPLANES

Dawn Patrols

World War I ended in 1918, but it wasn't until 1924 that Captain Flagg and Sergeant Quirt were immortalized in the play *What Price Glory?* by Maxwell Anderson and Laurence Stallings. It emphasized the profanity of the soldiers and the brutality and ugliness of war. But for those who had participated in the Great War, it also had nostalgic appeal.

Publishers didn't delay in mining the nostalgia for possible gold. (For the most part they ignored the profanity, brutality, and ugliness.) *War Stories* hit the newsstands in 1926; *Battle Stories* followed in 1927; and *Over the Top* and *Under Fire* in 1928.

Captain W.H. ("Billy") Fawcett was best known for *Captain Billy's Whiz Bang*, an under-the-counter collection of cartoons and off-color jokes. He was the editor of *Battle Stories* and had come by his captain's bars honestly. Most of the authors had fought in the Great War, and one of them, Arthur Guy Empey, had written two bestsellers: *Over the Top* in 1917 and *First Call* in 1918. The title of the first novel was used, probably with his permission, for the pulp of the same name, one to which Empey often contributed stories.

But the wave of nostalgia soon passed, and by the mid-'30s, when the country was in the midst of the Great Depression, nobody wanted to be reminded of the Great War, no matter how lighthearted and entertaining the memories. The war pulps largely vanished, revived occasionally for a few issues and then expired again.

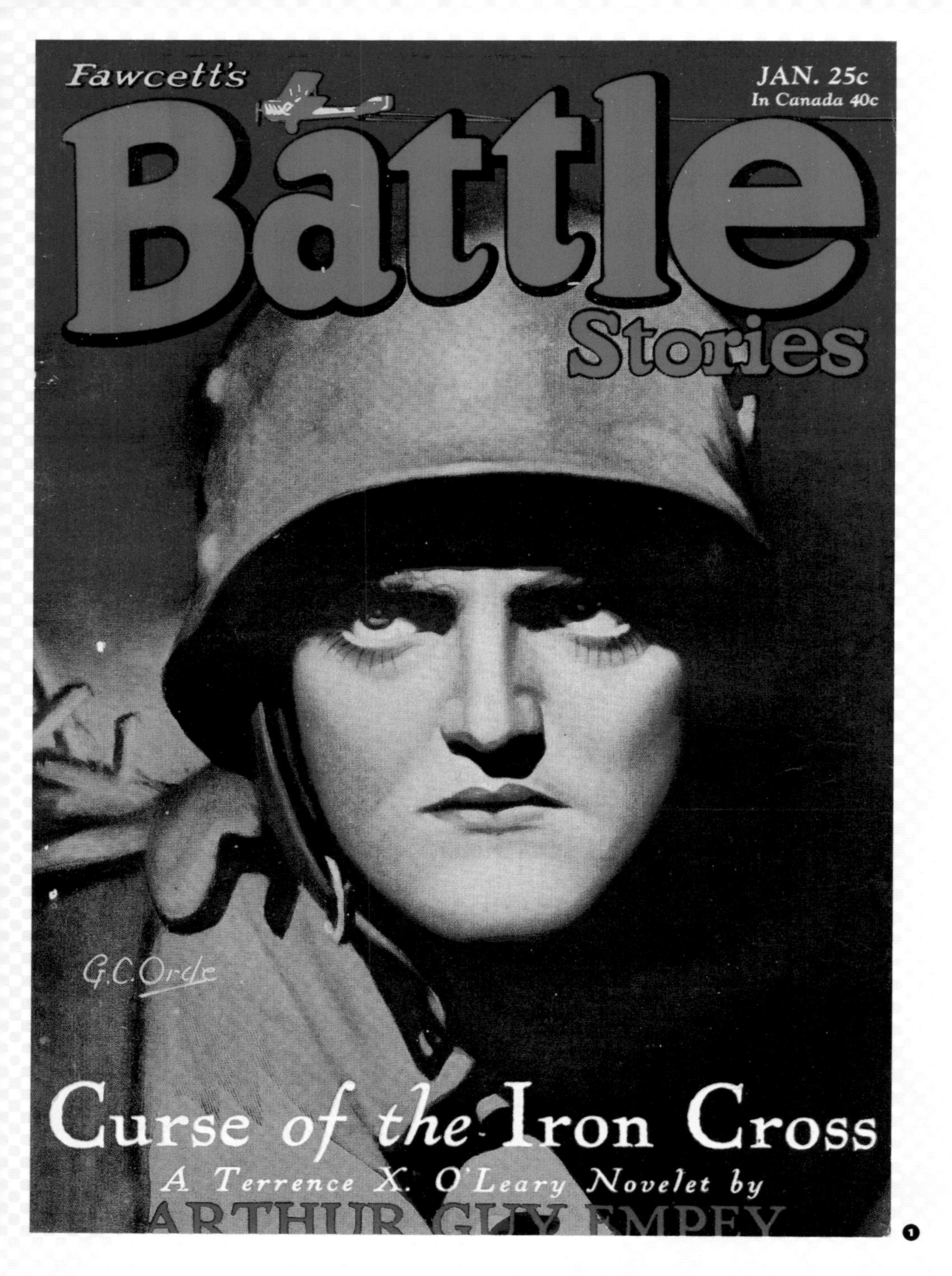

The more exotic air pulps had far greater staying power. *Air Stories*, the first of them, appeared in 1927, and was concerned more with flying than with dogfights. *Wings* also appeared in 1927, the year Lindbergh flew the Atlantic and the immensely popular film *Wings* starring Clara Bow, Richard Arlen, and Buddy Rogers (with Gary Cooper in a minor role), won the first film Oscar for Best Picture. (Clara Bow had little more than a cameo; the real "love" affair was between friends Arlen and Rogers.)

Wings (the film) wasn't responsible for the immortal cliché: "Would you send a kid in a crate like that up on a night like this?" But the aerial dogfighting scenes became the templates for dozens of air-war covers, from the leering German behind his twin machine guns firing directly at you, to planes going down in flames or a frightened pilot glancing behind him just as the enemy zoomed in for the kill.

❶ ••
Battle Stories
January 1932
G.C. Orde
All Quiet on the Western Front had been released two years earlier, and *Battle Stories* was quick to humanize the enemy.

❷ ••
Battle Stories
November 1928
Chester Sullivan
Bailing out of a gas bag on the Western Front.

❹ ••
WAR STORIES
February 16, 1928
Sidney Riesenberg
A touch of humor. The legend on the box car says it can carry forty men or eight horses.

❸ ••
WAR STORIES
May 23, 1929
Charles Durant
The first and most popular of the war pulp titles.

❸

❹

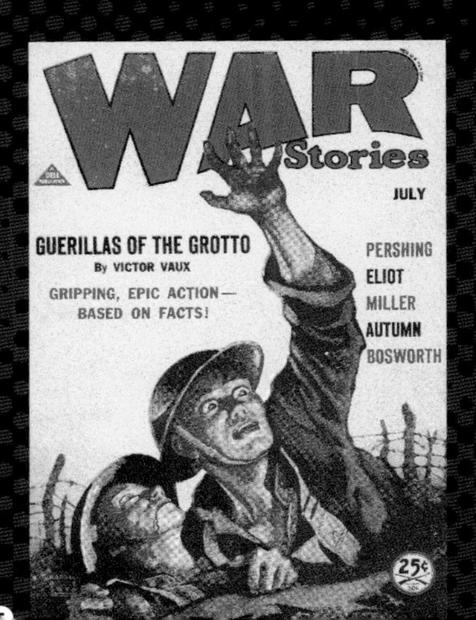

❺

❺ ••
WAR STORIES
July 1931
Rafael de Soto
A surprisingly grim cover for a war pulp. War wasn't all fun and games after all, and readership began to decline during the grim days of the Depression

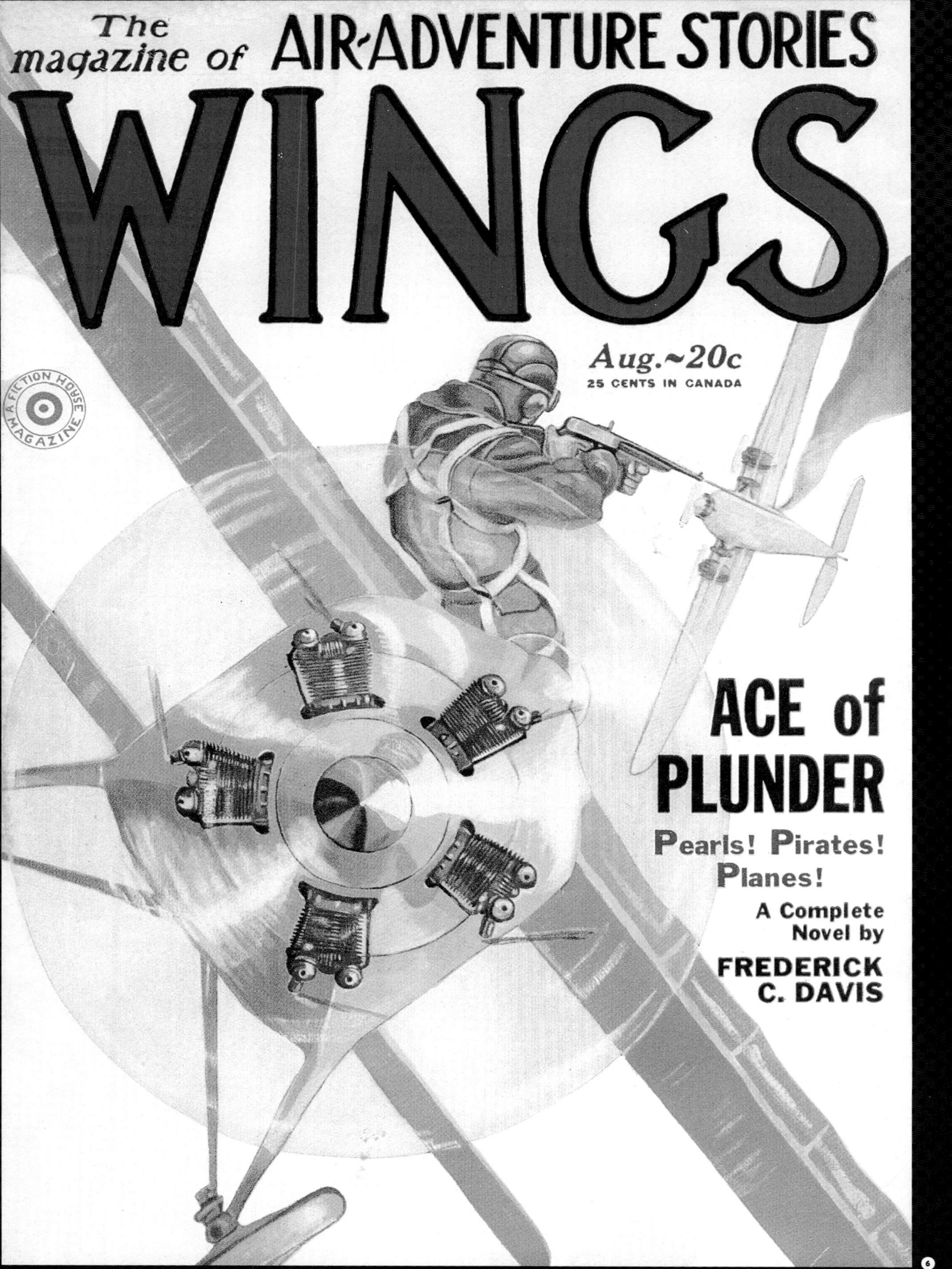

6 ••
WINGS
August 1929
Frank McAleer
A dramatic layout for an air pulp cover.

7 •••
NAVY STORIES
February 1929
Sidney Riesenberg
The first issue showed Zeppelins battling war ships. It probably never happened, but it was fun for the reader.

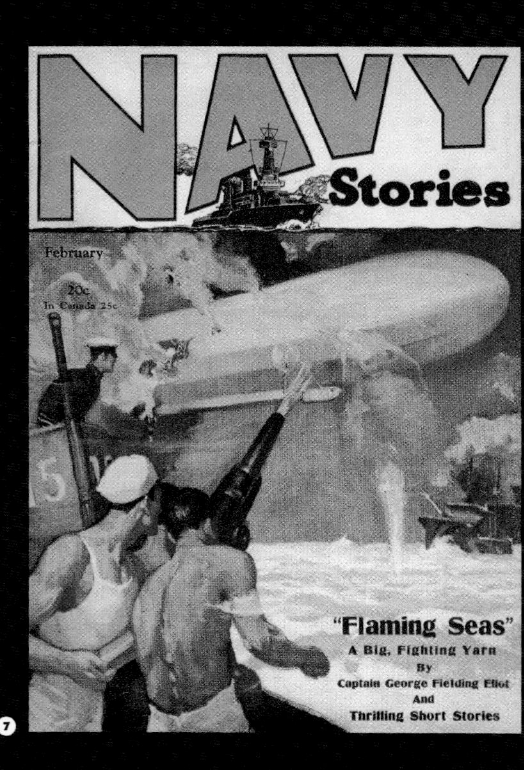

7

6

8 ••

AIR TRAILS
January 1929
Jerome Rozen
An early issue of *Air Trails* before the cover got a modern redesign.

9 •••

SUBMARINE STORIES
April 1929
Wendell Galloway
You couldn't leave out the "silent service" when fighting World War I.

AIR TRAILS
September 1931
Frank Tinsley
Air Trails had several incarnations: first, as an air pulp; second, a fact-and-model magazine; and last, a science magazine.

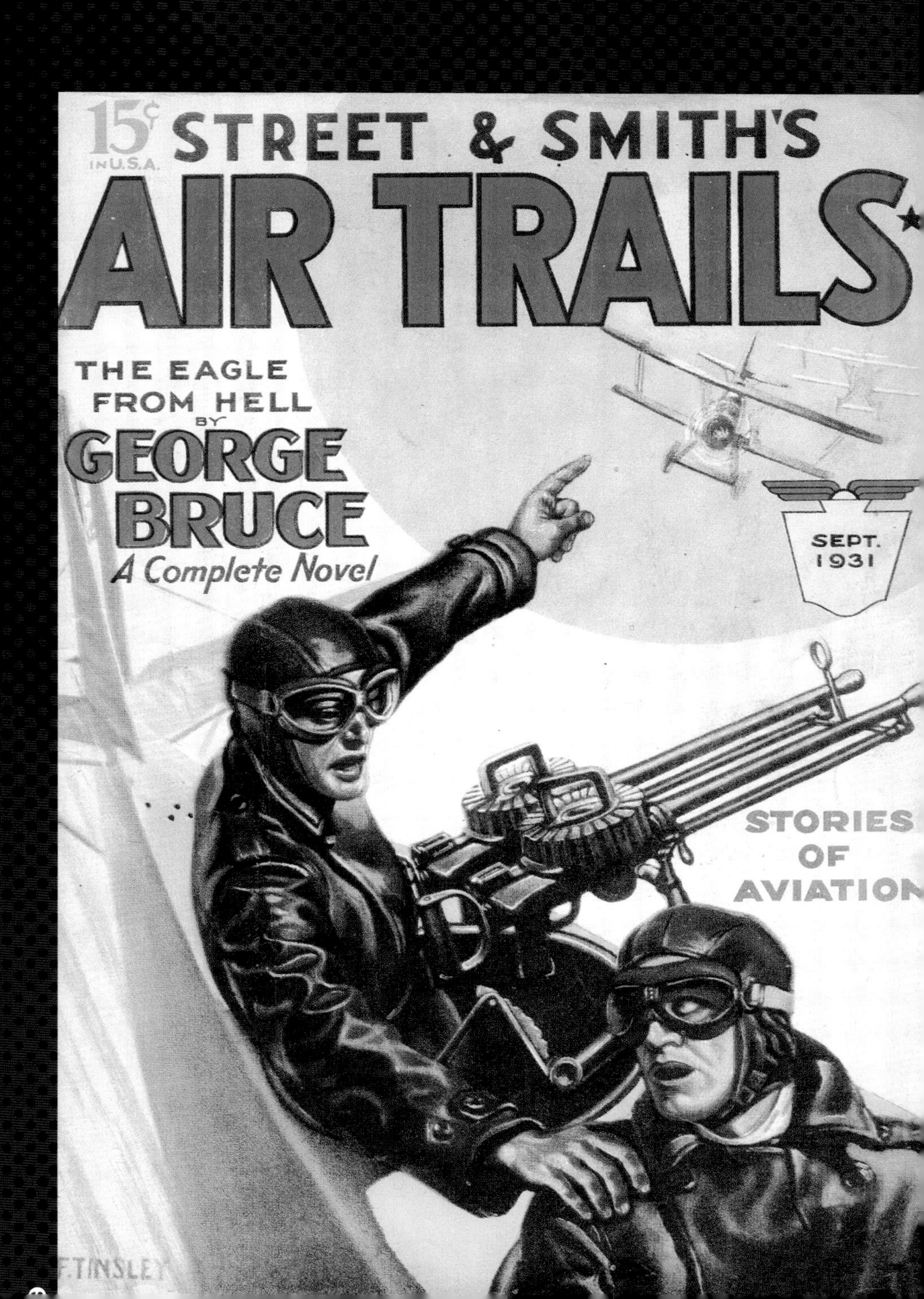

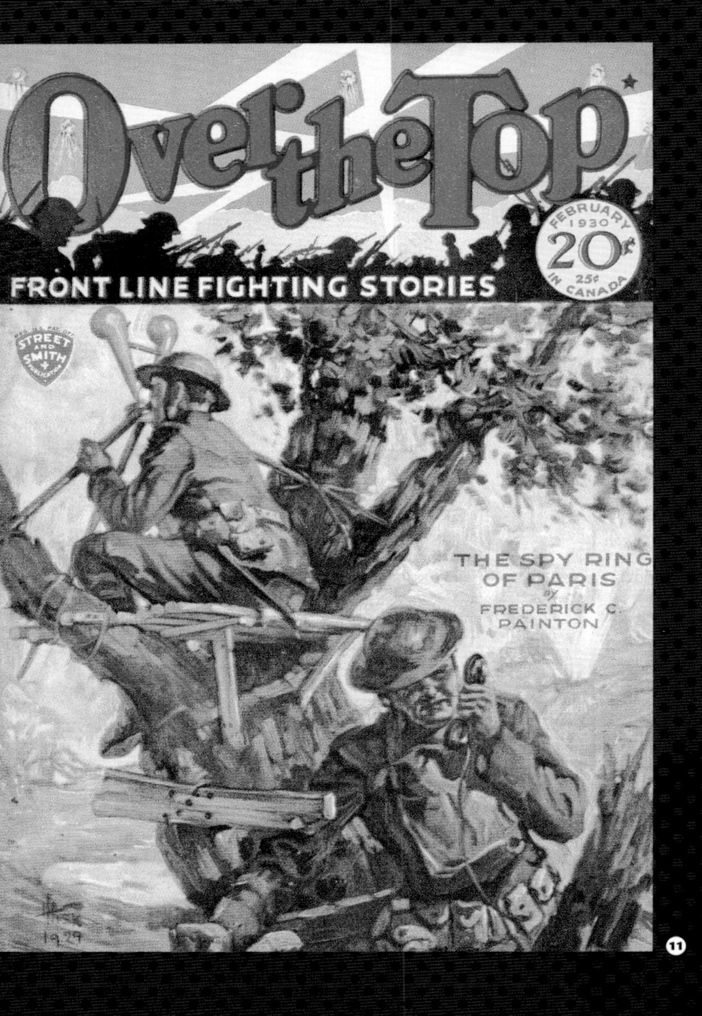

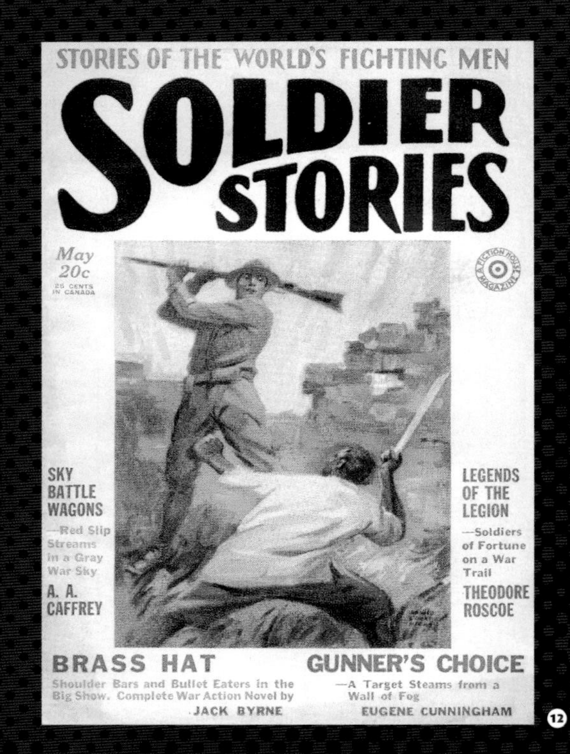

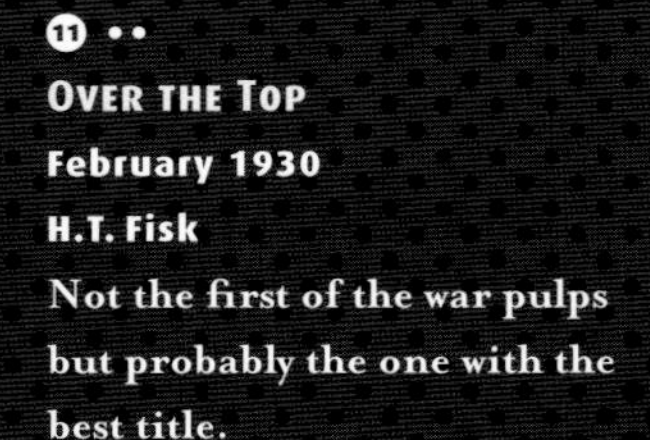

⓫ ••
Over the Top
February 1930
H.T. Fisk
Not the first of the war pulps but probably the one with the best title.

⓬ ••
Soldier Stories
May 1929
A.L. Hicks
Another short-lived war pulp.

⓭ •••
Under Fire
November 1928
Walter M. Baumhofer
Under Fire was a short-lived war pulp.

⓮ ••
Spy Stories
March 1929
Walter M. Baumhofer
The first issue profiled the most famous spy of all.

⓯ ••
Three Star Stories
April 2, 1929
Gerard Delano
Another view of the war from the German side.

Other publishers quickly jumped into the field with *War Birds*, *Sky Birds*, *Flight*, and *Eagles of the Air*, among others. Popular-science maven Hugo Gernsback even published an uneasy combination of air stories and science-fiction titled *Air Wonder Stories*. Other fledgling air pulps included *The Lone Eagle* (an obvious title), *Aces*, *Airplane Stories*, *Dare-Devil Aces*, *Flying Aces*, and so forth.

Like many of the writers for the war pulps, a number of the air-pulp authors were familiar with planes and flying. Arch Whitehouse had flown with the Royal Flying Corps, and Donald E. Keyhoe had served with World War I Marine aviation and was liaison to Lindbergh on a goodwill tour of America. Robert J. Hogan went to flight training but came down with flu in the big 1918 epidemic and never made it to the front, though later he became a sales manager and airplane demonstrator for Curtis-Wright. He named his most famous character, "G-8," for a Colorado ranch where he worked as a boy.

But the most popular air-war pulp writer of all was George Bruce, who probably added as much circulation to an issue of air pulp on whose cover he was featured as did "Race Williams" for *Black Mask* in the mystery field. Bruce's favorite plot usually revolved around the rich kid or the former quarterback—one who had everything going for him in civilian life or who had made his name in other fields—who comes in green to a squadron of veteran pilots and has to prove himself.

As with all pulps, the covers were posters for the magazine, and with the air pulps, like many of the westerns, the artist usually was admirably suited to the subject matter. Whether it was research or personal familiarity, few covers lacked at least a faint ring of authenticity.

But their appeal was based on far more than the echo of reality. The Spads and Sopwith-Camels and Jennys locked in mortal combat in the azure skies were exciting, and the grim-faced pilots, goggles on their foreheads and white silk scarves trailing behind, were glamorous. The more planes in the cover painting, of course, the greater the appeal to teenage readers. And the occasional battle between a plane and an observation balloon was a surefire grabber.

16

16 ••
THRILLING SPY STORIES
Fall 1939
Rudolph Zirn
Spy novels made it big after World War II but not during it.

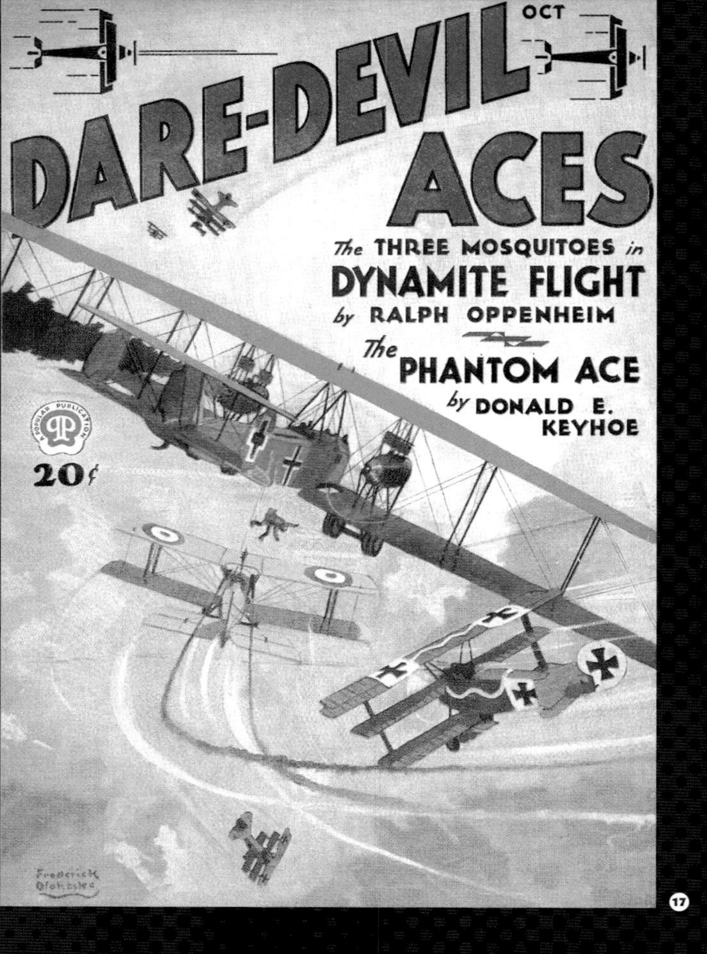

17

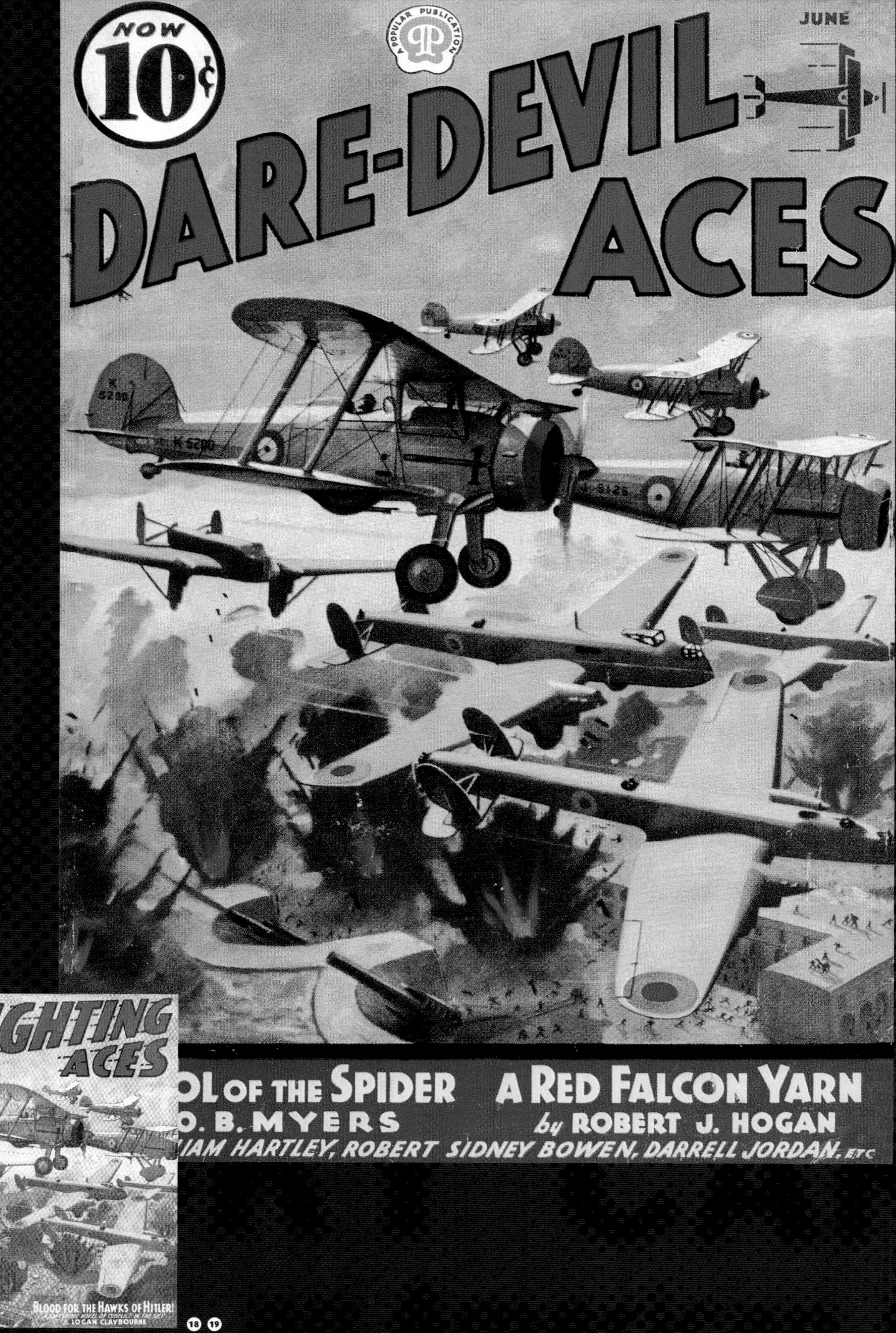

18 19

17 ••
Dare-Devil Aces
October 1932
Frederick Blakeslee
A classic World War I dogfight with German fighters protecting their bomber.

18 ••
Dare-Devil Aces
June 1937
19 •
Fighting Aces
November 1940
Frederick Blakeslee
Stories were sometimes reprinted but seldom cover paintings.

20 ••

Flying Aces
December 1928
Ray C. Wardel
The year 1928 was a great one for launching air pulps.

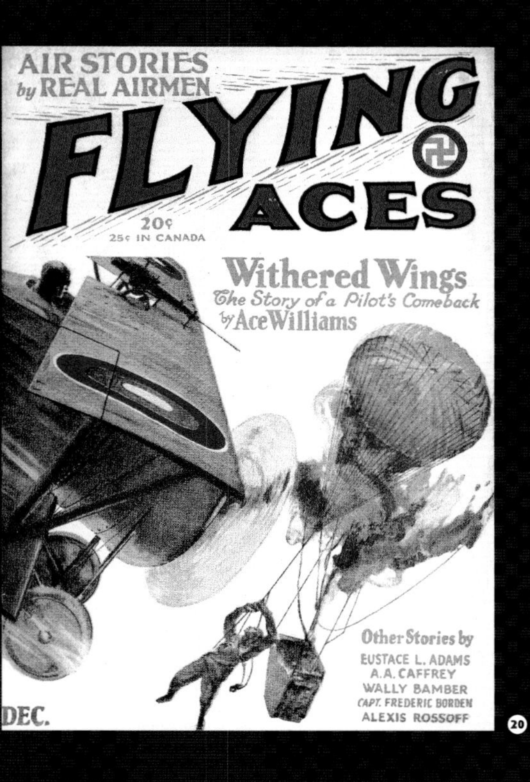

20

21 ••

Dare-Devil Aces
July 1933
Frederick Blakeslee
The more planes on the cover, the better the magazine sold.

21

22 ••
George Bruce's Contact
August 1933
Eugene M. Frandzen
There were five pulps named after George Bruce, a popular aviation author. Bruce edited, wrote for, and practically stapled the magazines himself.

23 ••
Air Stories
August 1927
Frank McAleer
The first issue of the first air pulp. Note the skywriting logo.

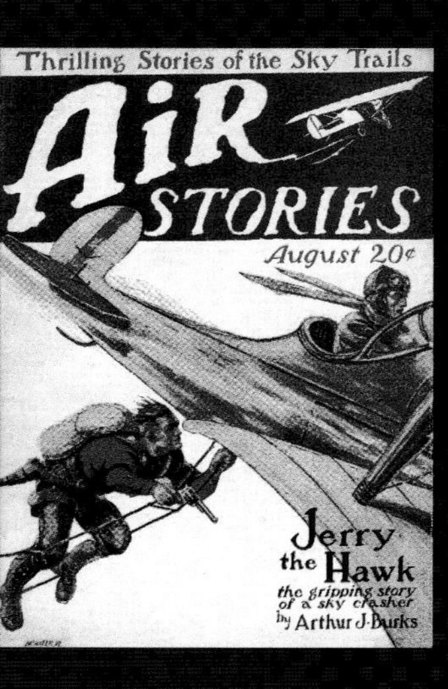

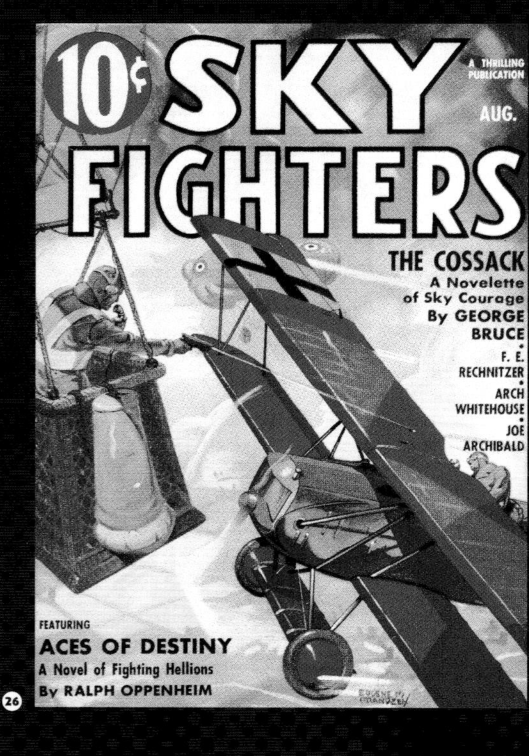

24 ••
Sky Birds
October 1931
C. Heurlin
Author Keyhoe not only predicted the start of World War II (for the U.S.) ten years later, he was one of the first to write about flying saucers.

25 •••
Zoom!
October-November 1931
Ray C. Wardel
The shortest and most expressive title in the air-war field.

26 ••
Sky Fighters
August 1936
Eugene M. Frandzen
A dogfight that probably never happened but made for a great cover.

27 ••

The Lone Eagle

December 1937

Eugene M. Frandzen

The Lone Eagle was named for Lindbergh, then changed its title to *The American Eagle* when Lindbergh opposed entry in World War II.

28 ••

Airplane Stories

February 1931

Eugene M. Frandzen

Artists seldom let impossibility stand in the way of a dramatic cover.

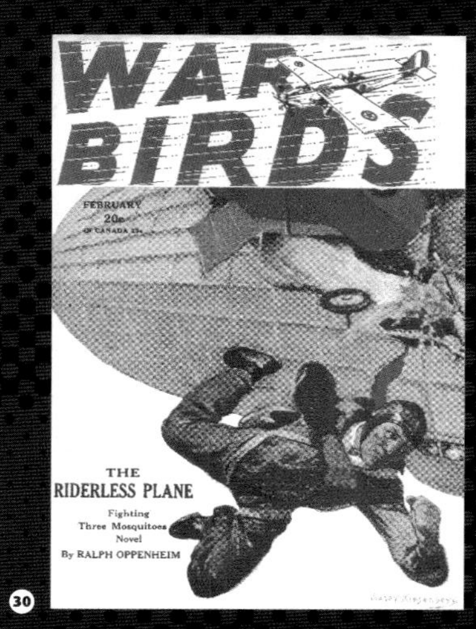

30

30 ••

War Birds

February 1930

Sidney Riesenberg

Gas bags vs. airplanes once again.

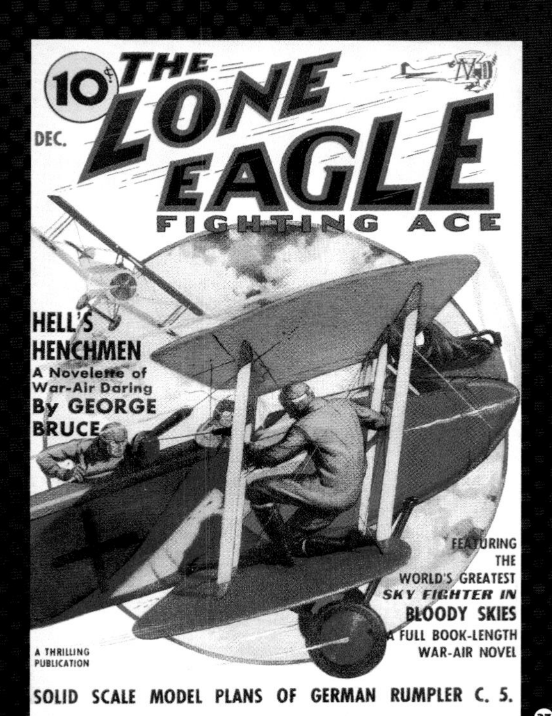

27

29 ••

War Birds

June 1934

Rudolph Belarski

Hero O'Leary moonlighted flying rocket ships.

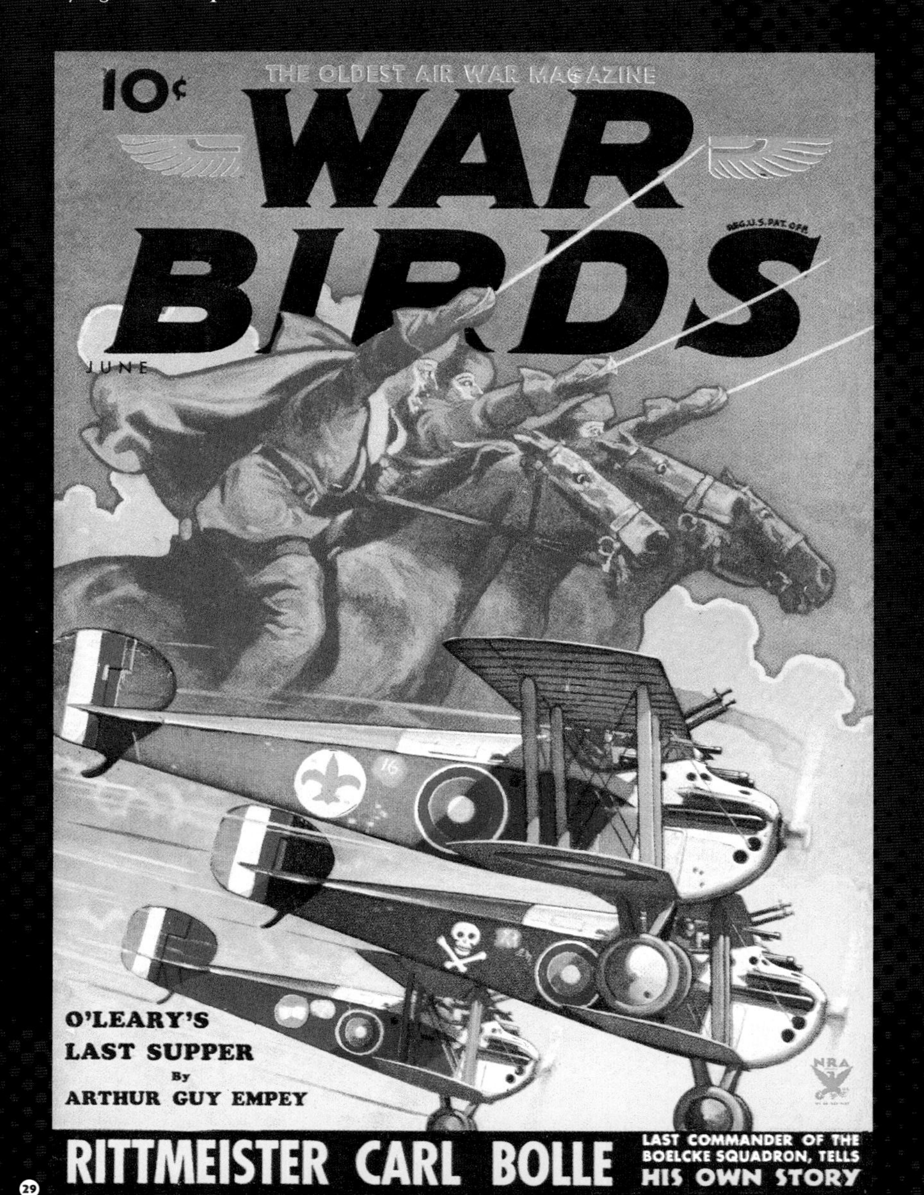

29

31

31 ••

Triple-X Magazine

July 1929

F.R. Glass

The magazine's gimmick was to combine air, war, and western genres on the same cover, and the results were unintentionally comic.

28

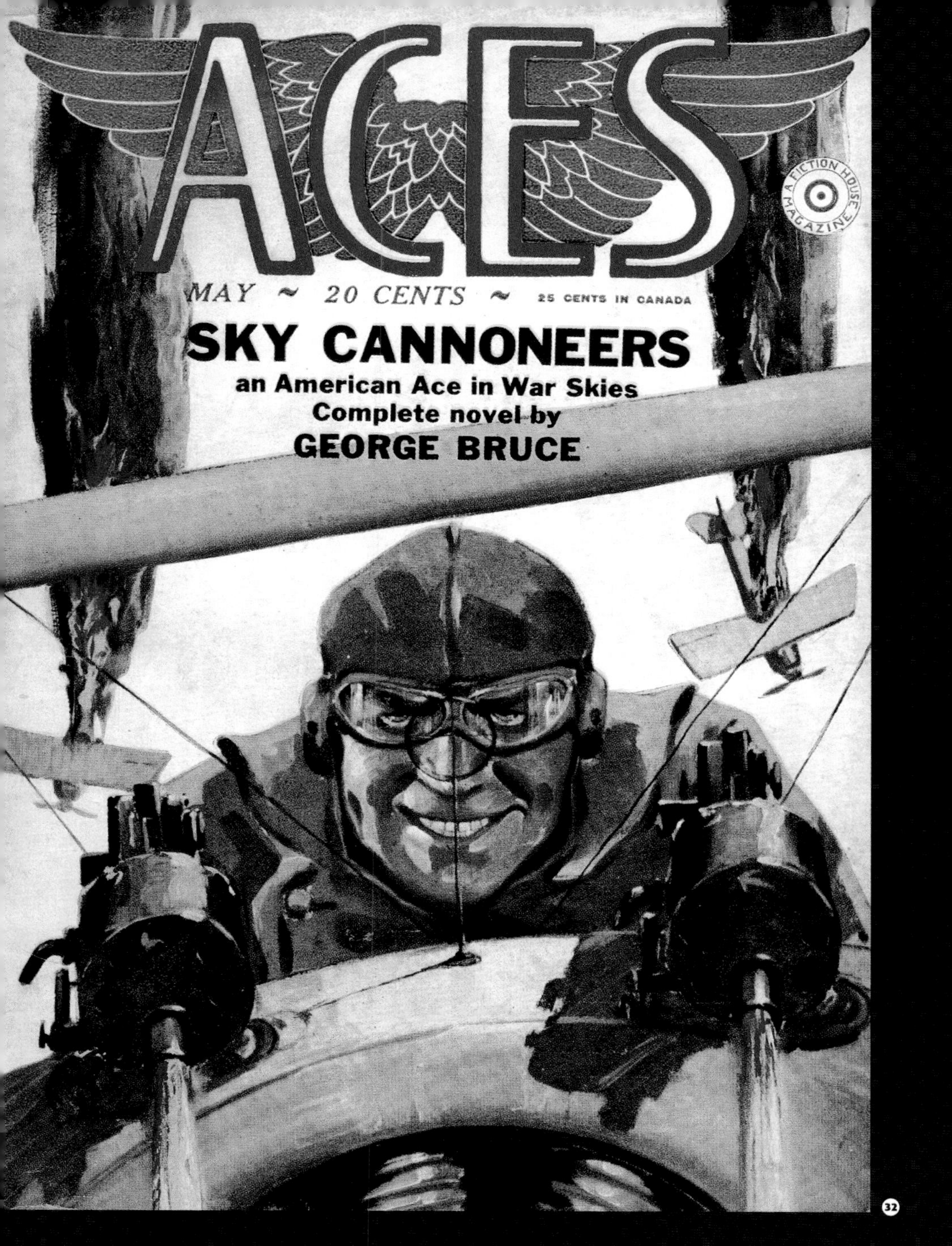

32 ••
Aces
May 1929
H.C. Murphy
He's got you in his sights,
and he's coming right at you!

34 ••
Aces
August 1929
Bertram Glover
A grimmer cover than usual.
The pilot is going down
in flames.

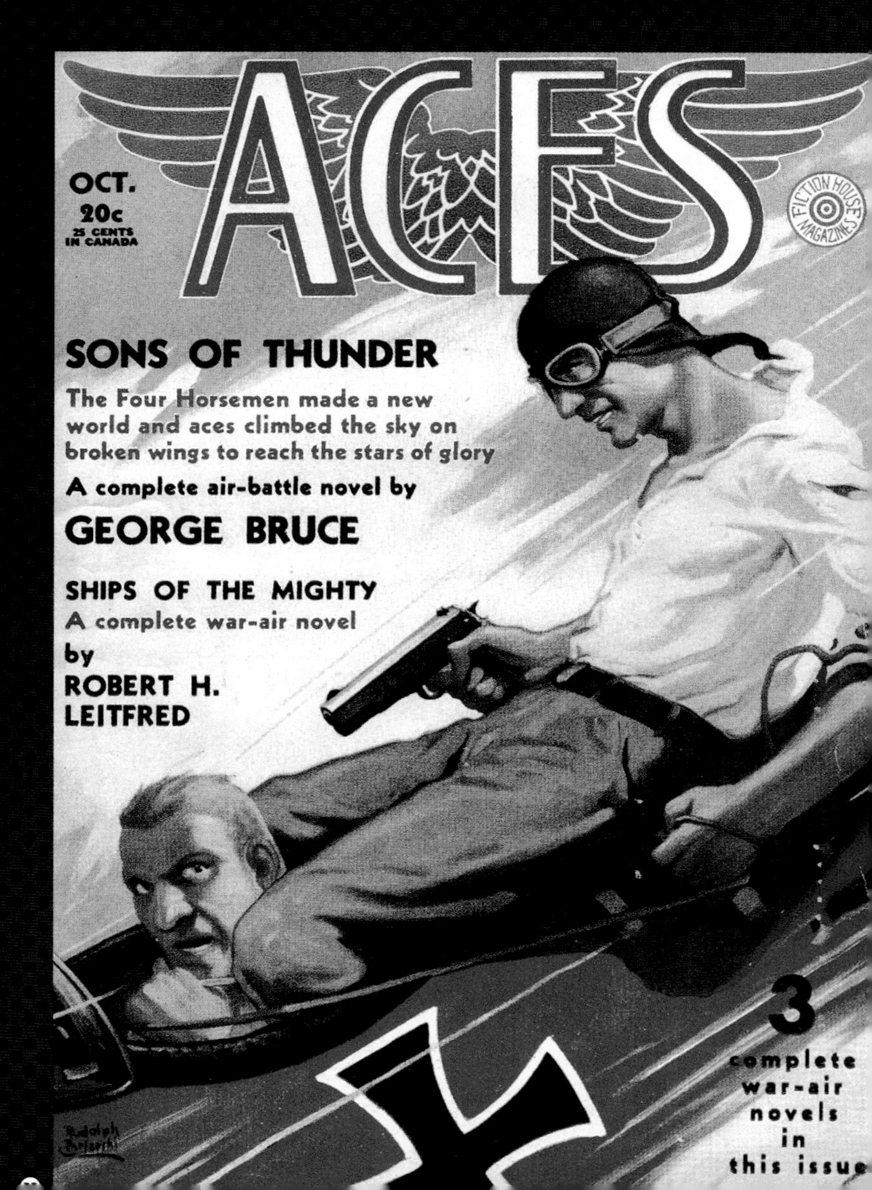

33 ••
Aces
October 1931
Rudolph Belarski
Take me to the nearest Allied
landing field!

Frank Tinsley generally was regarded as the best of the air-war illustrators, though Rudolph Belarski and Frederick Blakeslee weren't far behind. But perhaps the most attention-getting cover painting for an air pulp was the one that Eugene Frandzen did for *Airplane Stories*, showing a tiger crouched on the fuselage just behind the pilot. The concept was later lifted for an issue of *G-8 and His Battle Aces*.

By the start of World War II, the creaking biplanes and their hell-for-leather pilots firing their twin Vickers through the propeller had become dull stuff. A few of the pulps geared up to fight the new war. But fighting a war when nostalgia has gilded most of the grimmest memories and fighting one where the daily paper prints the latest casualty lists were two completely different matters. And with closed cockpits, the glamorous, grim-faced pilot had all but disappeared. It was now machine against machine, an impersonal fight at best.

Most of the air-war pulps hit the silk before the war even ended. As air-pulp historian Dale L. Walker put it: "A New Great War had made the Old Great War obsolete."

35 •
AIR WAR
March 1942
Rudolph Belarski
The pulps were finally fighting World War II. But as far as the covers went, the personal touch—the glamorous flying ace—was gone.

36 •
AIR ADVENTURES
December 1939
H.W. McCauley
The first air pulp to concentrate solely on World War II.

The Rocketeers Have Shaggy Ears

Science Fiction Addiction

Strangely enough, the pulp genre, which for many years had the fewest readers, also had the most fanatic ones. Fantasy is as old as fiction itself, and the story papers and dime novels published a fair amount of it, notably the "Frank Reade" and "Frank Reade, Jr." stories about "electric horses" and "steam men."

Early pulps like *Argosy* and *Blue Book* also printed science-fiction and fantasy, as did Street & Smith's short-lived *The Thrill Book*, published in 1919. But it remained for an immigrant from Luxembourg to publish the first magazine devoted solely to the genre.

Hugo Gernsback was intensely interested in radio and electricity and founded *Modern Electrics*, which in turn became *The Electrical Experimenter* and eventually *Science and Invention*. Though devoted to the latest gadgets and wonders of science, most of Gernsback's magazines also included stories of "scientific fiction"—many of which he wrote himself—in every issue.

The stories proved immensely popular, and Gernsback launched the over-sized *Amazing Stories* with the April 1926 issue. It was an immediate success, and Gernsback followed it with an annual (which printed Edgar Rice Burroughs's *The Master Mind of Mars* complete) and a quarterly.

1 ••••
Amazing Stories
February 1928
Frank R. Paul
New authors appeared in the magazine's third year. On the inside was the first appearance of Anthony "Buck" Rogers before he hit the comic strips.

2 •••
Amazing Stories
February 1927
Frank R. Paul
The first science-fiction magazine relied on reprints its first year. The cover was for Burroughs's *The Land That Time Forgot*.

3 •
Amazing Stories
August 1946
H.W. McCauley
Artist McCauley was famous for his "Mac" pin-up girls.

Along with its fiction, *Amazing Stories* published a readers' column and printed the addresses of correspondents. Readers began to contact one another, and within months an embryonic science-fiction "fandom" was born.

Initially the magazines were made up of reprints. They featured H.G. Wells, Jules Verne, and Edgar Allen Poe, as well as such relatively recent writers as Abraham Merritt, Murray Leinster, and Edgar Rice Burroughs, whose stories had previously been published in *Argosy* and *All-Story*.

Original manuscripts trickled in, among them *The Skylark of Space* by Dr. Edward Elmer Smith, who dominated the field for the next ten years. Smith's characters didn't restrict their adventures to the solar system but included the entire galaxy. And with that, the basic outlines of modern science-fiction were set.

Gernsback lost control of his magazines in 1929 but promptly replaced *Amazing Stories* and its quarterly with *Science Wonder Stories*, *Air Wonder Stories*, and *Science Wonder Stories Quarterly*. Unfortunately "science" wasn't much of a sales inducement when it came to fiction, and Gernsback soon dropped it, combining his two leading titles into simply *Wonder Stories*. He also started *Scientific Detective Stories* at about the same time but changed the tittle to *Amazing Detective Stories* for the same reason.

Greensback now was publishing much original material but, particularly in *Wonder Stories Quarterly*, was fond of reprinting German science-fiction novels. *Wonder Stories* itself went through several size changes, from "bedsheet" to pulp, back to bedsheet and then pulp again. Greensback paid relatively little—sometimes only on threat of lawsuit—but still managed to publish some of the more significant early science-fiction stories, including the stand-out "A Martian Odyssey" by Stanley G. Weinbaum.

There was no doubting the popularity of science-fiction, but it took a while for the general pulp houses to see its potential. The first was the Clayton chain. They printed their covers in groups, but in late 1929 were several short to fill the form or parent sheet. The publisher was anxious to add more titles on the cheap, and one of Clayton's editors, Harry Bates, suggested the jawbreaking *Astounding Stories of Super-Science* (January 1930). Bates and an assistant, Desmond Hall, became the editors.

❹ •
AMAZING STORIES
August 1937
Leo Morey
A splash of red and for once artist Morey had a standout cover.

Gernsback claimed science-fiction should teach. (We'll ignore Merritt, Burroughs, and Poe who never considered themselves to be teachers of much of anything.) Harry Bates thought science-fiction should be fun, with heroes and villains and lots of action. He offered his readers generous doses of all three. Bates and Hall, under the pen name of "Anthony Gilmore," even wrote their own science-fiction saga starring "Hawk Carse."

7

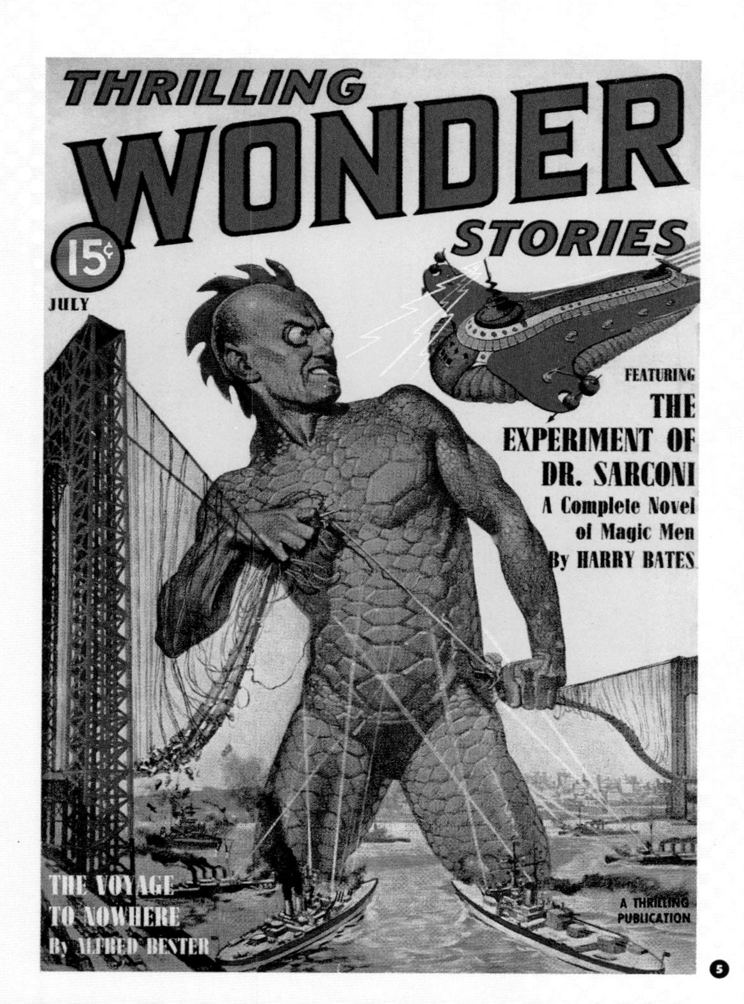

5

5 •
THRILLING WONDER STORIES
July 1940
Howard V. Brown
The magazine had started as *Science Wonder*, then just plain *Wonder* and finally it was *Thrilling Wonder*.

6 ••
WONDER STORIES
December 1932
Frank R. Paul
No other science-fiction illustrator captured the "sense of wonder" quite as well as artist Paul.

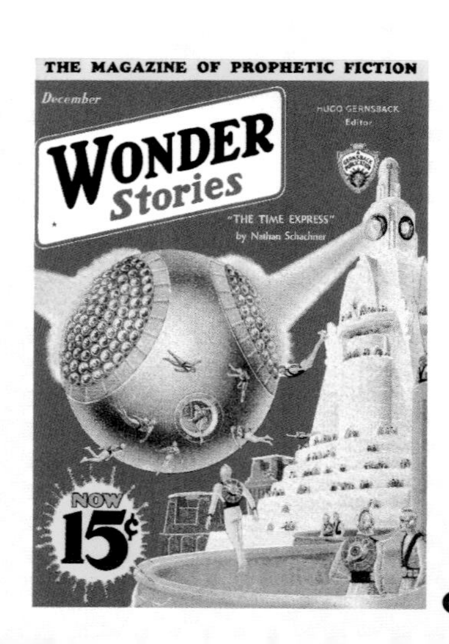

6

7 ••
WONDER STORIES
July 1931
Frank R. Paul
One of the more striking covers for *Wonder*: alien moths leaping into the "singing flame."

8 ••
SCIENCE WONDER STORIES
November 1929
Frank R. Paul
Publisher Gernsback lost control of *Amazing* in early 1929 but was back on the newsstands a month later with a new title.

8

9 ••
AIR WONDER STORIES
April 1930
Frank R. Paul
Combining air stories and science-fiction seemed like a natural. It wasn't. The magazine never sold well.

9

When Clayton foundered in 1933, Street & Smith bought *Astounding*. Editor F. Orlin Tremaine paid his writers promptly and well and encouraged new ideas, which he called "thought variants." With fresh blood among the authors and relatively sophisticated covers by artist Howard V. Brown, *Astounding* soon became the leader.

In late 1937 John W. Campbell, Jr., was appointed editor. Campbell attended M.I.T. and Duke University and contributed to the old *Amazing Stories*, where he competed with "Doc" Smith in writing epics of super science. He also had contributed to *Astounding*, for which he wrote a series of thoughtful, literate stories under the pen name of "Don A. Stuart."

Two classic science-fiction movies were based on stories by former editors of *Astounding*, which also published them. Harry Bates's "Farewell to the Master" became the movie *The Day the Earth Stood Still*, and Campbell's "Who Goes There?" was filmed—twice—as *The Thing from Another World* and *The Thing*.

Campbell was largely responsible for the "golden age" of science-fiction. Robert A. Heinlein, Isaac Asimov, A.E. van Vogt, L. Ron Hubbard, L. Sprague de Camp, Theodore Sturgeon, and Lester del Rey saw their most important stories published in his magazine.

By the early '40s science-fiction was flourishing, and the field became crowded with titles like *Thrilling Wonder Stories*, *Startling Stories*, *Astonishing Stories*, *Fantastic Adventures*, *Marvel Stories*, and so forth. No adjective was left unpublished. *Planet Stories*, known for its "space operas," printed Ray Bradbury's "Mars is Heaven" along with many of his other fine stories, as well as Keith Bennett's whimsically titled "The Rocketeers Have Shaggy Ears" (a lift from a bit of World War I doggerel called "The Cannoneers Have Shaggy Ears," referring to the donkeys used to carry explosives).

⑩ ••
Astounding Stories
May 1934
Howard V. Brown
A new editor and publisher and *Astounding* quickly became more sophisticated with the help of cover artist Brown, who had a real flair for the subject.

⑩

⑪ •
Astounding Science-Fiction
October 1939
Hubert Rogers
Author E.E. "Doc" Smith first appeared in the Gernsback *Amazing* but is best remembered for his "Lensman" stories in *Astounding*.

⑪

Astounding Science-Fiction
July 1940
Hubert Rogers
Artist Rogers painted one of the few sexy covers *Astounding* published—and right in the middle of editor John W. Campbell, Jr.'s "golden period."

Astounding Stories
May 1931
H.W. Wesso
Astounding invented the "bug-eyed monster" and became the longest-lived title in the field—but not because of its BEMs.

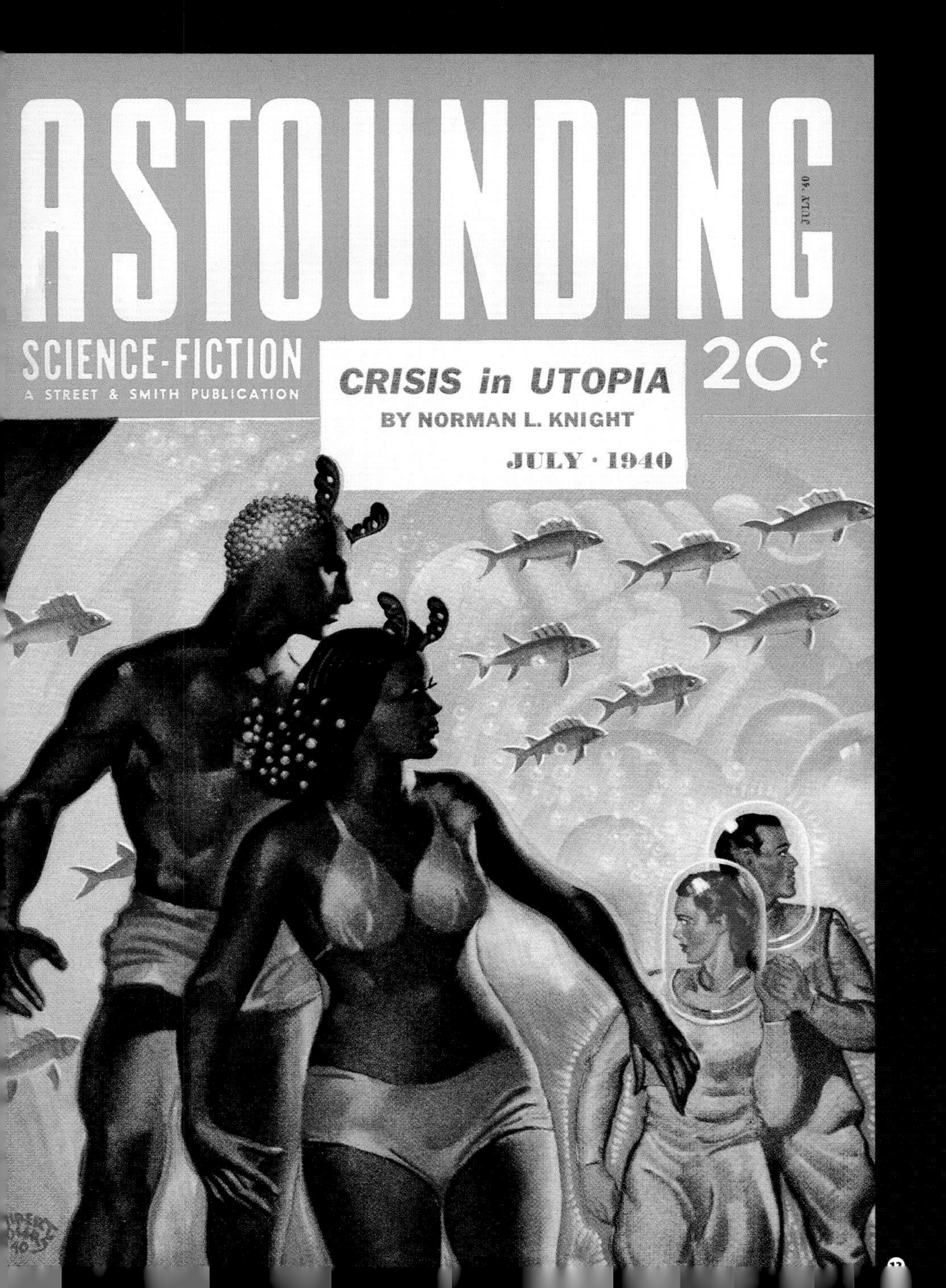

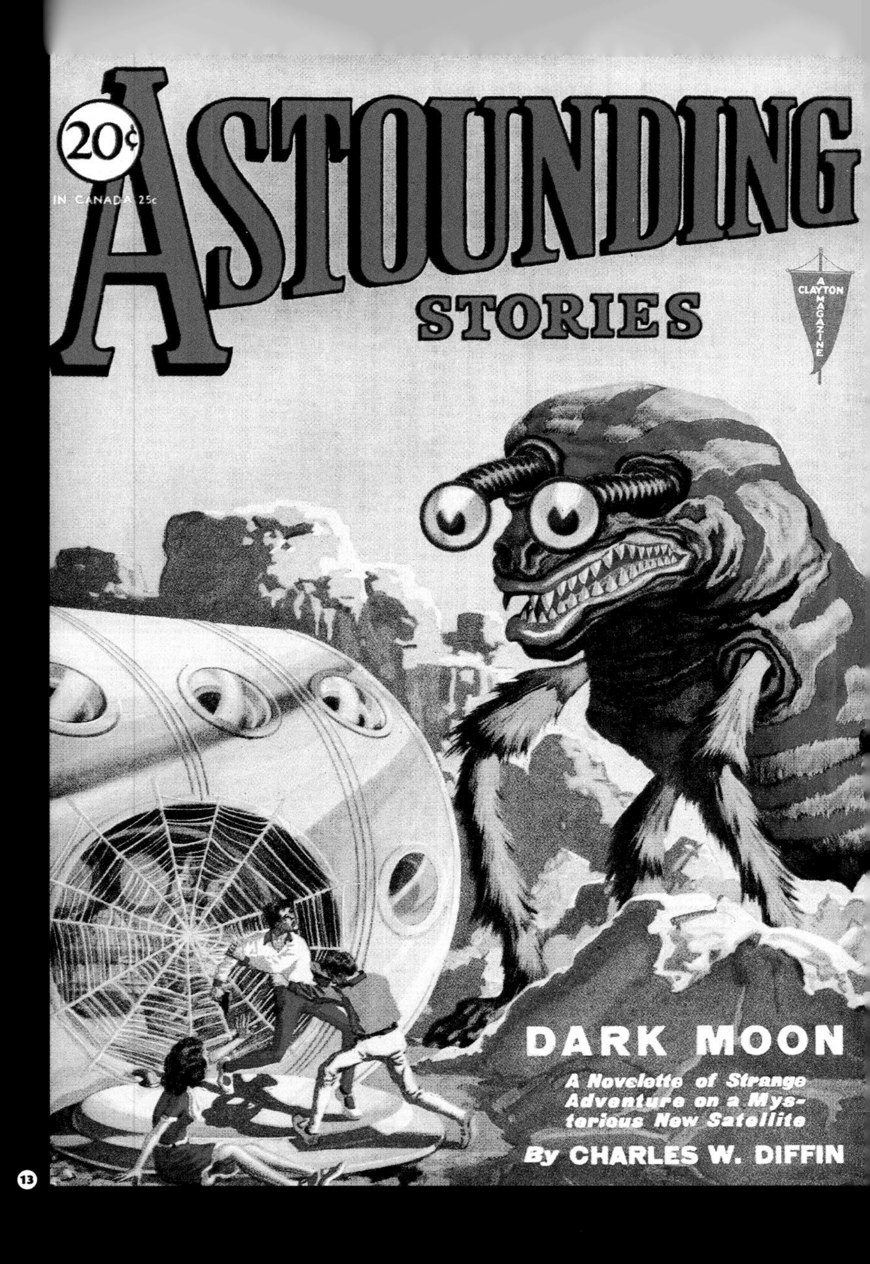

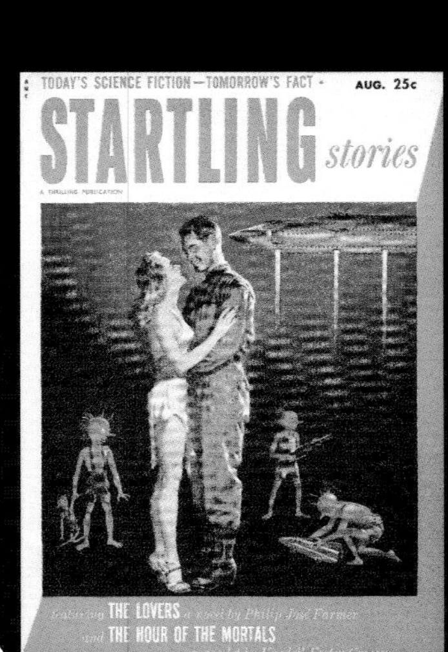

Startling Stories
August 1952
Earle K. Bergey
In "The Lovers" author Farmer wrote about sex in a frank and mature manner and created a science-fiction sensation.

15

15 •

Fantastic Adventures
October 1940
J. Allen St. John

The magazine was due to be discontinued, but sales zoomed with artist St. John's dinosaur cover.

16 •

Famous Fantastic Mysteries
October 1940
Virgil Finlay

The magazine was a huge success reprinting rare stories from the early *Argosy* and *All-Story*.

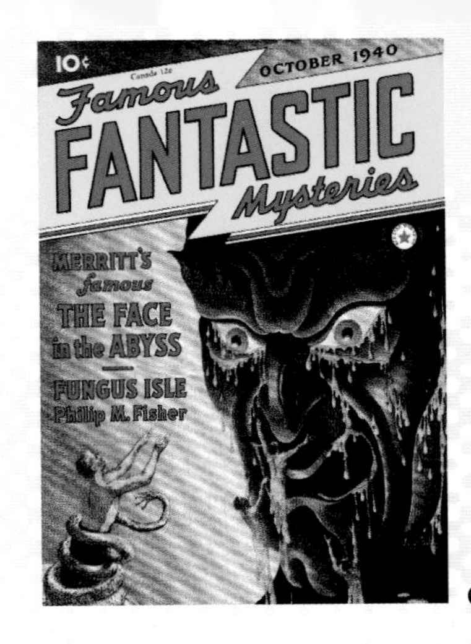

16

17 •

Fantastic Novels
November 1940
Virgil Finlay

Artist Finlay was one of the greatest stylists in the science-fiction and fantasy field and had a flair for painting beautiful women.

17

Much of the success of the field lay in its extremely vocal and highly active science-fiction fandom, which unceasingly proselytized for its favorite fiction. They held conventions and published amateur newsletters and magazines ("fanzines"), and many of them eventually became writers and editors in the field.

Perhaps the real strength of the genre was demonstrated when Street & Smith killed all its pulps in 1949. The single exception was *Astounding Science-Fiction*, now a healthy digest and role model for the dozens of other digest-sized science-fiction magazines that flooded the newsstands in the '50s and '60s. From the relatively minor role that science-fiction played in the pulps in the late '20s and mid-'30s, it now dominated the all-fiction field.

19

18

18 ••
Fantastic Adventures
January 1940
H.W. McCauley
A return to the large-format magazine of the early '30s featuring the ever-popular robot-on-wheels.

19 •
Famous Fantastic Mysteries
August 1942
Virgil Finlay
Artist Finlay's nudest—and most beautiful—cover painting.

DREAMER'S WORLDS—*Brilliant Novelette by* EDMOND HAMILTON

NOVEMBER

Weird Tales

15¢

A WITCH'S TALE

Specially Adapted From the Famous Radio Program

by

ALONZO DEEN COLE

+

A Drama of World Destiny—

THE BOOK OF THE DEAD

by

FRANK GRUBER

HENRY KUTTNER

—

MANLY WADE WELLMAN

—

AUGUST W. DERLETH

—

ROBERT H. LEITFRED

—

20

20 • •

WEIRD TALES

November 1941

Hannes Bok

Artist Bok captured the essence of the magazine in his cover.

21 • •

WEIRD TALES

August 1939

Virgil Finlay

When the magazine was sold to another publisher, readers claimed it had gone from the frying pan into the fire.

21

22

23

22 ••

Astonishing Stories

February 1940

Binder

The only ten-cent science-fiction magazine.

23 ••

Weird Tales

January 1937

Margaret Brundage

Artist Brundage reportedly used her daughters as models for her covers.

24

24 ••

Strange Stories

August 1939

Earle K. Bergey

A later competitor to *Weird Tales*, it featured thirteen stories in every issue and lasted exactly thirteen issues.

25 •••

Strange Tales

January 1932

H.W. Wesso

One of the few early competitors to *Weird Tales*. It never made it.

25

26

26 •••

Weird Tales

April 1934

Margaret Brundage

A run of *Weird Tales* is one of the most valuable to collectors. It introduced Robert E. Howard, H.P. Lovecraft, and Robert Bloch among many others.

Another genre that showed surprising staying powers was that of the weird-fantasy magazine. *Weird Tales* dated from 1923 and lasted until 1954 in its first incarnation, though it's been resurrected several times since. It was a product of the Rural Publishing Company, owned by Jacob Clark Henneberger and J.M. Lansinger, who also published *Detective Tales* and—surprise!—*College Humor*.

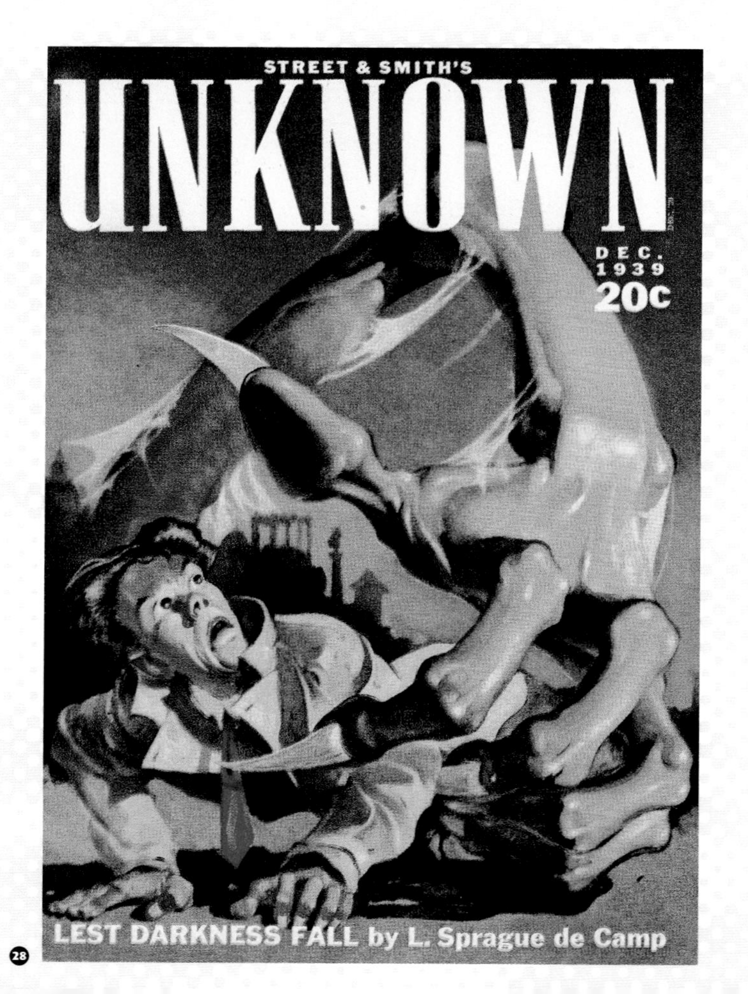

27 ••
Planet Stories
Spring 1942
Leydenfrost
Not the first but certainly the best of the bug-eyed monsters.

28 ••
Unknown
December 1939
Edd Cartier
Artist Cartier's cartoon style was ideally suited to the magazine.

㉙ ••
UNKNOWN
March 1939
H.W. Scott
The first issue. *Unknown* and its sister magazine *Astounding*, both edited by John W. Campbell, Jr., were probably the most anthologized pulps ever published.

㉚ •
FUTURE COMBINED WITH SCIENCE FICTION
October 1941
Hannes Bok
Artist Bok had one of the most unique styles in science-fiction.

The new magazine was edited by Edwin Baird for the first year and went through several size changes, ending up with the bedsheet "anniversary" issue in 1924 when the two partners split up. Lansinger took *Detective Tales* and editor Edwin Baird. Henneberger kept *Weird Tales* and the magazine's first reader, Farnsworth Wright.

Under Baird the magazine was relatively undistinguished. Under Wright, the magazine became... something else. It published the gothic fantasies and poetry of H.P. Lovecraft, the swords-and-sorcery adventure tales of Robert E. Howard, plus weird stories by August Derleth, Henry Kuttner, Ray Bradbury, Robert Bloch, and a host of others. In its early years it even published science-fiction by Edmond Hamilton, famous later for his creation of "Captain Future."

During its life and after, *Weird Tales* was to become the most anthologized pulp magazine of all time. It published fantasy, it published science-fiction, it published its own version of weird-menace material, and, perhaps most surprisingly of all, it published—literature.

Other titles in the weird-fantasy field were *Strange Tales*, a companion to the Clayton *Astounding* and early competitor to *Weird Tales*; *Strange Stories*, a later competitor; and especially *Unknown*, later titled *Unknown Worlds*. John W. Campbell, Jr., edited *Unknown Worlds* and *Astounding Science-Fiction*, and published weird fiction and fantasy with a modern face and an occasional sense of humor.

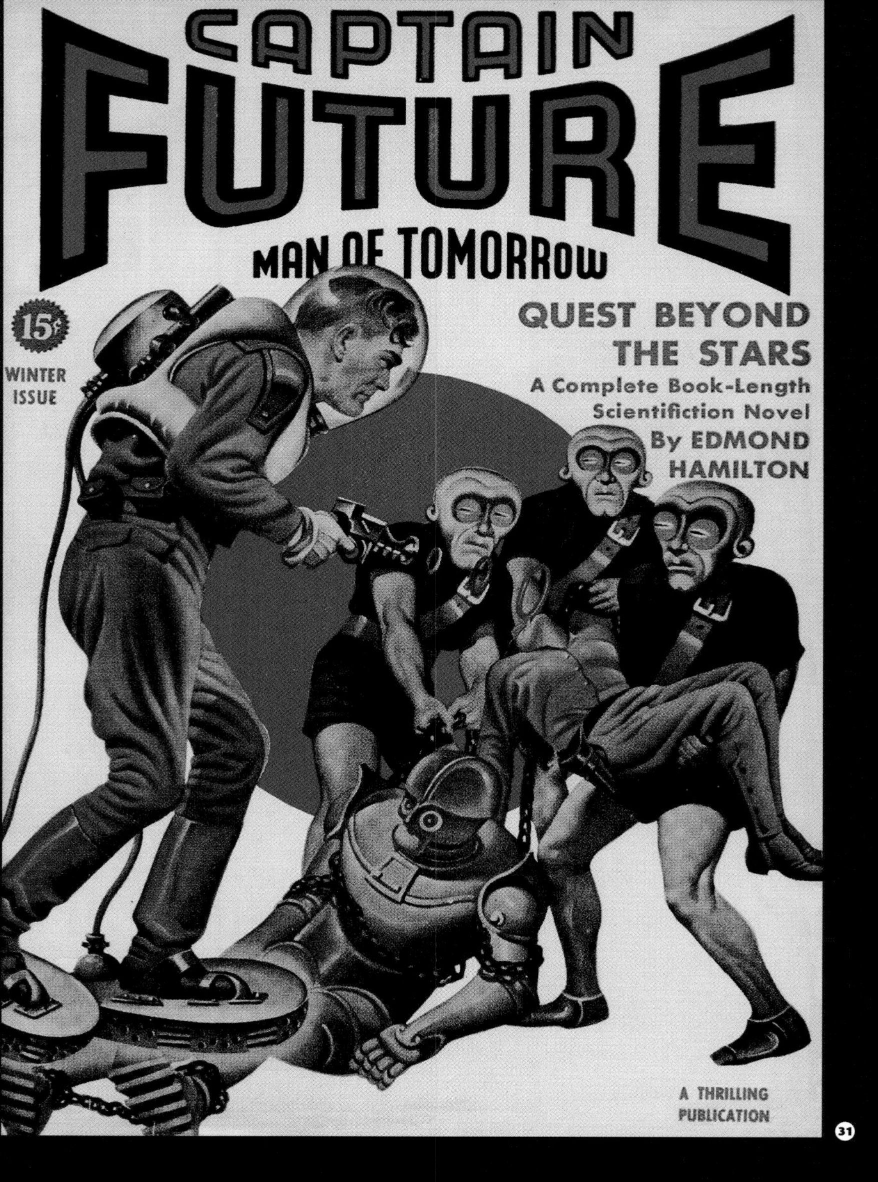

31

31 ••

Captain Future
Winter 1942
Earle K. Bergey
Captain Future was a science-fiction "hero" pulp.

32 •••

Miracle Science and Fantasy Stories
April-May 1931
Elliott Dold
Early, short-lived competition for *Amazing* and *Wonder* with a highly unusual cover by artist Dold.

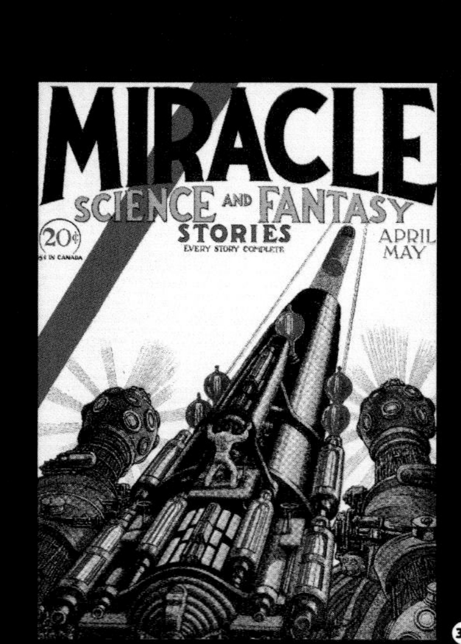

32

33 ••

Marvel Science Stories
April-May 1939
Norman Saunders
It was new bodies for old in this Saunders cover.

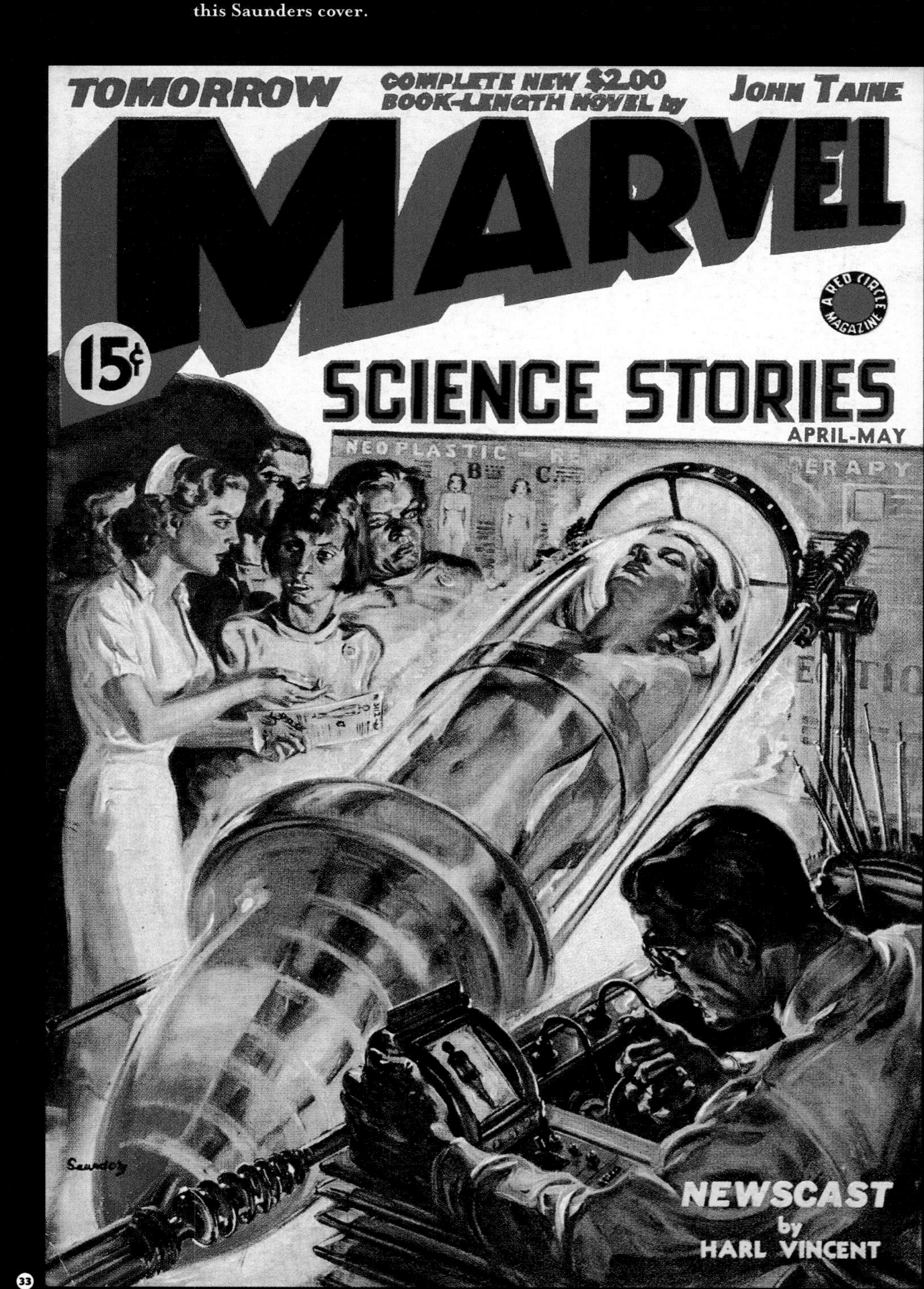

33

L. Ron Hubbard contributed many of his finest novels to *Unknown* (*Slaves of Sleep*, *Fear*, *Death's Deputy*), as did L. Sprague de Camp (*Lest Darkness Fall*) and Norvell Page (*But Without Horns*—a frightening superman story), who also wrote most of the novels for *The Spider*.

Unknown never made it through the war, but, like *Weird Tales*, after its death it received accolades by having many of its stories reprinted as hardback novels or in anthologies of classic fantasy fiction.

Of all the pulp genres, it was science-fiction and fantasy that had the most original and startling covers and interior illustrations, many of them painted or drawn by superb artists. In the letter columns, the readers noted—and praised—the artists almost as much as they did the writers.

Frank R. Paul was synonymous with Hugo Gernsback and illustrated every cover of Gernsback's early science-fiction magazines. Howard V. Brown was closely associated with the early years of Street & Smith's *Astounding* (he had painted many covers for Gernsback's *Science and Invention* earlier) and Hubert Rogers with Campbell's "golden age" of the same magazine.

Margaret Brundage and her nudes were a regular for *Weird Tales*, as was J. Allen St. John, who also painted all the covers for the Edgar Rice Burroughs Mars and Venus stories that ran in *Amazing Stories* and *Fantastic Adventures*. Virgil Finlay and Hannes Bok did notable work for *Weird Tales* and a dozen other magazines. And Edd Cartier was beloved by the readers of *Unknown* for his interior illustrations as well as his covers. (In addition, Cartier was highly respected for his interior work for *The Shadow*.)

Canvases by the science-fiction and fantasy artists and, in fact, paintings by all the better-known pulp artists, have sold for thousands of dollars. Perhaps the high-water mark was J. Allen St. John's cover for the issue of *Weird Tales* featuring the first installment of Jack Williamson's *Golden Blood*. A collector purchased it for $25,000—almost three hundred times what St. John was paid for it.

If the readers of the science-fiction and the fantasy magazines were more fanatical than the readers of other genres, the editor, authors, and artists had given them good reasons to be. For many science-fiction enthusiasts, reading, collecting, attending conventions, and publishing "fanzines" had become far more than a hobby.

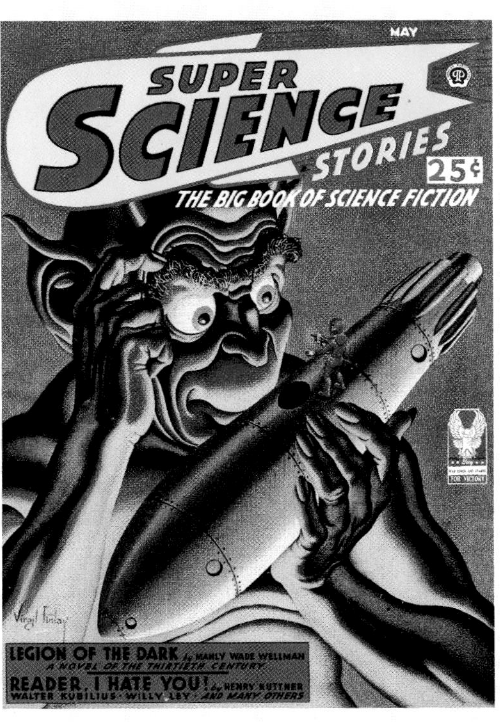

34 •
SUPER SCIENCE STORIES
May 1943
Virgil Finlay
Probably the only funny science-fiction cover ever published.

GORILLA OF THE GAS BAGS

From Adventure Stories to Zeppelin Tales

By the late '20s and early '30s, competition among pulp magazines had become fierce. Established titles such as *Argosy*, *Blue Book*, and *Western Story Magazine* dominated the market. There was money to be made in the "pulpwoods," and many publishers and would-be publishers were well aware of it. But how to compete? How to capture the public eye?

One of the answers in the never-ending quest for circulation was to find a niche market that you could have all to yourself, at least for a year or two. If the western field were overcrowded, perhaps there would be room for a magazine about Indians. And if *Gone With the Wind* fever was sweeping the country, perhaps readers would be interested in a magazine devoted solely to tales set in the Civil War period.

Sometimes a publisher or his editor would hit pay dirt. Harold Brainerd Hersey did when he came up with the unlikely combination of western and romance stories and created *Ranch Romances*, a title that turned out to be the most durable of all the pulps. Frank A. Munsey struck gold when he published *Railroad Man's Magazine*, a profitable title that had the field to itself for all its publishing life, its only competition coming from the model magazines. It finally died when the affection people felt for the 20th Century Limited had been replaced by that for Pan Am's China Clipper.

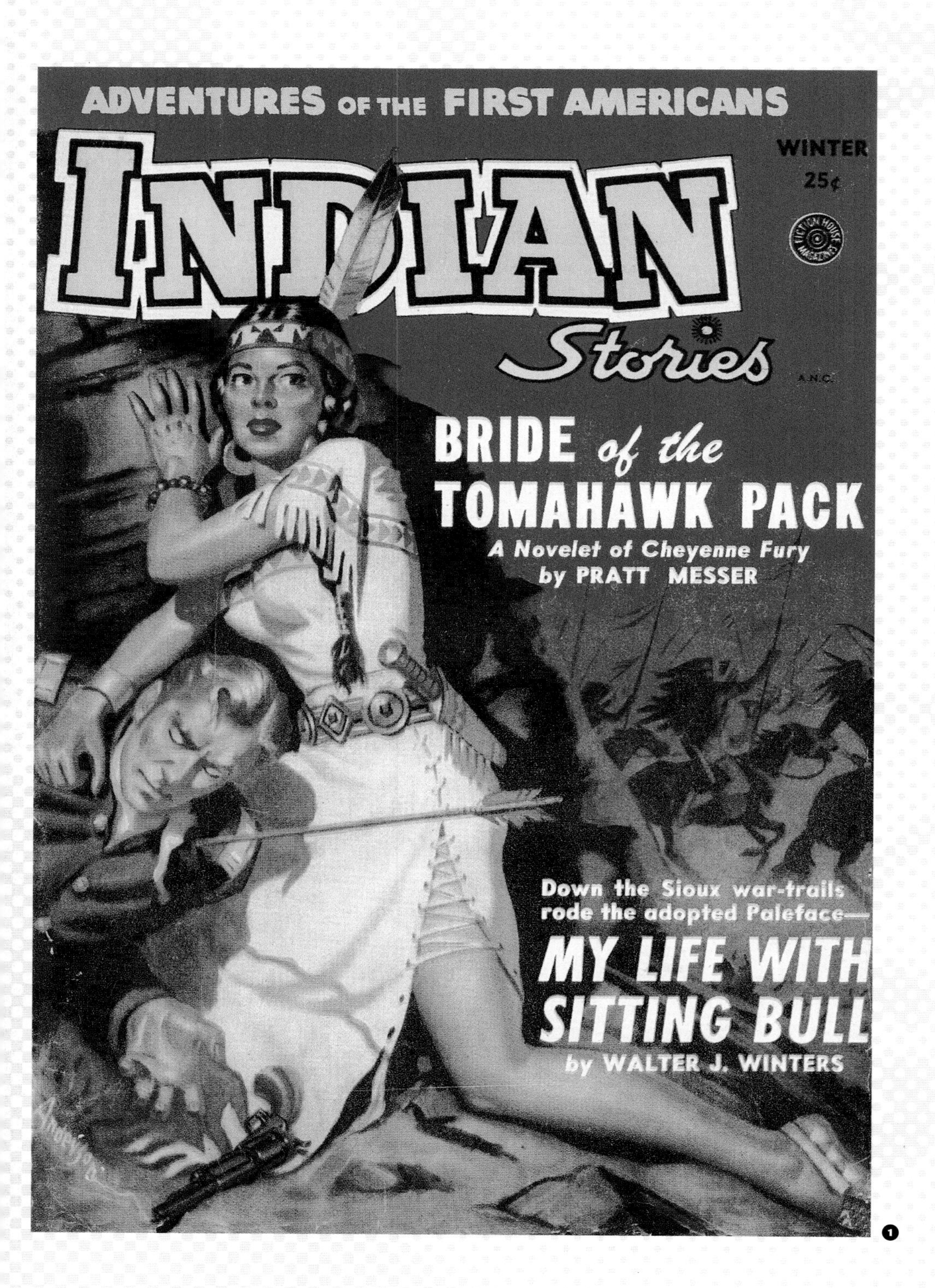

The niche market, of course, could be risky as well as profitable. Street & Smith launched *College Stories* in 1931 when going to college had become a vanishing possibility for most young Americans.

But one man left no stone unturned in his search for a specialized market. Harold Hersey, who had created the romance western, the first and most profitable niche, never gave up trying to create another. In his early days at Street & Smith, he was responsible for *The Thrill Book*, a would-be forerunner of *Weird Tales* and *Amazing Stories*. But Hersey was a young and inexperienced editor, and, while he may have had his convictions, he didn't have the courage of them. His approach was timid and vacillating; the magazine published more adventure stories than anything else; and it failed after sixteen issues.

(Size alone must have made the readers wonder just what they were buying. It had the dimensions and appearance of a dime novel for its first eight issues, that of a pulp for its last eight.)

1 ••
INDIAN STORIES
Winter 1950
Allen Anderson
If you had guessed that stories about Indians would be as popular as stories about cowboys, you would have guessed wrong.

2 ••
GOLDEN FLEECE
December 1938
Harold S. Delay
A "historical fiction" magazine that didn't do well in the '30s but probably would today.

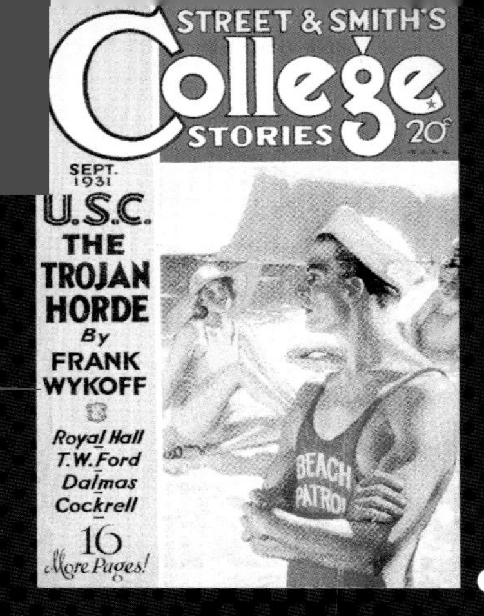

3 ••

College Stories
September 1931
Unknown
One of the authors on the inside was "Maxwell Grant," the "house name" of Walter Gibson for *The Shadow*.

4 ••

Civil War Stories
Spring 1940
Sidney Riesenberg
Gone with the Wind was the inspiration for this one-shot.

5 •••

Pirate Stories
March 1935
Joseph Sokoli
Publisher Gernsback's expertise was in science-fiction, not in pirate stories.

6 •

North-West Romances
Summer 1949
Allen Anderson
First published in 1925, by the late '40s the magazine relied on reprints by London and Service.

7 •••

Wild Game Stories
November 1926
Unknown
The idea was a natural, stories about hunting, but it never caught on.

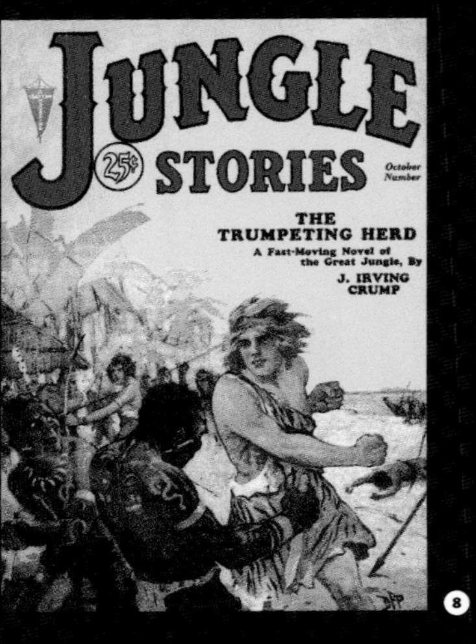

8 •••
Jungle Stories
October 1931
Domingo F. Periconi
Jungle Stories traded on the popularity of Tarzan.
The Lordsof the Jungle were always expert boxers.

9 ••
Ka-Zar
January 1937
H.W. Scott
Ka-Zar was one of the many short-lived imitators of Tarzan.

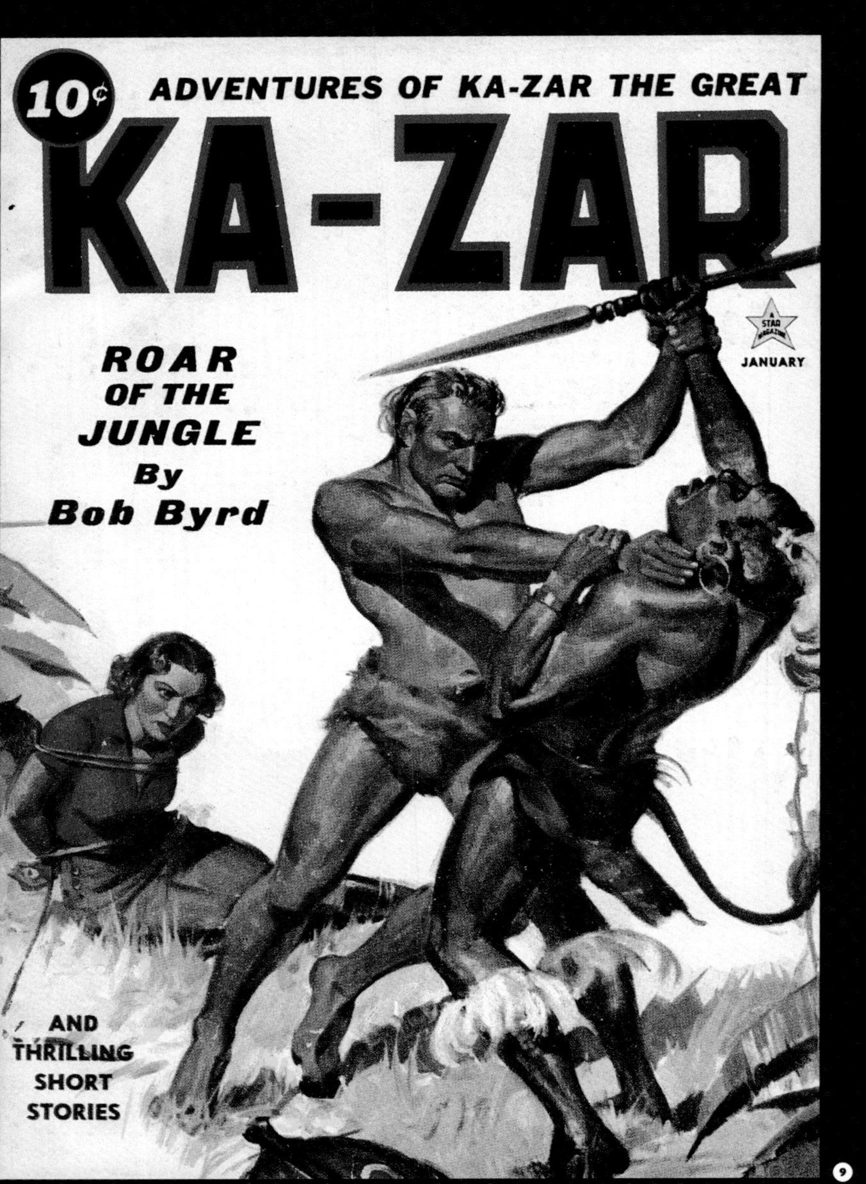

10 ••
Jungle Stories
Summer 1947
George Gross
Jane of *Tarzan of the Apes* was never this sexy.

Hersey's other attempts ran the gamut from modest successes to dismal failures. *Clues*, *Five-Novels Monthly*, and, of course, *Ranch Romances* were all successes. He largely invented the "gang" magazine—*Gangster Stories*, *Racketeer Stories*, *Mobs*, *Prison Stories*, *Murder Stories*, and so forth—and was responsible for creating *Outlaws of the West* and *Zoom!*, an aviation magazine. (Despite the titles of his gang magazines, Hersey always made sure the good guys won.)

Perhaps the least successful of Hersey's efforts were *Fire Fighters*, *Front Page Stories*, *Speed Stories* ("Stories of people going fast!"), *Courtroom Stories*, and *Speakeasy Stories*. Admittedly Hersey had a way with titles if not always the business acumen to sort out the losers from the winners.

⓫ •••
THRILLS OF THE JUNGLE
December 1929
Walter M. Baumhofer
The first and only issue.

⓬ •••
SHEENA QUEEN OF THE JUNGLE
Spring 1951
Allen Anderson
Equal opportunity for female versions of Tarzan. Sheena also starred in comic books.

⓭ ••

REAL DETECTIVE TALES

August-September 1925

James Stuart

Despite its title, *Real Detective* was all fiction. It was originally a companion magazine to *Weird Tales*.

⓯ •••

FIRE FIGHTERS

April 1929

Walter M. Baumhofer

One of the rarest of the pulp magazines.

⓮ •

MARRIAGE STORIES

February 1929

Unknown

Stories about *getting* married had appeal. Stories about *being* married didn't.

18 ••

SEA STORIES

August 1929

H.C. Murphy

Red sails in the sunset—
one of the last issues.

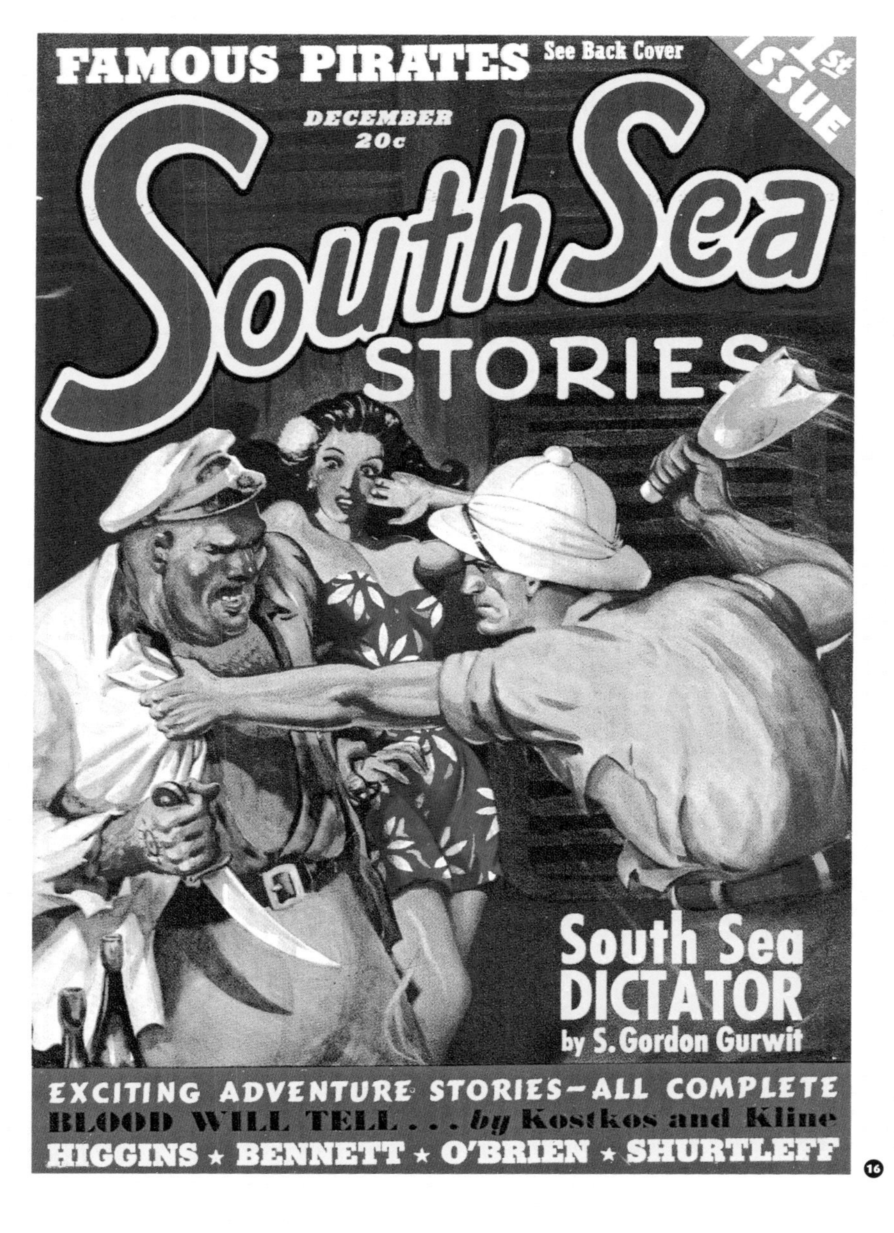

16

17

16 ••

SOUTH SEA STORIES

December 1939

Rod Ruth

Adventure in the South
Seas lost appeal once
World War II began.

17 •••

MOVIE ACTION MAGAZINE

June 1936

George Rozen

Movie Action Magazine featured
adaptations of movie scripts.

18

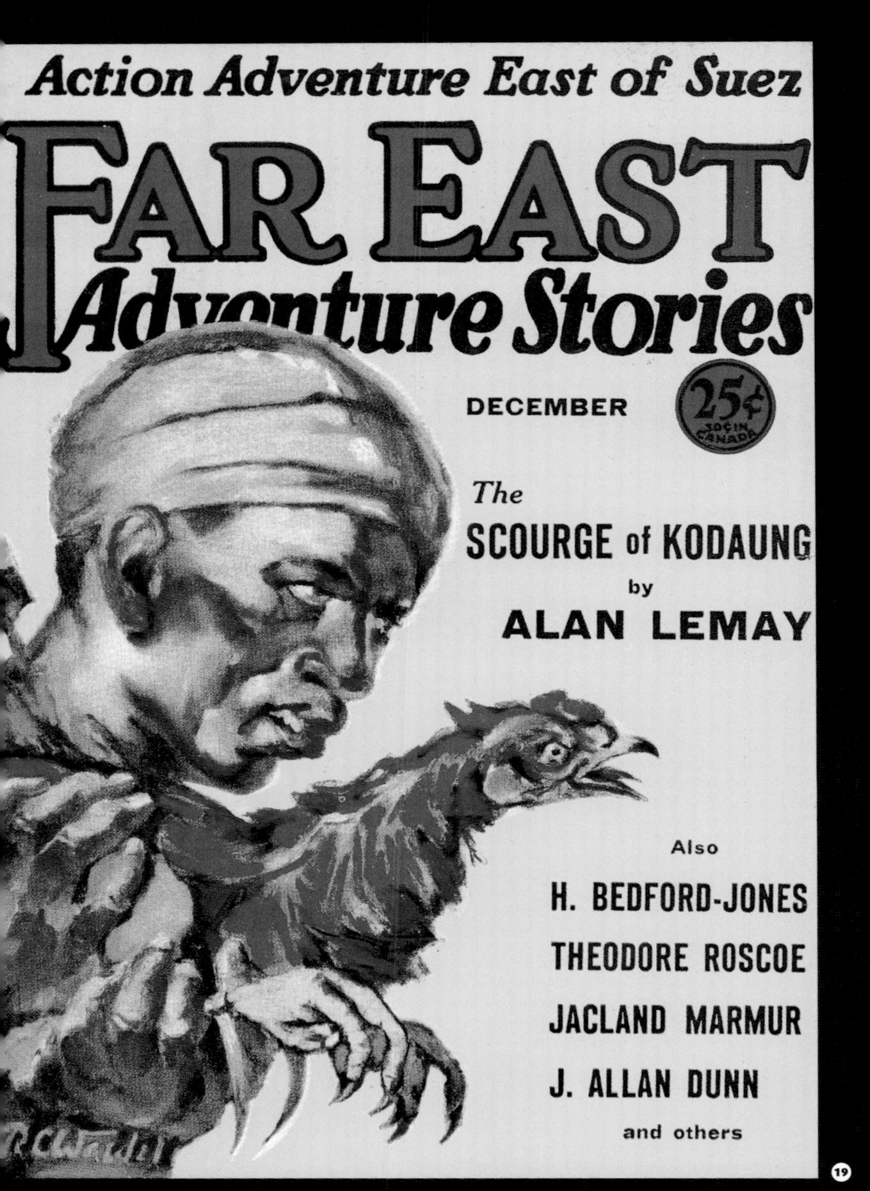

9 •••
AR EAST ADVENTURE STORIES
ecember 1930
ay C. Wardel
n exotic, short-lived
ompetitor to *Adventure*.

0 •••
HE MAGIC CARPET MAGAZINE
anuary 1933
argaret Brundage
riental Stories changes title.
he last few issues of *The Magic*
arpet sported a spectacular
nd evocative logo.

Other publishers also tried to hit the niche markets. Street & Smith successfully published *Sea Stories* for almost ten years where Hugo Gernsback later failed with *Pirate Stories* and *High-Seas Adventures*. *Wall Street Stories* had the misfortune of being published in 1929, the year of the stock market crash, even though the date on *Wall Street Stories* was February, and the market didn't crash until "Black Tuesday" in September. Perhaps the real reason was that, for the most part, the audience for pulps was teenagers and young adults, and neither had the money to invest in the market. Lacking the ability to invest in it, they probably also lacked any interest in reading about it.

Popular Engineering lasted a single issue, though its publisher must have had high hopes for it. *Argosy* had made stories about "high iron" and digging subway tunnels popular. Why not a magazine devoted to these topics? *Wild Game Stories* might have had a future—Lord knows there were enough hunters in America during the '20s—but the magazine itself was dull and amateurish. *Harlem Stories* was an interesting effort, presumably published by and for Black Americans, but racial stereotypes in the art and some of the fiction undoubtedly discouraged many would-be African American customers.

Oriental Stories, later retitled *The Magic Carpet Magazine*, was created to ease the financial burden on *Weird Tales*. It didn't, though it was a magazine with an intriguing author line-up and some of the most eye-catching covers on the newsstands. But other magazines devoted to stories of the Far East didn't make it either,

21 • • •

Oriental Stories

Autumn 1931

Lucille Holling

The magazine went through six different title designs in fourteen issues. This was one of the most striking (and the nudest!).

22 • • •

Oriental Stories

February-March 1931

von Gelb

A companion to *Weird Tales*, which later changed its title to *The Magic Carpet*. Unsuccessful, it rated as a noble effort.

22

21

23 • • • •

The Thrill Book

October 1, 1919

Unknown

This cover of *The Thrill Book* was later recycled as the first cover of *The Shadow*. An entirely different story by Jones, also titled "Mr. Shen of Shensi," later appeared in *Argosy*.

23

24 •••
Popular Engineering Stories
April 1930
W.C. Brigham
Tales of "high iron" and digging subways were carrying magazine specialization to extremes.

24

27

25

28

25 •••
Explorers
September 1929
Unknown
A skimpy sixty-four pages for a dime. The magazine didn't last long.

26 •••
Outdoor Stories
September 1928
Stockton Mulford
The last issue of a rare and little-known pulp.

26

27 ••••
The Thrill Book
October 15, 1919
James Reynolds
The magazine was a timid forerunner to *Amazing Stories* and *Weird Tales*.

28 ••
Foreign Legion Adventures
August 1940
Emmett Watson
World War II was upon us, and readers had lost interest in the Foreign Legion and the magazine that featured its stories.

29 •••
Front Page Stories
January 1932
Unknown
The title was probably inspired by the successful play and movie of the same name.

30 •••
Courtroom Stories
August-September 1931
Walter M. Baumhofer
Ahead of its time, an early magazine version of *Court TV*.

31 •••
New York Stories
April 1932
Unknown
New York was the only city to have a pulp named after it. There was no *Chicago Stories*, no *San Francisco Fables*, no *Boston Tales*.

31

29

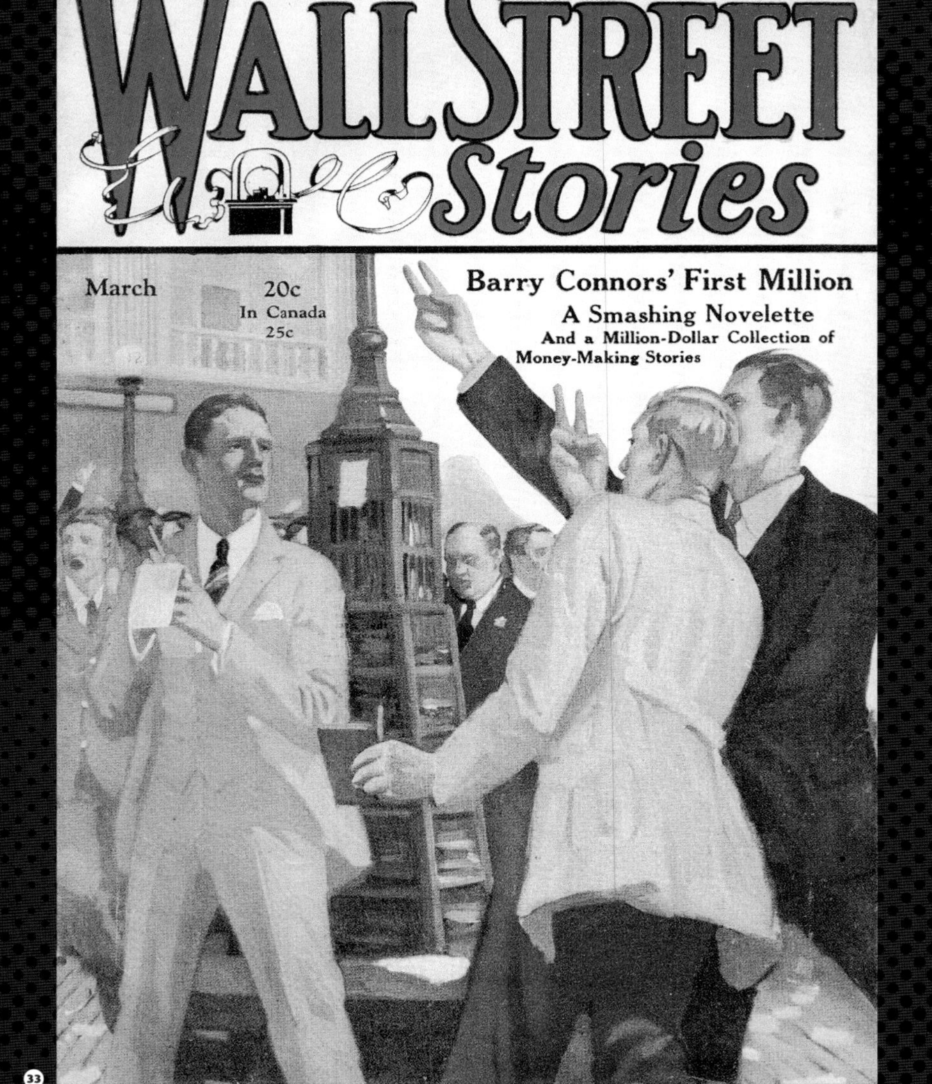

33

32

30

32 ••
Fame and Fortune Magazine
May 2, 1929
Unknown
Adventures in Making Money was fun in 1929—but only for a while...

33 ••••
Wall Street Stories
March 1929
Unknown
The magazine was a victim of bad timing. The market crashed in 1929.

Zeppelin Stories
June 1929
C.B. Colby
One of the strangest covers to appear on one of the strangest pulps—and one of the most valuable.

35 ••
Spicy Screen Stories
December 1935
R.A. Burley
A rare and expensive semi-pulp. There was no connection to the regular line of *Spicy* magazines.

36 •••
Harlem Stories
May 1932
Unknown
A rare semi-pulp, presumably edited for an African American audience. But the characters were stereotypes, and the magazine failed.

37 •••
Speed Stories
January 1931
Walter M. Baumhofer
Speed Stories was about "people going fast."

notably *Far East Adventure Stories*. It's a pity that *Oriental Stories*, a.k.a., *Magic Carpet*, didn't make the grade. As far as art and stories went, it deserved to.

Almost five years later, another Chicago magazine, *Golden Fleece*, a magazine of historical adventure, showed up on the newsstands. The contents looked suspiciously as if the publisher had bought the inventory of the discontinued *Oriental/Magic Carpet*. A well put-together pulp with trimmed edges and more-than-acceptable art work, it didn't last beyond nine issues.

Probably the most fascinating "high-concept" magazine of all was *Zeppelin Stories*, whose third issue featured the "Gorilla of the Gas Bags" cover. Published during the heyday of the air pulp, *Zeppelin* should have been a success. But it lasted a scant four issues and now is a rarity eagerly sought after by long-time collectors.

Few of them have the heart to tell newcomers that there never was a *Spicy Zeppelin Stories*.

38 ••
Ghost Stories
May 1930
Dalton Stevens
Ghosts were a favorite of cult groups in the '20s and early '30s—like UFOs are today.

AUTHOR! AUTHOR!

The Editors Tell it Like it Was

At the peak of their popularity the pulps were the biggest market in the world for short stories and "novels." They supported many very good writers, as well as some very bad ones. Most pulp writers wanted to sell to the slicks, and many of them did. But it's not their work in *Collier's* or the *Saturday Evening Post* for which most of them will be remembered. It will be for the tales they ground out for the munificent sum of a penny or two a word and frequently less.

Many started in the pulps and moved on to bigger and better things. C.S. Forester and his "Captain Hornblower" appeared in *Argosy* prior to the *Post*, as did Luke Short and Ernest Haycox. So did Max Brand with "Dr. Kildare," one of the most lucrative figures in fiction. In addition to the books and stories about him, film historian Leonard Maltin lists a total of sixteen movies about Kildare, with Lionel Barrymore playing crusty Dr. Gillespie in every one of them. And let's not forget the television series starring Richard Chamberlain.

Rafael Sabatini's "Captain Blood" and the "Sea Hawk" were regulars in *Adventure*. Both were made into films, the *Sea Hawk* twice with Errol Flynn starring in the talkie version. Agatha Christie's character of "Hercule Poirot" was featured in *Blue Book* long before he turned up in the PBS series. Zane Grey appeared in *Argosy* before the slicks, and Sax Rohmer made appearances in *Detective Story Magazine* as well as *Collier's*.

1 ••

Detective Story Magazine

December 31, 1921

John A. Coughlin

Sax Rohmer was the author of the famous Dr. Fu Manchu stories.

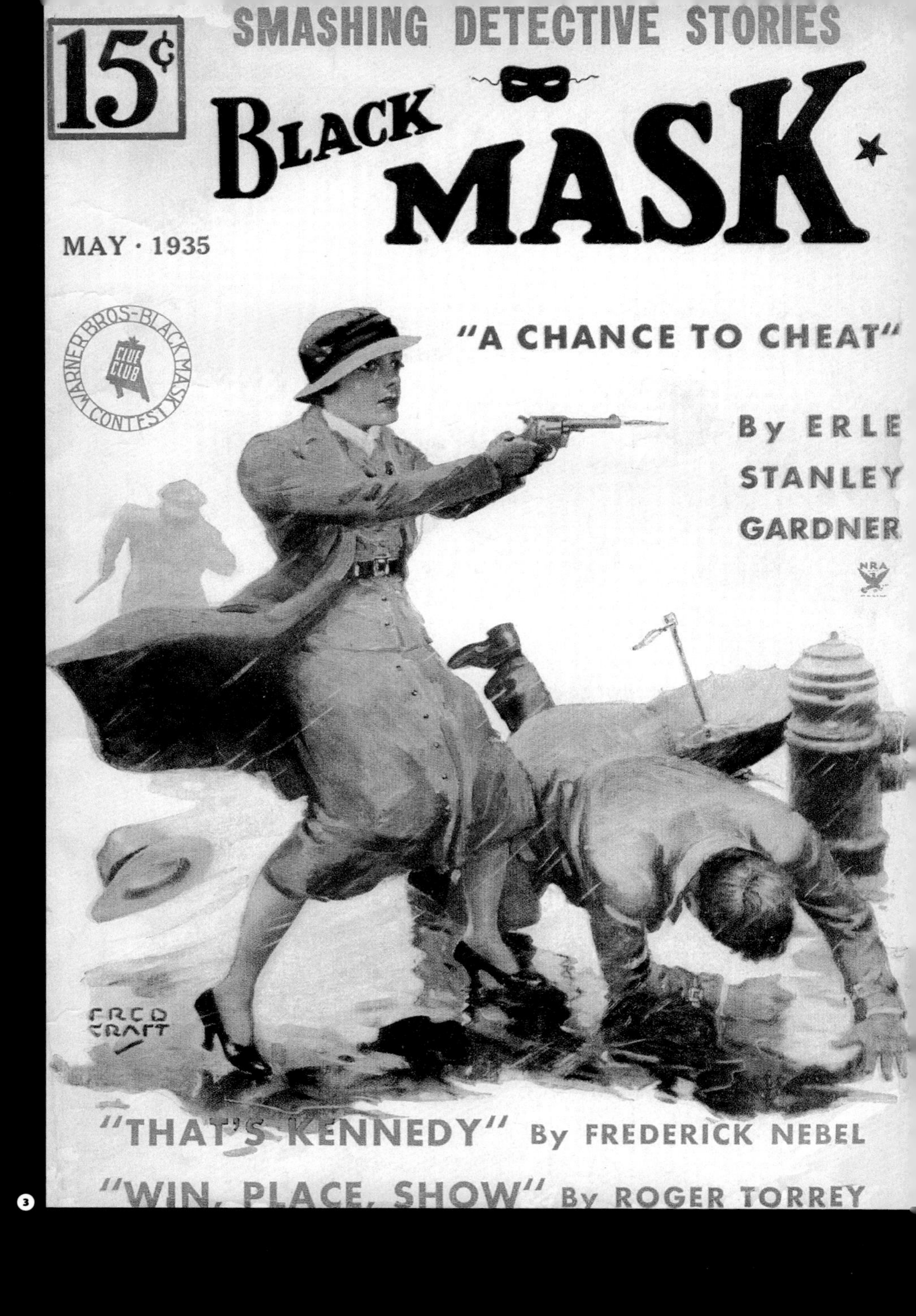

2 •

Argosy

December 3, 1938

Emmett Watson

Author C.S. Forester later "graduated" to the *Saturday Evening Post*.

3 ••

Black Mask

May 1935

Fred Craft

The number of novels written by Erle Stanley Gardner runs into the dozens— the number of copies printed into the millions.

Erle Stanley Gardner wrote millions of words for the pulps. Readers bought millions of copies of his books, and he was translated into thirty-two languages. Gardner was born in 1889 in Massachusetts, moved to California as a young man, and was admitted to the bar at twenty-one after studying law on his own. He was, by all accounts, an excellent lawyer but began writing fiction to make ends meet.

In 1932 Gardner created a young attorney named Ken Corning for *Black Mask*. A similar fighting attorney appeared in 1933 in his first novel, *The Case of the Velvet Claws*. The hero's name was Perry Mason. Gardner wrote some eighty Mason novels and oversaw the television series, personally choosing Raymond Burr for the lead. He even appeared as a judge in one of the episodes.

Another big producer for the pulps was Arthur J. Burks, known to bang out a short story in a single sitting. Burks, a former Marine officer, started writing in 1922 and earned all of $3.50. By the middle of the Depression he was turning out three million words annually and earning $50,000 a year.

"Max Brand" never really existed, of course. He was just one—though the most popular—pen name for Frederick Faust who lived in a villa overlooking the hills of Florence. In high school Faust had memorized some twenty thousand lines of Shakespeare and wanted to be a classical poet a la Chaucer or Milton. In his villa he wrote poetry in the morning using a quill pen on parchment. In the afternoon he banged out his westerns and other commercial fiction on a cheap portable typewriter.

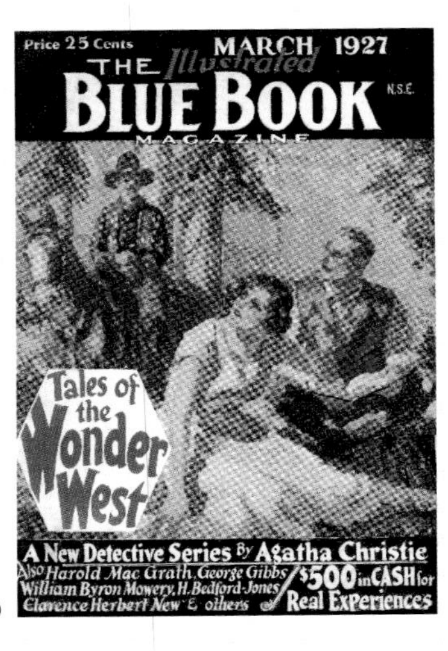

4 •
Adventure
July 1934
Walter M. Baumhofer
Like many pulp writers, Gardner couldn't keep away from the "yellow peril" as the theme for a novel.

5 •
Blue Book
March 1927
Laurence Herndon
Agatha Christie and her French detective Hercule Poirot were regulars in the old *Blue Book*.

6 •
ARGOSY
March 25, 1939
Marshall Frantz
Dr. Kildare was Max Brand's most popular character: the basis of a popular TV series and before that some sixteen films, all of them starring Lionel Barrymore as Dr. Gillespie with Lew Ayres and other actors playing Dr. Kildare.

6

Faust was something of a Jekyll/Hyde writing personality. As Faust he was contemptuous of his pulp fiction, though the writer in him probably admired its narrative flow. As "Max Brand" he probably considered Faust a pompous bore.

Faust was a correspondent in Italy during World War II. He insisted on going in with the first invasion wave at the "boot" and was hit in the chest by a shell fragment. Although wounded he crawled out under enemy fire to get ammunition for a trapped gunner and died moments later.

Frederick Faust died as much a hero as any of those he wrote about. And "Max Brand," "David Manning," "George Owen Baxter," "John Frederick," "George Challis," "Evan Evans," and more than a dozen other popular authors died with him.

"Talbot Mundy," actually an Englishman named William Lancaster Gribbon, had run away to India at an early age where he promptly earned a reputation as a shady character. He came to the United States in 1909, and, after being hospitalized from a beating by some gamblers, caught religion and turned to writing. "Jimgrim" and his other tales of India appeared almost exclusively in *Adventure*.

An author beloved by editors because he was as versatile as he was prolific was Lafayette Ron Hubbard. The quintessential pulp writer, L. Ron Hubbard was born in 1911, raised in Montana, and learned to ride as soon as he could walk. Far more than most pulp writers, he lived the adventures he wrote about, traveling a quarter of a million miles

❼ • •
Romance
May 1929
Edgar Franklin Wittmack
Despite featuring Talbot Mundy on the cover and publishing authors identified with male-oriented fiction, *Romance* was intended for women.

❽ •
Adventure
November 15, 1930
Hubert Rogers
Talbot Mundy was a mainstay of *Adventure*, specializing in stories about India.

❾ •
Western Story Magazine
February 13, 1932
Baldy McCowen
Every author listed on the cover was actually Frederick Faust, better known as "Max Brand," King of the Pulps.

❼

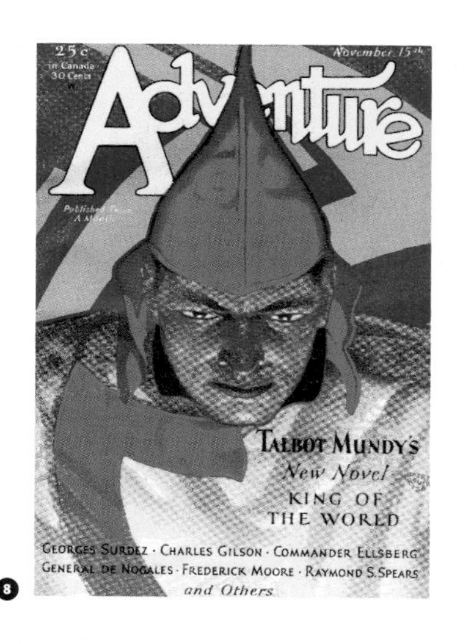

❽

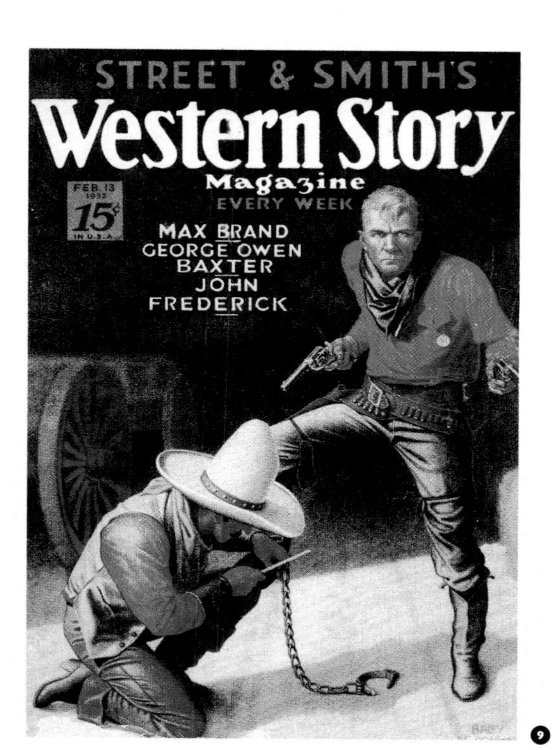

❾

❿

❿ •
Adventure
August 15, 1935
Walter M. Baumhofer
With a new publisher and editor, Mundy returned to *Adventure*. His stories about "Tros" made up a novel longer than *Gone with the Wind*.

⓫ •
Argosy All-Story Weekly
February 2, 1929
Robert A. Graef
Mundy wrote historical romances as well as stories about India.

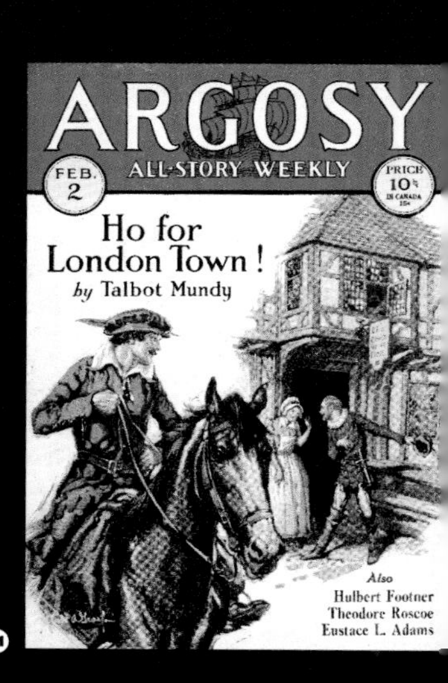

⓫

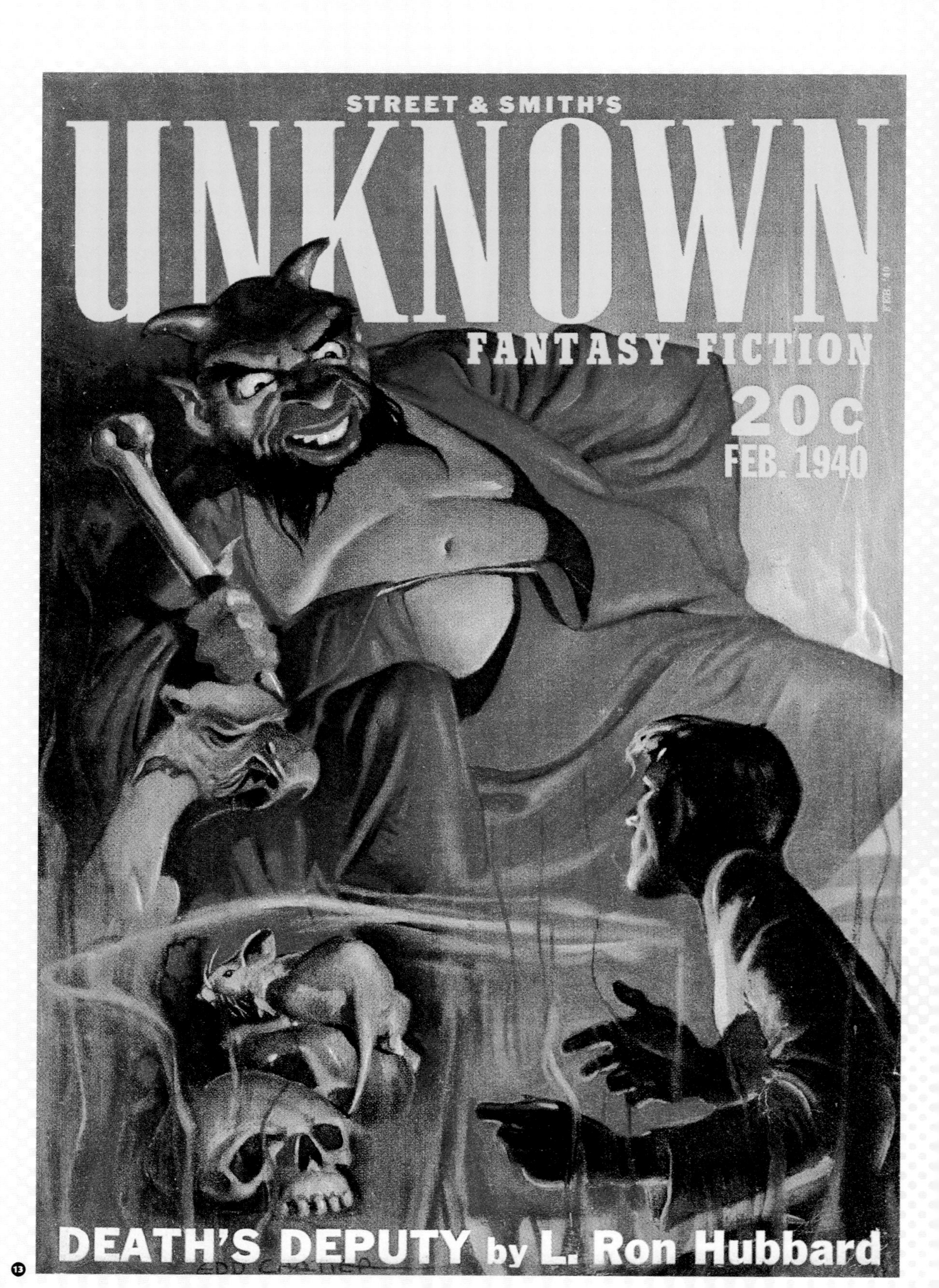

⓬ ••
UNKNOWN
July 1939
H.W. Scott
Slaves of Sleep was Hubbard's most popular novel for *Unknown*.

⓭ ••
UNKNOWN
February 1940
Edd Cartier
Hubbard's *Death's Deputy* featured a knock-out cover by artist Cartier.

throughout the Far East before he was nineteen. He explored the jungles of Polynesia, lived with natives in Mongolia, and gained introductions to some of the sages of China.

When he returned to the United States, he became a barnstorming aviator, sailed aboard a four-masted schooner, and served on Navy vessels. He started writing fiction in 1933 and sold heavily to the pulps: *Top-Notch*, *Thrilling Adventures*, *Romantic Range*, *Cowboy Stories*, *Western Story Magazine* (his name was featured above the title at least once), and *Five-Novels Monthly*, as well as the air, mystery, and sports pulps.

There's not much doubt that the management of Street & Smith suggested Hubbard as a contributor when John W. Campbell, Jr., took over *Astounding* in late 1937 and was looking for new writers. Hubbard was immensely popular in other Street & Smith pulps and had amazing versatility. Could he write science-fiction? He had never tried, but eventually it was in the science-fiction and fantasy pulps that he made an enduring reputation—and it became the field he loved most.

He contributed a number of stories to *Astounding*, including the classic *Final Blackout*, though it was for *Unknown* that he consistently did his best work. For it he wrote *Slaves of Sleep*, *Death's Deputy*, *Typewriter in the Sky*, and *Fear*, a classic novel that showed a thorough grasp of human psychology. Hubbard was a classic "high-concept" writer when it came to science-fiction and fantasy. But he was as adept in handling action and suspense in those fields as he was in the others for which he wrote.

14 ••
Astounding
April 1940
Hubert Rogers
Hubbard's *Final Blackout* was a science-fiction classic.

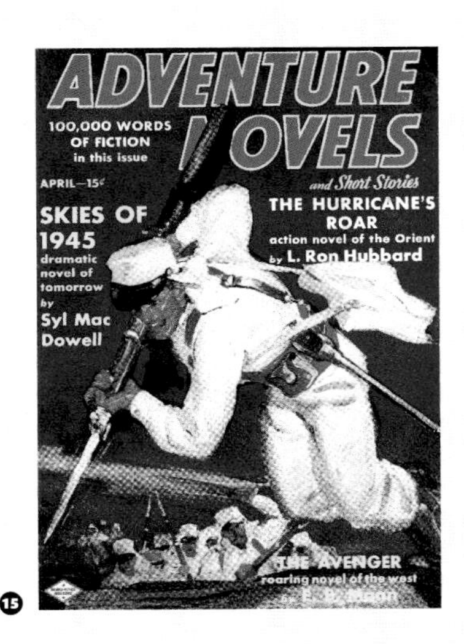

15 ••
Adventure Novels
April 1939
Unknown
Living an adventurous life provided background and story ideas for author Hubbard.

After World War II (he served in the Navy and was wounded, invaliding out in 1945) he returned to writing. But the pulps were dying, and Hubbard had bigger things in mind. In 1950 he wrote articles about a new "science of the mind" called "Dianetics" and later a bestseller with the same title. Soon after, he created Scientology.

When the pulps died, some writers concentrated on books, others wrote for the movies, and a surprising number became television scriptwriters.

But it remained for Hubbard to found a religion.

Edgar Rice Burroughs didn't start writing until he was thirty-seven. He had failed at everything else, and writing was a last resort. His first novel, *Under the Moons of Mars*, was serialized in *All-Story* under the pen name of "Norman Bean" (a typographical error of his intended byline pun of "Normal Bean"). His second novel, *Tarzan of the Apes*, appeared under his own name and made history. In it Burroughs created a character who was to rank with Sherlock Holmes in popular appeal.

Burroughs wrote some twenty-four books about Tarzan, plus numerous others in his Mars, Venus, and "Pellucidar" series (the latter about a land at the earth's core). Like "Heinie" Faust, Burroughs, too, served as a war correspondent—this time in the Pacific theater.

⓰ ••
Western Romances
December 1937
Norman Saunders
Next to fantasy and science-fiction, Hubbard was probably most proficient at Westerns—even romantic ones.

⓱ •••
Top-Notch
November 1935
Tom Lovell
Name a foreign locale, and chances were that Hubbard had been there at one time or another.

op-Notch
ctober 1935
.G. Harris
uthor Hubbard was heavily
eatured on covers for *Top-Notch*
nd *5 Novels Monthly* during the
niddle '30s.

Argosy
October 3, 1936
V.E. Pyles
Hubbard wrote for the general pulps as well as the fantastic.

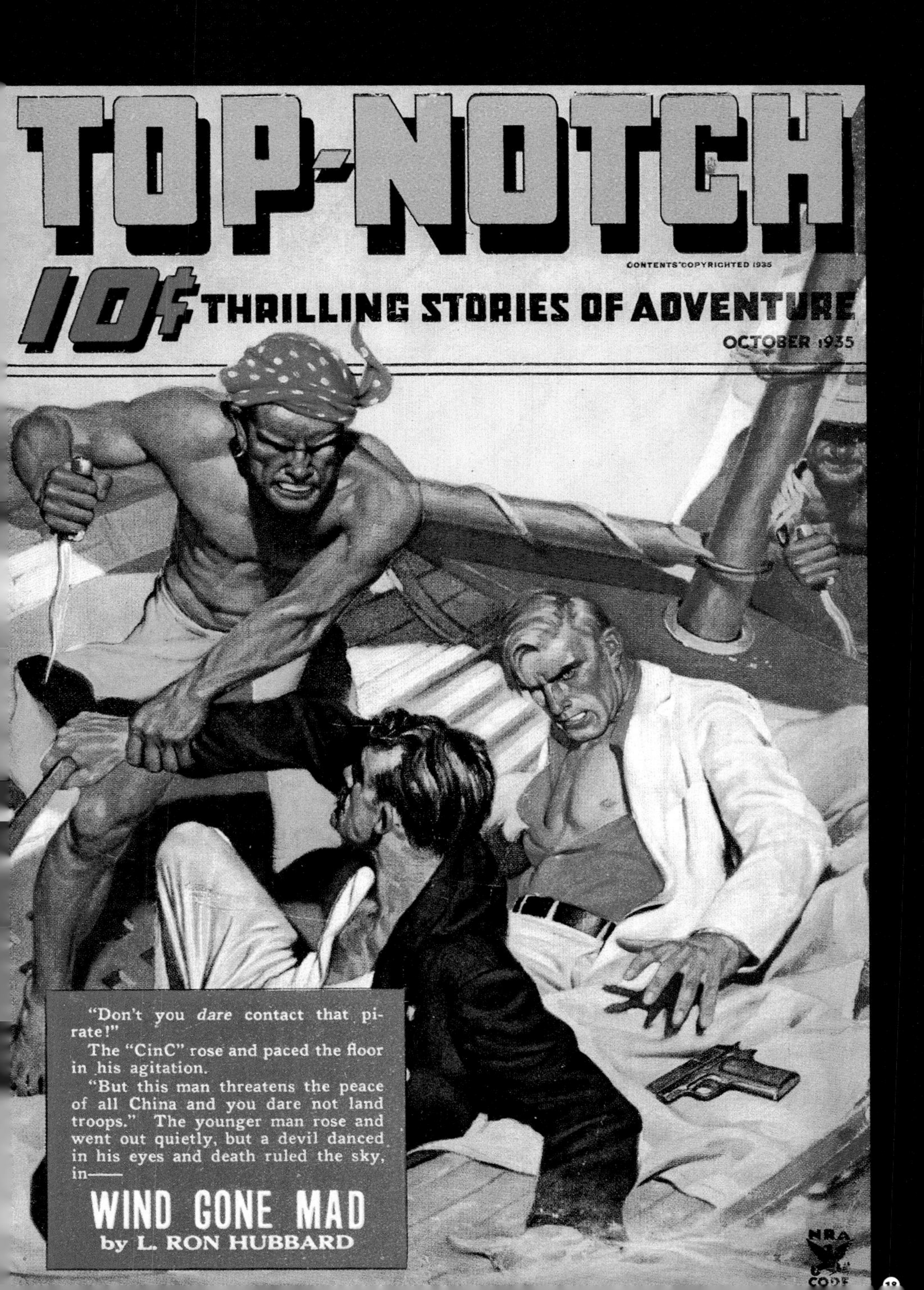

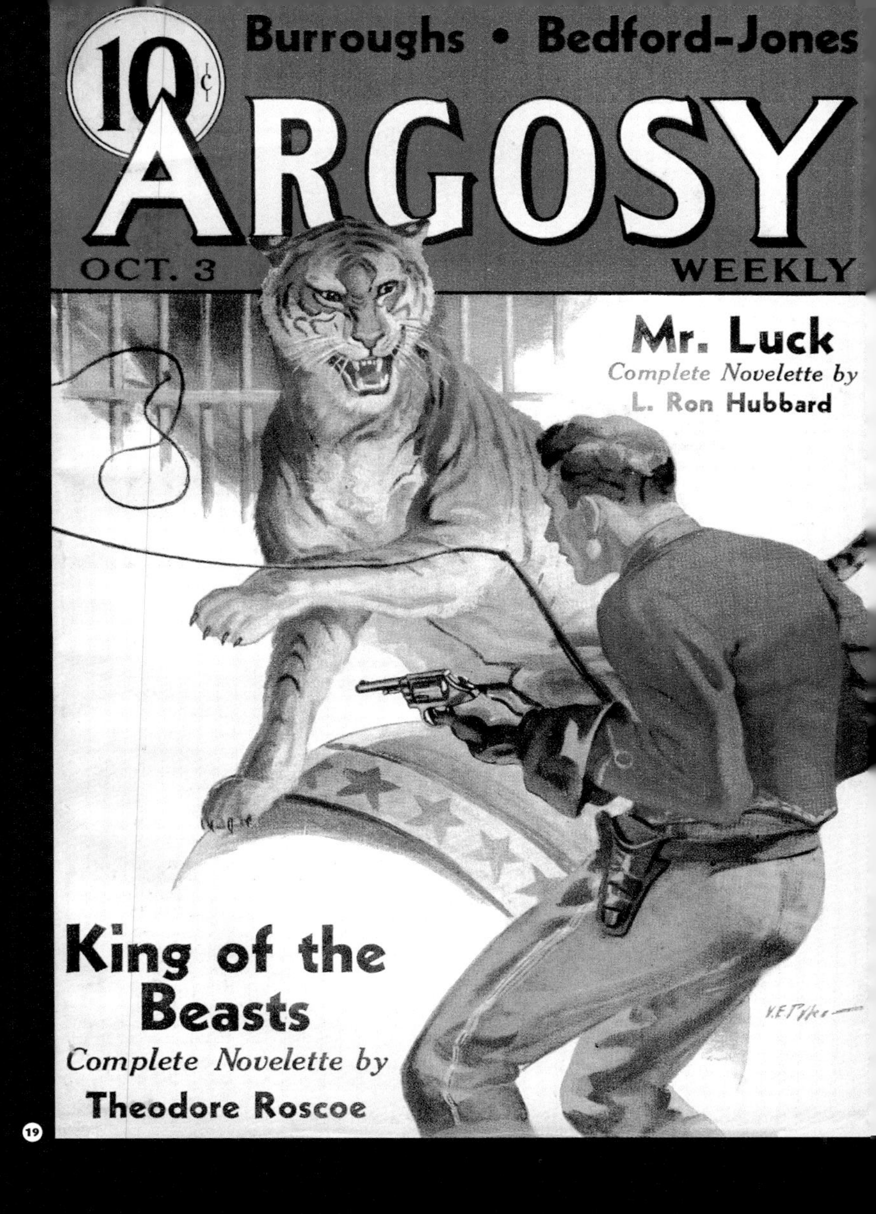

19

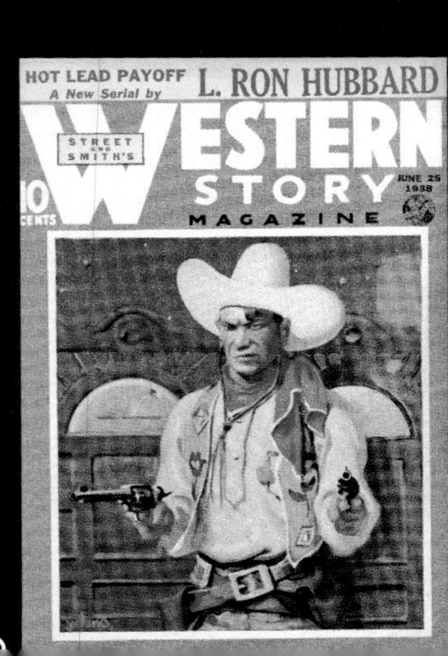

20 ••
Western Story Magazine
June 25, 1938
Gerard Delano
Proof of Hubbard's popularity was the publisher's decision to run his name above the magazine title.

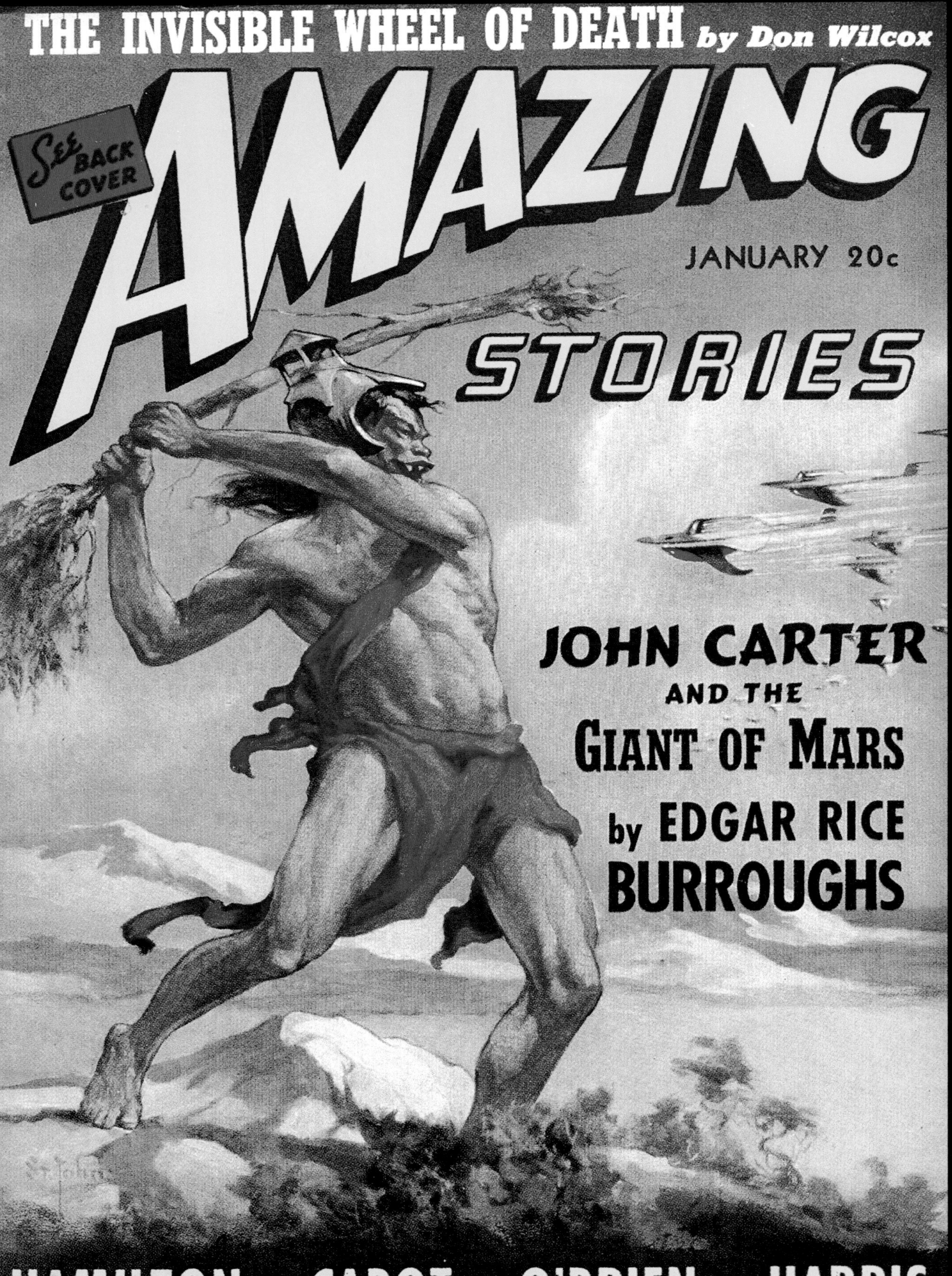

21

21 • •
AMAZING STORIES
January 1941
J. Allen St. John
A dramatic St. John cover marked Burroughs's return to writing his "Martian" stories for the pulps.

22 • • • •
NEW STORY MAGAZINE
June 1913
N.C. Wyeth
For some reason the editors of *Argosy* didn't think author Burroughs was worth a raise after the success of *Tarzan of the Apes*. The editor of *New Story* offered more money for the sequel and was overjoyed at the chance to publish the author.

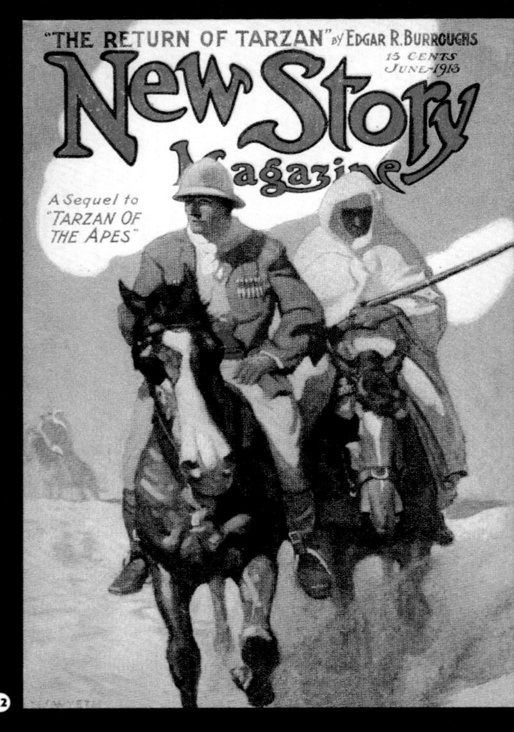

22

23 ••••
Amazing Stories Annual
1927
Frank R. Paul
The rare and valuable annual featured Burroughs's *The Master Mind of Mars* complete in one issue.

23

26

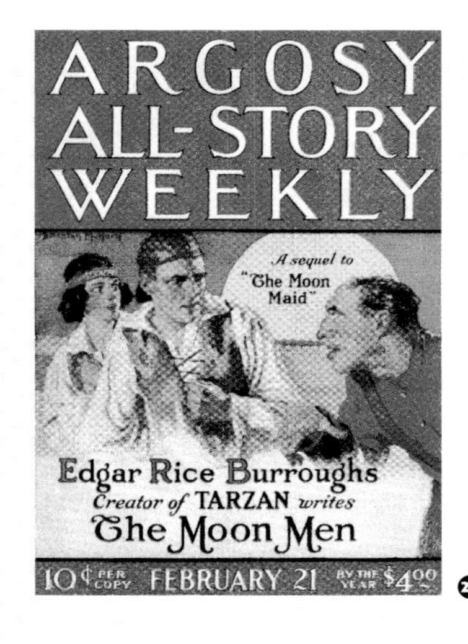

24

27

24 ••
Argosy All-Story Weekly
February 21, 1925
Stockton Mulford
The Moon Men was a parable about Communists ruling the U.S.—and the favorite novel of many Burroughs fans.

25

25 ••
Fantastic Adventures
March 1941
J. Allen St. John
Burroughs's "Venus" stories weren't nearly as popular as his other series.

26 ••
Blue Book Magazine
May 1930
Laurence Herndon
Second in popularity only to Tarzan were Burroughs's *Martian* novels.

27 ••
Blue Book Magazine
October 1931
Laurence Herndon
With his novels about Tarzan, Edgar Rice Burroughs became one of the all-time stars of the pulp magazines.

Black Mask
October 1934
Fred Craft
Raymond Chandler went from the pulps to fame with private eye Philip Marlowe and novels and films like *The Big Sleep*.

28 ••••
Black Mask
March 1930
J.W. Schlaikjer
The Glass Key was one of Dashiell Hammett's most famous novels.

29

30
Black Mask
April 1928
Fred Craft
A retouched cover of *Black Mask* was a prop in the film *Hammett* (Francis Ford Coppola, executive producer). The name "continental op" never appeared on a real cover.

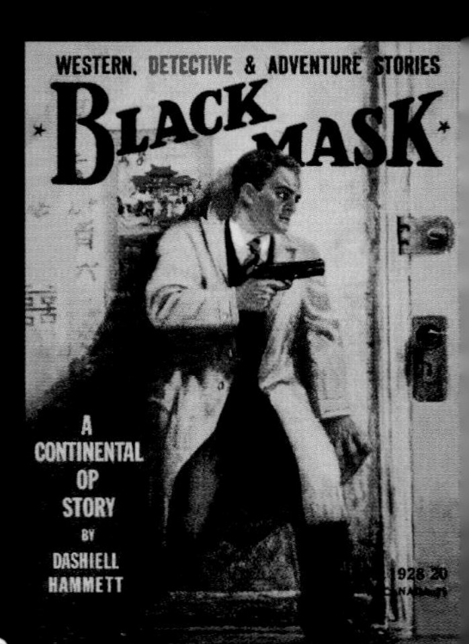

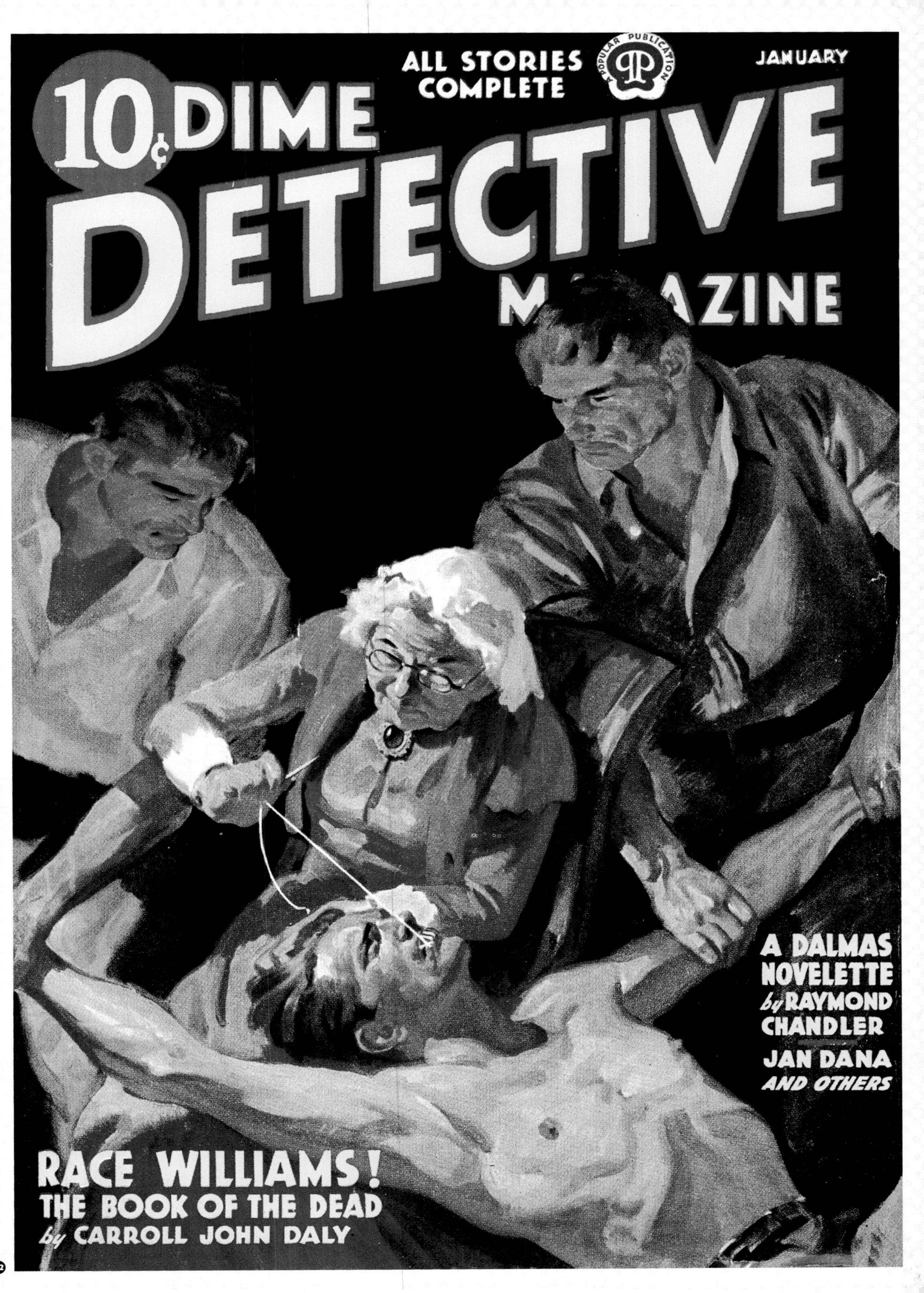

31 •••

Black Mask
November 1927
Fred Craft
"Poisonville" was later published as part of Hammett's novel *Red Harvest*.

32 •••

Dime Detective Magazine
January 1938
Walter M. Baumhofer
Chandler published more stories in *Dime Detective* than he did in *Black Mask*, with which he is usually associated.

Dashiell Hammett used his background as a Pinkerton operative from 1915 to 1922 to lend a gritty reality to his stories about hard-boiled "private eyes." More than any other writer, he made the reputation of *Black Mask*. With the publication of *The Maltese Falcon*, which introduced Sam Spade, he made his own as well. As novelist Joe Gores put it, the difference between Hammett and other detective writers was that "Hammett was not a writer learning about private detectives; he was a private detective learning about writing."

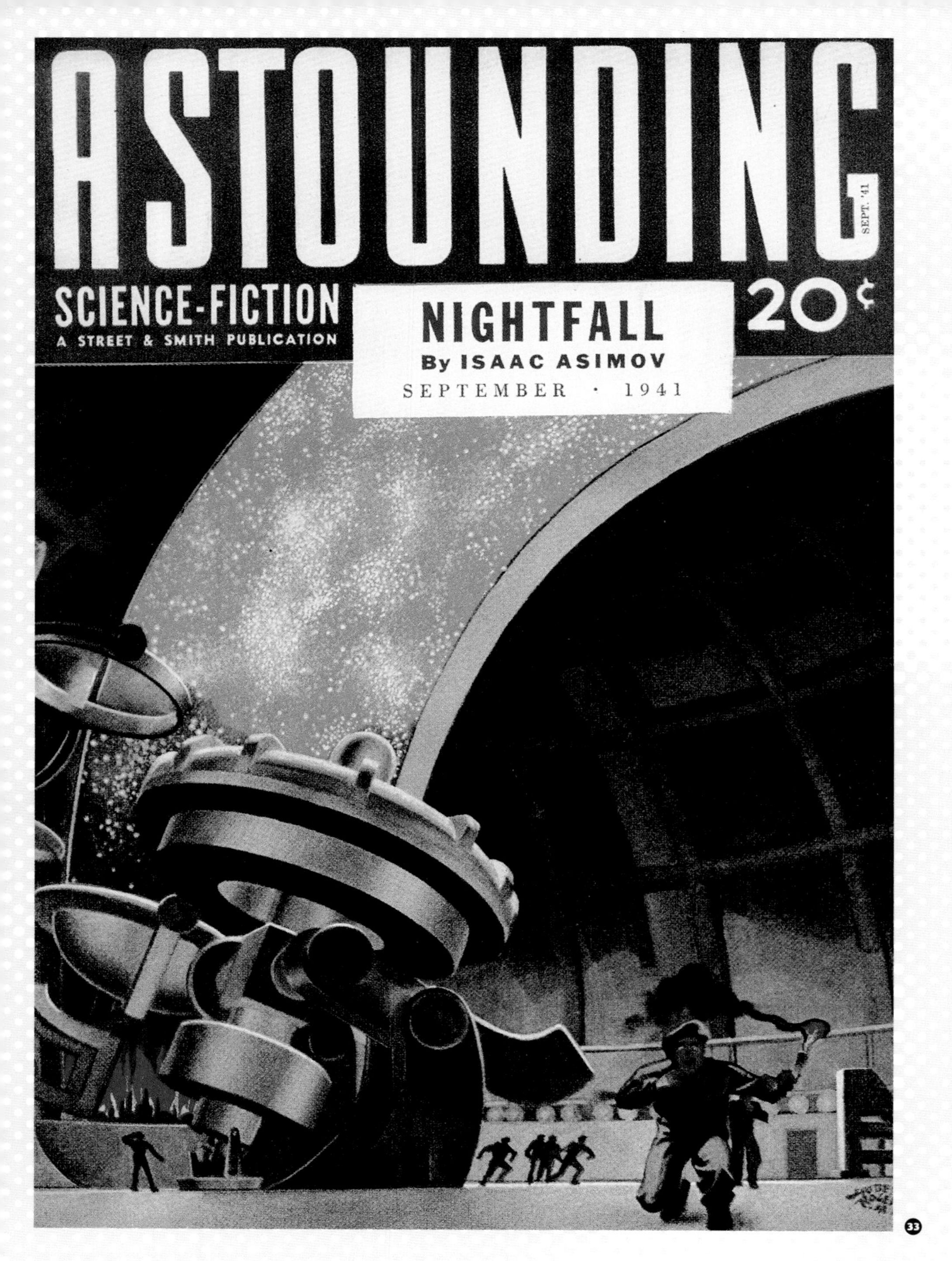

33 •
Astounding Science-Fiction
September 1941
Hubert Rogers
Isaac Asimov was to become a famous science popularizer and one of the most prolific writers the United States has ever known.

34 •
Astounding Science-Fiction
February 1940
Hubert Rogers
Heinlein was the most popular science-fiction writer of his day and the "gold standard" to whom many modern writers are compared.

Hammett's last book was *The Thin Man*, which became a hugely successful film series starring William Powell and Myrna Loy. His later attempts to write "serious" fiction failed, and Hammett's reputation today rests on the Continental Op, Sam Spade, and the Thin Man.

Raymond Chandler wrote a scant twenty or so stories for *Black Mask* and *Dime Detective* before turning to novels. *The Big Sleep* introduced Philip Marlowe and made Chandler famous. In 1946 it was made into a film starring Humphrey Bogart as Philip Marlowe and Elisha Cook, Jr., in a supporting role. Both had starred earlier in a film version of Hammett's *The Maltese Falcon* with Bogart playing Sam Spade and Cook the role of Wilmer, villain Sidney Greenstreet's murderous sidekick.

Chandler went on to write a series of novels about Philip Marlowe, all enormously popular. Nobody before had so successfully captured the seedy side of life in Southern California. Chandler later became a screenwriter but hated it. Writing novels remained his primary interest.

Writers featured by the pulps in the '30s and '40s included Cornell Woolrich (author of the short story made into the film *Rear Window* starring Jimmy Stewart), and Robert Bloch (who wrote for *Weird Tales* and whose novel *Psycho*, based on a real series of murders in a small Wisconsin town, was directed by Alfred Hitchcock), and science-fiction writers Robert Heinlein, Isaac Asimov, and Arthur C. Clarke. Later Clarke collaborated on the screenplay for the Stanley Kubrick film *2001: A Space Odyssey* based on Clarke's short story "The Sentinel."

35 •
Amazing Stories
March 1944
J. Allen St. John
Robert Bloch was best known for his novel *Psycho* but got his start writing for the pulps.

36 •
Shock
March 1948
Unknown
John D. MacDonald's "Travis McGee" novels would become bestsellers.

37 ••••
EIRD TALES
ugust 1928
.C. Senf
obert E. Howard starred
n the cover but inside
as also the first story by
ourteen-year-old Thomas
anier "Tennessee" Williams.

38 •
TARTLING STORIES
ovember 1948
arle K. Bergey
uthor Clarke is best
nown for *2001—A Space Odyssey*
ased on his short story,
The Sentinel." He helped write
he screenplay for the movie.

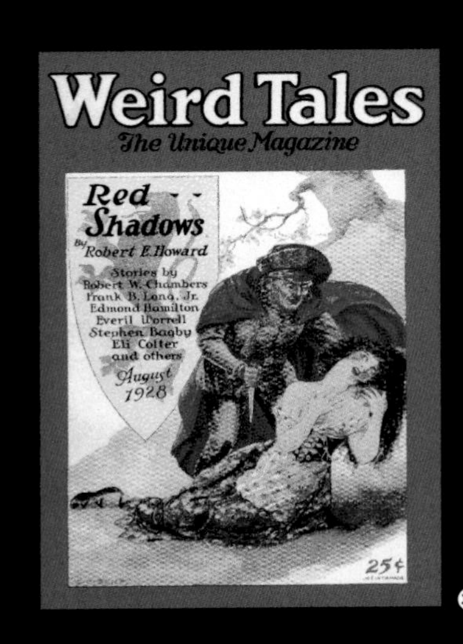

37

38

Ray Bradbury wrote segments of *The Martian Chronicles* for *Planet Stories* (and contributed to *Dime Mystery* as well as the slicks) and had many stories televised on *The Twilight Zone*. Robert E. Howard wrote for *Weird Tales*, *Thrilling Adventures*, and *Fight Stories*, among others. A suicide at an early age, he never saw his "Conan" stories made into films starring Arnold Schwarzenegger. H.P. Lovecraft, another writer for *Weird Tales*, was to serve as an inspiration for many modern horror writers, including Stephen King, and also had stories made into films. Like Howard, his fame was largely posthumous.

Toward the end of the pulp era, John D. MacDonald, who had yet to write about "Travis McGee," was writing in almost every pulp genre but was best known for his mysteries and science-fiction. Elmore Leonard, currently famous as a mystery novelist, wrote westerns (one of them was made into the movie *3:10 to Yuma* starring Glenn Ford). Louis L'Amour, one of the last great western authors, was writing adventure, sports, and mysteries, as well as westerns. (L'Amour wrote *Hondo* starring John Wayne—the first western in 3-D!).

39

39 ••
THRILLING ADVENTURES
December 1936
Rudolph Belarski
Howard wrote adventure and sports stories as well as fantasies.

By the mid-'50s the pulps had withered and died. The writers scattered, some to do books and others to write scripts for films and television. Robert Leslie Bellem wrote segments of *Perry Mason*, *The Lone Ranger*, *Charlie Chan*, *77 Sunset Strip*, and a dozen others. Tommy Thompson, a former western writer, became a story editor on *Bonanza* and made sure his friends in the western field had a chance to write for the show. W.T. Ballard wrote segments of *Shannon*, *Manhunt*, and *Wild Bill Hickock*, while Frank Bonham, another western writer, wrote scripts for *Wagon Train*, *Tales of Wells Fargo*, *Death Valley Days*, and so forth.

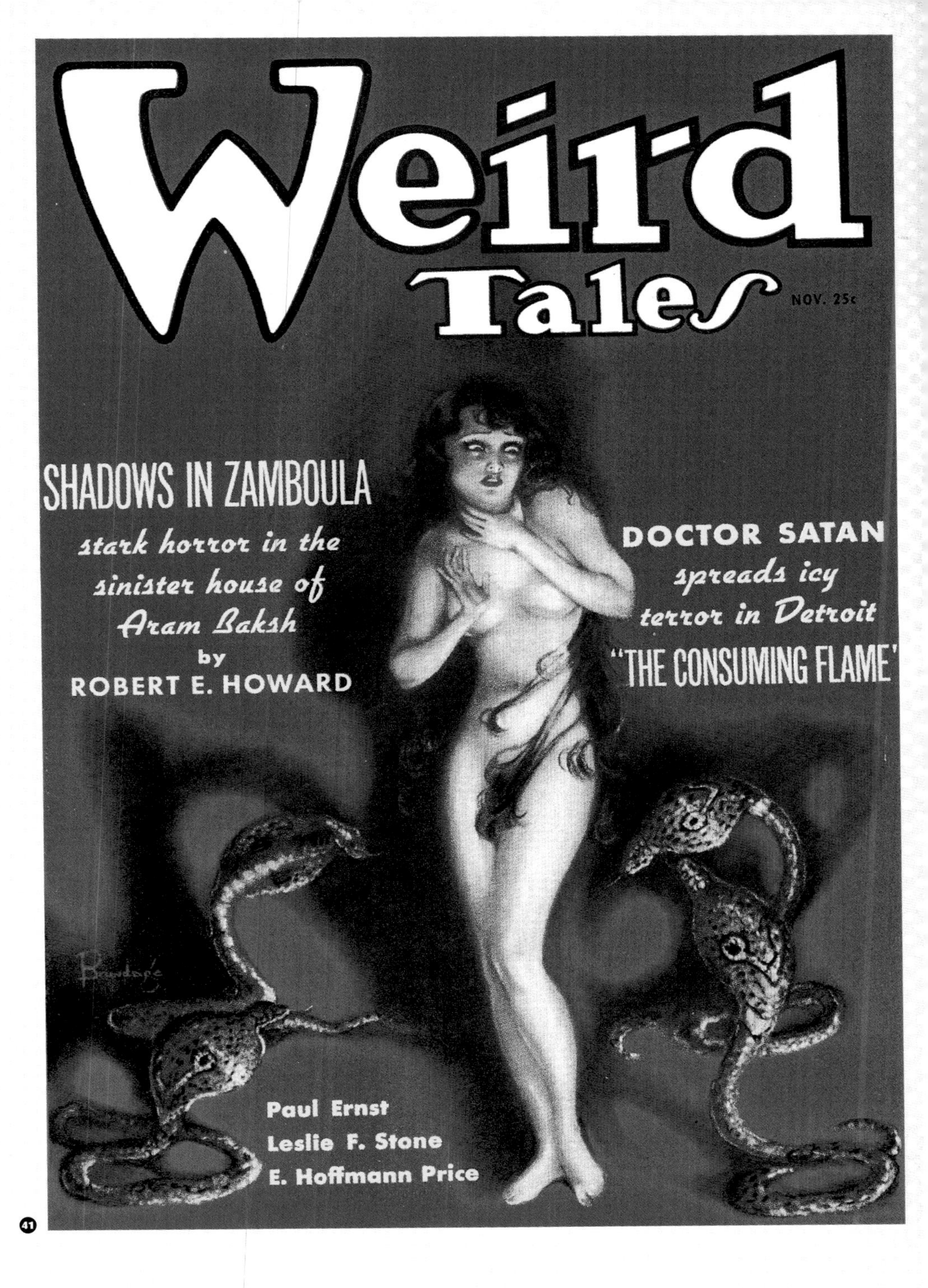

41

40

40 •
PLANET STORIES
January 1954
Kelly Freas
Ray Bradbury became one of the country's leading fantasy writers. *Planet Stories* published many of his *Martian Chronicles*. Leigh Brackett wrote the screenplays for *The Big Sleep* and *The Empire Strikes Back*.

41 •••
WEIRD TALES
November 1935
Margaret Brundage
Author Howard created *Conan the Barbarian*, later filmed with Arnold Schwarzenegger playing Conan. A review of a recent movie about Howard compared his life to that of Ernest Hemingway.

Roy Huggins, a detective-story writer discovered by editor Howard Browne of *Mammoth Detective* and *Mammoth Mystery*, originated *77 Sunset Strip*, *Cheyenne*, *Surfside 6*, and *The Rockford Files* and brought Browne out to Hollywood to write for the shows. Pulp writers Frank Gruber, Steve Fisher, Walker Tompkins, and many others also wrote for films and TV.

It was no mistake that the writers who had contributed so heavily to the glory days of the pulps were largely responsible for some of the best years of film and television. It was in the pulps that beginning writers learned the rudiments of story telling—and could be paid while they learned. And it was in the pulps where fantastic flights of fantasy and wild tales of adventure would inevitably lead to those twin icons of popular culture, *Star Wars* and *Raiders of the Lost Ark*.

The pulps had their faults—bad writing was as prevalent as good and they mirrored their times in their insensitivity to race and a frequently adolescent attitude toward women—but when they were good, they were very good. The readers who curled up with them back then and faithfully bought issue after issue of *The Shadow* or *G-8* did so for the same reasons that lines form around the block today to see *Independence Day* or the latest James Bond or Star Trek movie or scan *TV Guide* so they won't miss their favorite show.

In the last analysis the pulps simply were a helluva lot of fun. As Charles Beaumont, a contributor to *Twilight Zone*, once wrote in *Playboy*: "The pulps weren't good, *they were great!*"

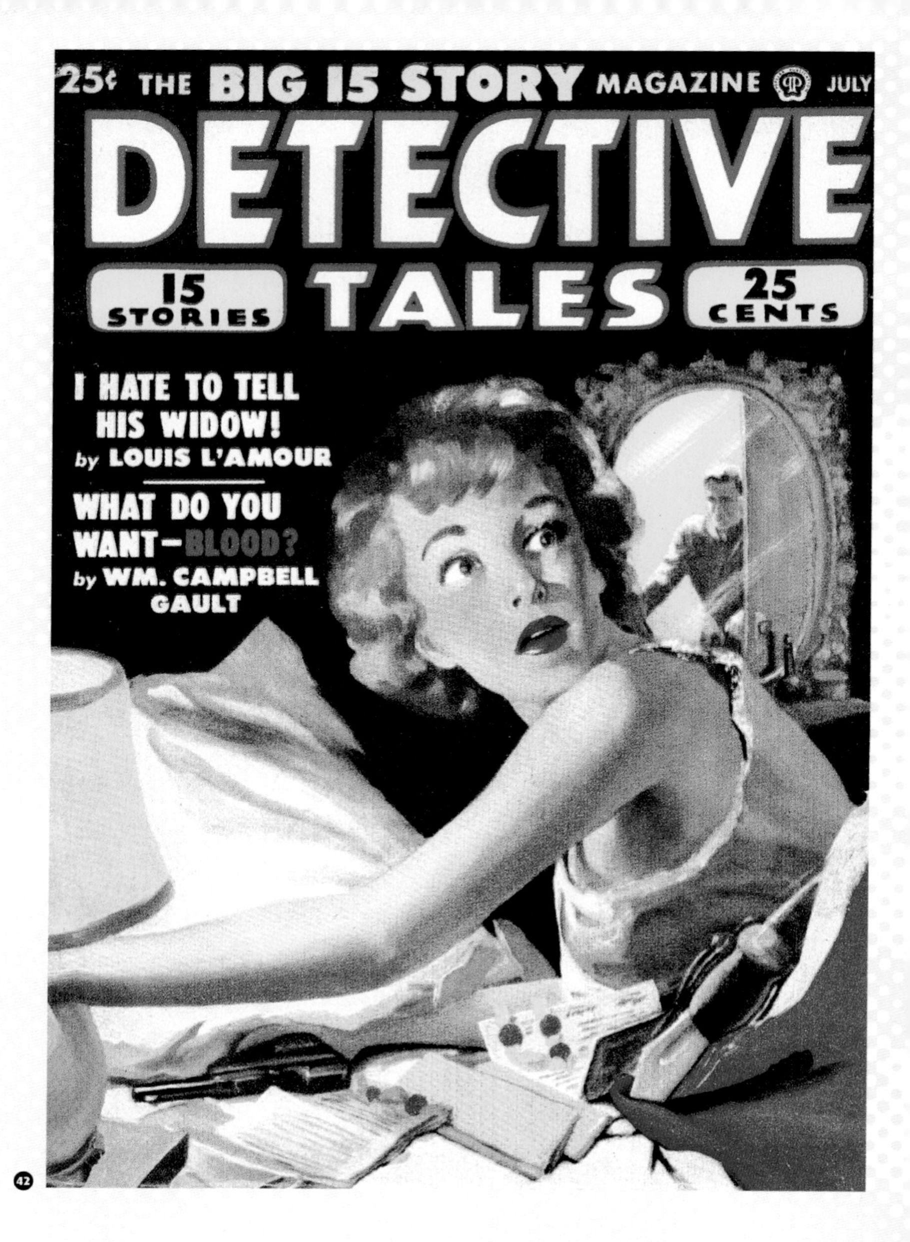

42 •
DETECTIVE TALES
July 1949
Unknown
Louis L'Amour was to become America's most famous modern writer of Western stories.

43 •
DETECTIVE FICTION WEEKLY
March 12, 1938
Rudolph Belarski
Woolrich also wrote under the name of "William Irish" and penned the story later filmed as *Rear Window*.

44 ••
Astounding Stories
February 1936
Howard V. Brown
Lovecraft was more closely identified with *Weird Tales*, but two of his best novels appeared in *Astounding*.

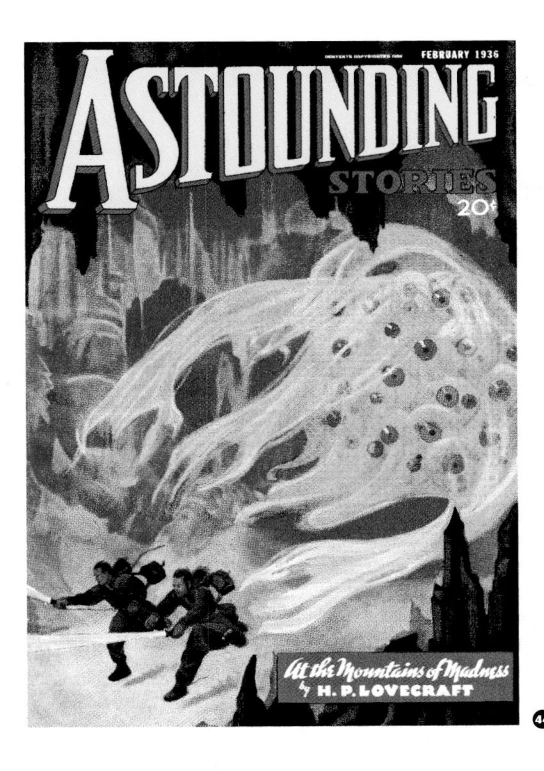

44

45 ••
Weird Tales
May 1941
Hannes Bok
H.P. Lovecraft was the greatest horror-story writer of his time.

45

PULPLIOGRAPHY

Dealers in Pulp Magazines and Related Material

For those interested in purchasing and collecting pulp magazines, Adventure House, owned and operated by John Gunnison, has specialized in pulp material since 1985 and comes highly recommended. Adventure House issues bi-monthly reprints of novels and collections of short stories, ranging from the adventures of Tarzan to the exploits of Operator #5. From time to time it issues collateral material such as its latest CD-ROM titled *Lurid Lasses*, a collection of pulp art in the style of the *Spicys* of the 1930s. Adventure House also deals extensively in buying and selling pulps.

Address: Adventure House, 914 Laredo Rd., Silver Spring, MD 20901.

Web page: *http://www.adventurehouse.com/index.htm*.

Weinberg Books, Inc., operated for years by Robert and Phyllis Weinberg, occasionally handles pulps as well as new hardcover books in the mystery, horror, and science-fiction fields plus books and periodicals about the pulp era. Catalogs available.

Address: Weinberg Books, Inc., 15145 Oxford Dr., Oak Forest, IL 60452.

Other recommended dealers: David Alexander, Box 273086, Tampa, FL 33618. (Ask for catalog.) Dark Star Books, 231 Xenia Ave., Yellow Springs, OH 45387. Jack Deveny, 6805 Cheyenne Trail, Edina, MN 55435. (Jack puts out several catalogs a year.) Claude Held, P.O. Box 515, Buffalo, NY 14225. Graham Holroyd, 19 Borrowdale Dr., Rochester, NY 14626. Robert Madle, 4406 Bestor Dr., Rockville, MD 20853. (Ask for catalog.) R.F. Wald, 5 Becket, Lake Oswego, OR 97035. Ray Walsh, Curious Book Shop, 307 E. Grand River, East Lansing, MI 48823.

Many other dealers, of course, sell through the mails or operate bookstores that carry a selection of pulps. Dealers who set up in the "huckster" rooms at science-fiction, mystery, and comic-book conventions frequently handle pulps. Other sources are antique shops and paper shows.

The price of paper collectibles depends on condition as well as rarity. Copies with white paper and uncreased covers go for a premium. If possible, check the magazine in person and look for clipped coupons, missing pages, water damage and stains, warping, rusted staples, spine damage, and so forth. Prices vary widely from dealer to dealer.

If you have found a small treasure trove in the attic and wish to sell instead of buy, any of the above-named dealers would be glad to quote you a price. They will want to know titles, dates, and approximate condition and paper quality. Do not write them offering Grandfather's collection of *National Geographic* or *Life*. (You could also write the editors of this book for a dealer near you. No guarantee, but we'll do our best.)

MANHATTAN
November 1932
A magazine stand outside Grand Central Station.

Libraries for Research

The San Francisco Academy of Comic Art shelves the largest public-access pulp collection in the world. You may visit the collection weekdays and weekends, but make an appointment with the director, Bill Blackbeard. Students and teachers may request copies of covers, texts, and selected issues. You may purchase a brochure covering the Academy collection by sending three dollars to SFACA, 2850 Ulloa St., San Francisco, CA 94116.

In larger cities the public library sometimes will house a donated collection of pulp magazines. Unfortunately many of these collections are deteriorating. Better sources are university libraries specializing in popular culture and having the will and resources to preserve them. The University of Texas at Austin has extensive holdings in the popular culture field, as does Stanford, University of Florida, University of California at Los Angeles, and, perhaps most especially, the Popular Culture Library at Bowling Green State University. The archives of Street & Smith, one of the major publishers of story papers, dime novels, and pulp magazines, are housed at Syracuse University.

Some universities hold collections of manuscripts and biographical information on particular authors, but we haven't room to list them all. We urge readers to research them on their own.

An Informal Bibliography

The number of books on various aspects of popular culture is enormous, and we could continue for pages and only scratch the surface. It was, of course, not the purpose of this book to present a detailed, scholarly overview of the field.

Specific books about the pulps that we enjoyed reading include *The Pulp Jungle* by Frank Gruber, an author's-eye view of what it was like to write for the pulp magazines; *Pulpwood Editor* by Harold Hersey, an editor's-eye view of the same subject; *The Way the Future Was* by Frederik Pohl, a recent autobiography by a man who was—and is—one of the foremost science-fiction writers and a top editor in the field for many years.

The Fiction Factory by Quentin Reynolds is a history of pulp publisher Street & Smith from the story-paper days through dime novels and the pulps to *Charm* and *Mademoiselle*. *Cheap Thrills* (retitled *An Informal History of the Pulp Magazine* when published in paperback) by Ron Goulart is a highly readable, overall look at the field.

On a specialized basis, there is *The Black Mask Boys* by William F. Nolan, a collection of stories from the magazine by representative authors plus an informative essay about the history of the magazine itself. *The Dime Detectives* by Ron Goulart is something of a history and analysis of the pulps told from the viewpoint of the detective field. *The Shudder Pulps* by Robert Kenneth Jones does much the same thing for the "weird menace" magazines of the 1930s.

The Weird Tales Story, edited and written by Robert Weinberg, is a history of the magazine and its authors with a number of black-and-white illustrations showing the covers and the interior artwork—a must for anyone interested in the pulps.

Yesterday's Faces by Robert Sampson is an exhaustive six-volume study of the heroes and villains of the pulps. (Published by the Bowling Green State University Popular Press, Bowling Green, OH 43403. Send for catalog.) Then there is Tony Goodstone's *The Pulps*, a collection of fiction from the pulps along with a selection of cover photographs.

Biographies of individual authors are also available, such as William F. Nolan's *Max Brand: Western Giant* and Richard A. Lupoff's *Edgar Rice Burroughs: Master of Adventure*. Check up on your favorite author at the library.

We should also mention especially a "semi-professional" magazine published by Douglas Ellis titled *Pulp Vault* (Tattered Pages Press, 6942 N. Oleander Ave., Chicago, IL 60631, ten dollars). A large-sized publication of one-hundred-sixty pages, the issue numbered "12/13" contains John Locke's staggering index of every pulp title that was ever published, including details such as number of issues and date of first and last issue. This for more than a thousand titles and close to thirty-five thousand different issues.

What Are They Worth?

We've resisted the temptation to turn *Pulp Culture* into a price guide for several reasons. Price guides reflect the opinions of a single individual (usually a dealer hoping to make a killing) and go out of date far too quickly. On the other hand, it's natural to wonder whether those old magazines in the attic constitute a treasure trove or trash.

As with any collectible, "value" depends primarily on condition, rarity and demand so let's see how they interact.

Condition: Is the paper white, or near white, or is it browning and brittle? Is the spine bright and intact or is it faded with pieces missing? Is the front cover bright with no creases or tears or chips? Is there a back cover? Has the magazine been repaired with tape? No pages or ads torn out?

A beat-up copy of an otherwise highly collectible magazine may sell for a few dollars while one in pristine condition will go for ten to fifty times that. Remember, few people collect waste paper.

Rarity: *Argosy* and *Blue Book*, very popular magazines which sold in the hundreds of thousands and were published for decades, are not nearly as valuable as, say, *Zeppelin Stories* or *The Scorpion* or *Vice Squad Detective* which sold relatively few copies and lasted only an issue or two.

First issues are usually more expensive than others although last issues may also command a premium. And, obviously, older dates cost more than later ones.

Demand: A magazine may be rare but if nobody wants it, it's not going to command much of a price. Among the pulps there is a high demand among collectors for *The Shadow*, *Weird Tales*, *Black Mask*, *The Spider*, *Operator #5*, and *G-8 and His Battle Aces*, among others.

There is also a demand for certain authors and their presence may increase the value of a magazine considerably. Most issues of *Argosy* and *All-Story* are modestly priced, but those issues containing stories by Edgar Rice Burroughs or L. Ron Hubbard command a premium. Issues of *Weird Tales*, always costly, are even more so if they feature stories by Robert E. Howard or H.P. Lovecraft. *Black Mask* is another collectible where prices escalate if issues contain Dashiell Hammett or Raymond Chandler.

In General: Be prepared for the realities of the marketplace. Dealers pay as little as possible and sell for as much as possible. That's the nature of the system.

Sport story and love story magazines are usually at the bottom of the collecting heap. They don't sell for very much, not many people want them and not many dealers even carry them. The "general" pulps like *Argosy*, *Blue Book*, *Adventure*, *Short Stories* and *The Popular Magazine* sell for anywhere from five dollars to twenty-five dollars depending on condition, date, and what authors are in them. The "shudder pulps" (*Horror Stories*, *Terror Tales*, *Dime Mystery*, etc.) can cost a hundred dollars and up—again, depending on date and condition though *Dime Mystery* usually goes for less.

The "hero" pulps—magazines devoted to the exploits of a single individual (*The Shadow*, *Doc Savage*, *G-8 and His Battle Aces*, *Operator #5*, etc.)—can also take the wind out of a hundred dollar bill if they're "sharp" copies (as can issues of *Spicy Mystery*, *Spicy-Adventure*, etc.). Early issues will go for more—sometimes much more—and later issues less.

And then there are the super stars. Probably the rarest and most valuable of all the pulps is the October 1912 issue of *The All-Story* with *Tarzan of the Apes* complete. A copy in just "good" condition went in a recent auction at Sotheby's for close to $5,000. Estimates of a copy in "fine" condition with near-white paper, range from $8,000 on up. *The All-Story* was a popular magazine but that particular issue is much in demand by Burroughs collectors and pulp collectors in general. Here, demand is the overriding factor.

Runner-ups in value are the first issue of *Weird Tales* which has sold in "fine" condition for as much as $4,000 and the first issue of *The Shadow* where a dealer recently listed an issue in "good-very good" at $3,800.

Ratings: This is not a price guide but having come this far we should give you some idea of the relative values of the magazines shown here. Let's use the bullet system:

• $5 to $25
•• $26 to $100
••• $101 to $250
•••• $251 to $1000
••••• More than $1000

That gives you a lot of leeway—but remember, price depends on condition, rarity, and demand!

One small warning: Years ago collecting "dime novels" was a huge hobby with some dime novels costing hundreds of dollars. And then, almost overnight, the hobby collapsed. Visit any dusty second-hand bookstore and you'll find copies on the back shelves still bearing outrageous prices. Or talk to any former comic book collector who was convinced at the age of 12 that his comic book collection would pay for his college tuition.

That said, collecting pulps is a great hobby—and a lot of fun. And maybe we'll see you at the next convention!

"Wall of Pulps"
January 1998
Magazines from the collection of Frank M. Robinson.
Photograph by Daniel Nicoletta.

Acknowledgements

The authors wish to thank Author Services, Inc., and Fred Harris, Gary Diederich, William Desmond, Doug Ellis, Brian Emerich, Dan Gobbett, Tom Kicinski, Richard Meli, William F. Nolan, Bill Pronzini, Darrell Richardson, Dick Wald, and Malcolm Willits for generously lending rare copies of magazines from their files. A special thanks to Bill Blackbeard of the San Francisco Academy of Comic Art, John Gunnison, John Locke, and Steve Miller for not only lending valuable issues from their collections but also for contributing invaluable information and advice.

Our special gratitude to Conde Nast Publications; Argosy Communications, Inc.; Davis Publications; TSR, Inc.; Robert Weinberg; and Keith Deutsch for their permission to reprint the covers of magazines for which they hold the copyrights.

All Street & Smith magazines reprinted courtesy of Conde Nast Publications. Titles of Street & Smith magazines at date of original copyright included *Air Trails, Astounding Science-Fiction, The Avenger, Bill Barnes Air Adventurer, Clues Detective Stories, College Stories, Complete Stories, Cowboy Stories, Crime Busters, Detective Story Magazine, Doc Savage, Dynamic Adventures, Excitement, Fame and Fortune, Far West, The Feds, Love Story Magazine, Movie Action Magazine, Nick Carter Magazine, Outdoor Stories, Over the Top, Pete Rice Magazine, The Popular Magazine, Sea Stories, The Shadow, The Skipper, Sport Story Magazine, Tip-Top, Top-Notch, Unknown, Western Story Magazine, The Whisperer, Wild West Weekly, The Wizard*. Copyright ©1922, 1924, 1927, 1928, 1929, 1930, 1931, 1932, 1933, 1934, 1935, 1936, 1937, 1938, 1939, 1940, 1941, and 1949 Street & Smith Publications/The Conde Nast Publications, Inc.

All covers from the following magazines: *Ace G-Man Stories, Ace-High Western, Adventure, All Aces Magazine, All-Story, All-Story Love Stories, Argosy, Argosy All-Story Weekly, Astonishing Stories, Blue Steel Magazine, Bull's-Eye Western Stories, Captain Satan, Captain Zero, Dare-Devil Aces, Detective Action Stories, Detective Fiction Weekly, Detective Tales, Dime Adventure, Dime Detective Magazine, Dime Mystery Magazine, Dime Western Magazine, Double Detective, Dr. Yen Sin, Dusty Ayres and His Battle Birds, .44 Western Magazine, Famous Fantastic Mysteries, Fantastic Novels, Fifth Column Stories, Fifteen Sports Stories, Fighting Aces, Foreign Legion Adventures, Gang World, G-8 and His Battle Aces, Horror Stories, Love Short Stories, The Mysterious Wu Fang, The Octopus, Operator #5, Pioneer Western, Railroad Stories, Rangeland Romances, Red Star Adventures, The Secret 6, Shock, The Spider, Sports Novels, Strange Detective Mysteries, Super Science Stories, 10 Story Mystery, 10 Story Western, Terror Tales, Thrilling Mysteries, Western Rangers*—Trademark and Copyright ©1998 Argosy Communications, Inc. All rights reserved. Argosy Communications, Inc., is the successor-in-interest to Popular Publications, Inc., Fictioneers, Inc., The Frank A. Munsey Company, and the Red Star News Company.

Astounding Stories cover from January 1934 issue: Copyright ©1934 by Street & Smith Publications, Inc.; renewed 1961 by Conde Nast Publications, Inc.; renewed 1988 by Davis Publications, Inc. Reprinted by permission of Davis Publications, Inc.

All This and Conventions, Too!

Occasional auctions and small conventions catering to the readers and collectors of pulp magazines are scheduled around the country. The great grand-daddy of them all, "Pulpcon," meets during the summer usually on a Midwest university campus. Over its several days collectors buy and sell magazines; one of the highlights is the auction of rare collectibles. Housing is available through the university. For information write Pulpcon, Box 1332, Dayton, OH 45401.

Frank M. Robinson and Lawrence Davidson

New York
December 1935
The pulps on sale would be worth a mint today.